Cooking for Applause

Produced By
Backers of The Repertory Theatre of St. Louis

Proceeds from *Cooking for Applause* will be used to support the cultural and educational activities of The Repertory Theatre of St. Louis.

Library of Congress Catalog Card Number: 80-82835
ISBN 0-9605504-0-2

To order copies of *Cooking for Applause*
send check for $12.95 plus $1.50 for postage and handling to:
Cooking for Applause
P.O. Box 28090
St. Louis, MO 63119

First Printing February 1981 12,500 copies

Printed by
S.C. Toof & Co.
Memphis, Tennessee

Introduction

Theatre folk have ever loved to eat well—be it meals between performances, a late supper after the show, or a very late brunch the morning after.

Falstaff, the agreeable gourmand who inhabits three of Shakespeare's plays, loves his food as much as anyone. His bill of fare for an evening's work in the Boar's Head Tavern reads as follows:

Item. A capon . . . . 2 s. 2 d.
Item. Sauce . . . . 4 d.
Item. Sack, two gallons . . . . 5 s. 8 d.
Item. Anchovies and sack after supper . . . . . . 2 s. 6 d.
Item. Bread . . . . ½ d.

(Henry IV, Part I)

A prodigious amount of sack for a most prodigious character!

Whether we prepare food for energy or for aesthetic satisfaction, we are always ***Cooking for Applause*** in the theatre. The artistry of the master chef is very much akin to that of the actor, the writer, the designer, or the director.

Cooking for Applause is vibrant proof of the resourcefulness and ingenuity of those who work with the theatre as volunteers. Without their creativity, we in the theatre could not exist. A superb act of the imagination, this book will lead to fine work on the stage as it benefits The Repertory Theatre of St. Louis.

May the standing ovations around your dinner table be as exhilarating and as satisfying as the performances at "The Rep".

And may all your Falstaffs be merry and full!

Wallace Chappell
Artistic Director

Foreword

Just as a good play is the product of playwright, director, designers, cast and crew, this book is the product of many dedicated performers: The Backers, a support group of The Repertory Theatre of St. Louis, and its friends.

ACT I opened with Backers preparing meals for actors to comply with Equity union rules requiring that meals with a choice of two hot entrees be provided actors on evenings when there are two performances. The Backers met that challenge and were rewarded with applause from the casts.

ACT II followed this acclaim as the Backers exchanged and improved recipes they were gathering from "Welcome Back" parties, "Thank you" luncheons, and annual potluck dinners with the idea of compiling a cookbook. Four years of collecting, culling, testing and tasting followed, always with an eye for effective, dramatic and outstanding dishes.

In ACT III section chairmen were selected and full-color graphics were produced. As the production moved to its climax, many volunteers worked together to organize materials, devise a format, type copy, proof and re-proof recipes, compile the index and re-check all the final proofs for printing.

Thanks to the concerted efforts of many people, and the financial support of the corporate Board of Directors, the drama ends with *Cooking for Applause* in your hands. We hope that with the help of this cookbook applause, bravos and encores will greet your culinary efforts.

Backers of The Repertory Theatre of St. Louis

Chairman
Suzy Wahl

Editor
Anne Leopold

Business Manager
Donna Nussbaum

Policy Committee
Nancy Forsyth
Joanne Kohn
Phyl Maxwell
Mary Tureen

Testing Chairmen

Appetizers
Tricia Reay

Soups
Marilyn Steinbrecher

Eggs and Cheese
Carolyn Clarke

Salads
Nancy Monson
Tina Burke

Vegetables
Madeline Stribling

Pasta
Joan Goodson
Peggy McClellan

Fish and Seafood
Joyce Driemeyer

Poultry
Barbara Ferrenbach

Beef
Madeline Monat

Ground Beef
Joanne Kohn
Mary Tureen

Pork
Carol Drennan

Lamb and Veal
Beverly Clarkson

Breads
Etta Taylor

Desserts
Virginia Schreiber

Restaurant
Sarajoan Rezak

Advisors
Charline Baizer
Bebe Scott
Marcia Bernstein

Graphics
Beverly Rife
Stan Gellman Graphic Design

Committee

Kathryn Allison
Ann Augustin
Marilyn Bell
Joanne Berger
Judi Bettendorf
Penelope Biggs
Judy Champ
Ivy Conerly
Karen Corbett
Jean Countryman
Hope Edison
Nancy Forsyth
Margo Friedman
Bess Gardner
Jean Goding
Adele Grace
Betty Gunther
Tad Hamilton
Florence Hardcastle
Marilyn Helmholz
Terry Hieken
Jane Horner
Nancy Kaegel
Vivian Kirk
Jinny Klein
Suzanne Koster
Jean Lange
Lois Leith
Lee Leopold
Patti Lewis
Phyl Maxwell
Elaine McCammon
Barbara Mennell
Linda Mills
Nancy Oglesby
Garie Perry
Pat Richter
Jere Rieser
Joan Robertson
Kathleen S. Rogers
Jane Ross
Pat Schoeffel
Audrey Senturia
Glenn Sheffield
Shirley Sher
Gwen Springett
Marleah Strominger
Betty Suttle
Dee Thompson
Joan Thulin
Valerie Walch
Jeffrey T. Wehling
Marian Wuest
Sally Wurdack

Our sincere appreciation to all who submitted recipes. We regret we were unable to include all of them due to similarity and lack of space.

Table of Contents

Appetizers

Bleu Cheese Chutney Spread

2 (3 ounce) packages cream cheese, softened
3 ounces bleu cheese, crumbled
¼ cup butter, softened
¼ cup finely chopped onion
1 to 2 Tablespoons milk
½ teaspoon curry powder
¼ teaspoon salt
3 Tablespoons chutney

Combine cream cheese, bleu cheese, butter, onion, milk, curry powder and salt in blender. Blend until creamy. Add chutney and blend a few seconds. Refrigerate 24 hours. Remove from refrigerator 1 hour before serving. Makes 1½ cups.

Wilma Martin

Capaccio

10 Tablespoons olive oil
¼ cup red wine vinegar
½ cup freshly grated Parmesan cheese
6 Tablespoons Dijon mustard
2½ Tablespoons Worcestershire sauce
2 Tablespoons minced garlic
1 teaspoon salt
½ teaspoon freshly ground pepper
1 pound beef tenderloin, thinly sliced
Freshly grated Parmesan cheese (garnish)

Combine oil and vinegar. Add cheese, mustard, Worcestershire sauce, garlic, salt and pepper and blend until thick and smooth. Overlap beef slices in petal design on pottery plate. Spread with sauce. Top with additional cheese if desired.

Mrs. Ray Patrick

Cheese-Stuffed Dates

1 (3 ounce) package cream cheese, softened
1 Tablespoon pickle relish
1 Tablespoon mayonnaise
1 teaspoon minced chives
1 teaspoon minced green onions
Dash Tabasco
Salt and freshly ground pepper to taste
½ pound pitted dates
½ cup finely ground pecans
1 teaspoon paprika

Combine cream cheese, pickle relish, mayonnaise, chives, onions, Tabasco, salt and pepper. Mix until well blended. Stuff dates with cheese mixture. Combine pecans and paprika. Roll dates in pecan mixture. Refrigerate. Makes 25.

Elaine George

Jellied Ham with Parsley

6 cups diced cooked ham
4 cups hot clarified chicken stock
1 cup minced parsley
¼ cup dry white wine
1 Tablespoon tarragon vinegar

Mix ham with 2 cups stock. Press into 9 x 13-inch baking dish. Chill until set. Add parsley, wine and vinegar to remaining 2 cups stock. Chill, but just before it sets, stir and pour over ham mixture. Chill until set. Cut into squares. Serves 8.

Clarified Chicken Stock:
4 cups chicken stock
1 egg white, beaten frothy
1 egg shell, crushed

Clarified Chicken Stock:
Whisk egg white and egg shell into cool stock. Simmer 5 minutes. Strain.

Margie Bornell

Rumaki

½ pound chicken livers
1 (8 ounce) can water chestnuts, drained
½ cup butter, softened
6 slices crisp bacon, crumbled
1 Tablespoon Kikkoman soy sauce
1 teaspoon dry mustard
1 teaspoon onion salt
½ teaspoon nutmeg
Dash cayenne

Simmer chicken livers until tender, about 20 minutes; drain. Put livers and water chestnuts through medium blade of food chopper or chop roughly in food processor. Add butter, bacon, soy sauce, mustard, onion salt, nutmeg and cayenne. Refrigerate. Soften at room temperature 1 hour before serving. Makes 2 cups.

Jane Ross

Smoked Beef Rollups

1 (2½ ounce) jar smoked beef
1 (8 ounce) package cream cheese
¼ cup sour cream
¼ cup horseradish
3 Tablespoons finely chopped onion
2 Tablespoons mayonnaise
Garlic powder to taste
Worcestershire sauce to taste

Separate beef into slices. Combine cream cheese, sour cream, horseradish, onion, mayonnaise, garlic powder and Worcestershire and blend well. Spread on beef slices and roll up. Makes about 20.

Claudette Richmond

Ribbon Pâté

Aspic:

1 cup water
2 beef bouillon cubes
1 Tablespoon unflavored gelatin
1 Tablespoon lemon juice

Aspic:

Combine water, bouillon cubes and gelatin in small saucepan. Heat, stirring constantly, just until gelatin dissolves. Put ¼ cup gelatin mixture and lemon juice into 6-cup mold.

Cheese Mixture:

2 (8 ounce) packages cream cheese
½ cup sour cream
1 Tablespoon grated onion

Cheese Mixture:

Combine cream cheese, sour cream, onion and ¼ cup gelatin mixture. Stir until smooth.

Ham Mixture:

2 (4½ ounce) cans deviled ham
¼ cup sweet-mustard relish

Ham Mixture:

Combine ham, relish and ¼ cup gelatin mixture. Blend well.

Liver Mixture:

2 (4½ ounce) cans liver pâté
¼ cup mayonnaise
2 Tablespoons chopped parsley

Liver Mixture:

Combine liver pâté, mayonnaise, parsley and ¼ cup gelatin mixture. Stir until smooth.

Topping:

3 large pitted black olives, sliced

Topping:

Place mold in sinkful of ice water. Arrange olive slices on aspic in mold. Spoon half the cheese mixture into mold. Spoon ham mixture into mold. Spoon remaining cheese mixture into mold. Spoon liver mixture into mold. Wait until each layer is sticky firm before adding next layer. Remove mold from ice water. Cover with foil. Refrigerate until firm. Serves 24.

Mrs. J. Bruce McBrayer

Country Pâté

1 pound ground pork
½ pound ground veal
2 yellow onions, sliced
2 cloves garlic, minced
⅓ cup brandy
⅓ cup white wine
1 teaspoon thyme
Salt and white pepper to taste
Bacon

Combine pork, veal, onions and garlic in bowl. Combine brandy and wine; pour over meat. Add thyme, salt and pepper. Cover and marinate in refrigerater overnight. Regrind meats in meat grinder or food processor. Line terrine or loaf pan with bacon. Pack with pâté mixture. Place terrine or loaf pan in larger pan with water halfway up the side. Bake at 350°F for 1½ hours. Remove from oven and weight with bricks until cool. Refrigerate. Makes 1 pound pâté.

Empire Cafe and Charcuterie

Crab Mold

¼ cup cold water
1 teaspoon unflavored gelatin
2 (8 ounce) packages cream cheese
1 (6 ounce) package frozen king crab meat, thawed, drained, cut up
1 (2 ounce) jar pimientos, chopped, drained
2 Tablespoons sherry
¾ teaspoon salt
⅛ teaspoon freshly ground black pepper
¼ cup snipped parsley, divided

Sprinkle gelatin over cold water to soften, set over hot water, and stir until dissolved. Stir in cream cheese, crab meat, pimientos, sherry, salt, pepper and 2 Tablespoons parsley. Pour mixture into a 3-cup ring mold. Refrigerate until set, about 4 hours. Unmold and garnish with remaining parsley. Makes 3 cups spread.

Melita Hopkins

Dip Louis

¾ cup mayonnaise
¼ cup thick French dressing
3 ounces bleu cheese
¼ cup ketchup
3 Tablespoons chili sauce
2 Tablespoons horseradish
1 Tablespoon lemon juice
1 Tablespoon onion juice
1 clove garlic, minced
1 or 2 dashes Tabasco
Salt to taste
1 or 2 (4½ ounce) cans shrimp, drained

Combine mayonnaise, French dressing, cheese, ketchup, chili sauce, horseradish, lemon juice, onion juice, garlic, Tabasco and salt in blender. Blend until smooth. Remove mixture from blender, and stir in shrimp. Makes 2 cups.

Garie Perry

Lomi Lomi

1 pound salmon
¾ cup fresh lime juice
¾ cup fresh frozen coconut milk
¼ cup chopped dry onion
2 teaspoons salt
1 teaspoon freshly ground pepper
½ teaspoon sugar
4 dashes Tabasco
3 cups chopped tomatoes

Cut salmon into pieces ⅕ inch thick and ¾ inch wide. Combine salmon, lime juice, coconut milk, onion, salt, pepper, sugar and Tabasco in large stainless steel bowl. Marinate for 6 hours in refrigerator, mixing ingredients from time to time. Mix in tomatoes when ready to serve. Serve in Bluffer shell on snow ice. Serves 15 to 20.

Trader Vic's

Pickled Shrimp

2 pounds jumbo shrimp
1 Tablespoon shrimp boil spices
1 cup olive oil
⅓ cup white wine vinegar
2 onions, thinly sliced
2 teaspoons sugar
2 teaspoons celery seed
2 teaspoons Worcestershire sauce
1 teaspoon salt
½ teaspoon dry mustard
4 bay leaves
3 dashes Tabasco

Cook shrimp in 2 quarts boiling water with shrimp spices. Peel, devein and put in bowl. Combine oil, vinegar, onions, sugar, celery seed, Worcestershire sauce, salt, mustard, bay leaves and Tabasco. Pour over shrimp. Cover and refrigerate for at least 24 hours. Once a day stir or shake to recoat shrimp. Makes 32 to 40.

Tricia Reay

Smoked Trout Pâté

¾ to 1 pound smoked trout, deboned
2 Tablespoons fresh lemon juice
Freshly ground Szechuan pepper to taste
½ pound unsalted butter

Put fish, lemon juice and pepper in food processor with steel blade in place. Process with a few on/off turns. Add butter, cut into pieces, and process into a smooth paste. Pack into ceramic fish mold and refrigerate several hours. Unmold and serve with whole grain wheat crackers. Serves 6 to 8.

Joyce Driemeyer

Artichoke and Spinach Dip

2 (8½ ounce) cans artichoke hearts, drained
1 (10 ounce) package frozen chopped spinach, cooked and squeezed dry
1 cup mayonnaise
¼ cup parsley, minced
2 large shallots, minced
1 large clove garlic, minced
2 Tablespoons fresh lemon juice
2 Tablespoons snipped fresh chives
2 teaspoons dillweed
1 teaspoon salt
Freshly ground pepper to taste
Raw vegetables

Purée artichoke hearts and spinach. Combine with mayonnaise, parsley, shallots, garlic, lemon juice, chives, dillweed, salt and pepper. Mix well in food processor or in batches in blender. Put in bowl, cover and chill overnight. Serve with raw vegetables. Makes 3 cups.

Jean Lange

Caviar Mousse

2 Tablespoons cold water
1½ teaspoons unflavored gelatin
¾ cup sour cream
3 hard-boiled eggs, halved
¼ cup chopped onion
3 Tablespoons mayonnaise
4 teaspoons lemon juice
1½ teaspoons salt
½ teaspoon Worcestershire sauce
¼ teaspoon white pepper
2 or 3 drops Tabasco
2 ounces black caviar

Sprinkle gelatin over cold water to soften; set over hot water and stir until dissolved. Cool. Blend sour cream, eggs, onion, mayonnaise, lemon juice, salt, Worcestershire sauce, pepper and Tabasco until puréed. Stir gelatin into sour cream mixture and gently but thoroughly fold in caviar. Pour into 2-cup mold and chill, loosely covered, for at least 3 hours. Serve with pumpernickel bread. Makes 2 cups.

Tricia Reay

Caviar Supreme

¼ cup cold water
1 Tablespoon unflavored gelatin

Soften gelatin in cold water. Set bowl over hot water to liquefy.

Egg layer:
4 hard-boiled eggs, chopped
½ cup mayonnaise
¼ cup parsley, minced
¾ teaspoon salt
Freshly ground white pepper to taste
Dash Tabasco

Egg layer:
Combine eggs, mayonnaise, parsley, onion, salt, pepper and Tabasco with 1 Tablespoon dissolved gelatin. Spread into bottom of 1-quart soufflé dish which has been lined with foil extending 4 inches beyond rim on 2 sides and lightly oiled. Smooth top of mixture with spatula.

Avocado layer:
2 medium avocados
1 large shallot, chopped
2 Tablespoons fresh lemon juice
2 Tablespoons mayonnaise
½ teaspoon salt
Freshly ground pepper to taste
Dash Tabasco

Avocado layer:
Purée 1 avocado and dice 1 avocado. Combine with shallot, lemon juice, mayonnaise, salt, pepper, Tabasco and 1 Tablespoon dissolved gelatin. Spread mixture evenly over egg layer.

Sour cream and onion layer:
1 cup sour cream
¼ cup minced onion
1 (3½ or 4 ounce) jar black or red caviar
Fresh lemon juice

Sour cream and onion layer:
Mix sour cream, onion and remaining 2 Tablespoons gelatin. Spread carefully over avocado layer. Cover dish tightly with plastic wrap and refrigerate overnight. Just before serving, place caviar in fine sieve and rinse gently under cold running water. Sprinkle with lemon juice. Drain well. Lift mold out of dish with extended foil. Transfer to serving dish using wide spatula. Spread caviar over top. Serves 12 to 16.

Mrs. Martin Caldwell

Avocado Dip Con Queso

3 avocados, mashed

6 Tablespoons mayonnaise, divided

1 Tablespoon lemon juice

¾ cup sour cream

1 (1¼ ounce) package taco seasoning mix, or 3 Tablespoons taco sauce

½ cup grated Cheddar cheese

½ cup grated Monterey Jack cheese

3 green chiles, chopped

1 large or 2 small tomatoes, chopped

1 bunch green onions, chopped

Taco chips

Combine avocados, 2 Tablespoons mayonnaise and lemon juice. Spread on serving plate. Combine sour cream, 4 Tablespoons mayonnaise and taco seasoning or sauce and spread over avocado mixture. Combine Cheddar cheese, Monterey Jack cheese and chiles; sprinkle over sour cream mixture. Combine tomatoes and green onions and sprinkle over top. Serve with taco chips. Serves 8.

Judith Davis

Olive Eyes

1 (7 ounce) bottle large stuffed olives, drained

2 (8 ounce) packages cream cheese, softened

1 cup finely chopped walnuts or pecans

Wipe olives dry. Roll a generous Tablespoonful of cream cheese around each olive and cover evenly. Roll olives in nuts. Chill. Roll with hands to press nuts in. Cut each olive crosswise so pimiento shows in center of circle. Cover and chill. Makes 44 to 48.

Mildred Trotter

Snail-Stuffed Mushrooms

1 (7 ounce) can snails, drained
¾ cup olive oil
¼ cup white vinegar
2 Tablespoons coarsely chopped chives, divided
1 teaspoon minced fresh parsley
1 clove garlic, minced
24 medium mushroom caps, lightly sautéed in butter and lemon juice

Place snails in bowl. Combine oil, vinegar, 1 Tablespoon chives, parsley and garlic and blend well. Pour over snails and chill for at least 1 hour. Drain snails and place in mushroom caps. Sprinkle with remaining chives. Serve cold. Makes 24.

Tricia Reay

Water Chestnut Dip

1 cup sour cream
1 cup mayonnaise
½ cup finely chopped water chestnuts
¼ cup thinly sliced green onions, including tops
1 Tablespoon Kikkoman soy sauce
1 Tablespoon finely chopped parsley
1 teaspoon ginger
1 clove garlic, crushed
Pinch salt

Combine sour cream and mayonnaise thoroughly. Add water chestnuts, green onions, soy sauce, parsley, ginger, garlic and salt. Refrigerate overnight. Makes 2½ cups.

Jane Selcer

Baked Brie

1 whole well-ripened Brie cheese, about 2 pounds
1 cup slivered almonds

Place cheese in oven-proof serving dish. Sprinkle almonds over top. Bake at 300°F for 20 minutes, until cheese is soft and almonds are brown. Serve with crackers and fruit. Serves 12.

Donna Nussbaum

Boereg

2 (10 ounce) packages refrigerated crescent rolls
1½ pounds Muenster cheese, coarsely grated
¾ cup chopped parsley
1 egg, beaten
3 Tablespoons melted butter
½ teaspoon garlic salt
½ teaspoon salt
½ teaspoon freshly ground pepper

Separate crescent roll dough into squares; pinch diagonal seams together. Roll each square as thin as possible without tearing. Combine cheese, parsley, egg, butter, garlic salt, salt and pepper in bowl and mix well. Spread filling on half the squares, leaving ½ inch around edges. Cover with remaining squares and seal edges with fork. Make slits on top. Bake at 375°F about 15 minutes until brown. Cut into squares. Makes 24.

Katrina Young

Hot Olive Canapés

1 cup mayonnaise
1 (4.2 ounce) can chopped ripe olives, well drained
½ cup chopped green onions
¼ cup grated Cheddar cheese
¼ teaspoon curry powder
Dash Tabasco
Salt and freshly ground pepper to taste
6 English muffins, split

Combine mayonnaise, olives, green onions, cheese, curry powder, Tabasco, salt and pepper. Spread on muffins; cut each muffin into quarters. Bake at 450°F for 10 minutes. Makes 48.

Nancy S. Forsyth

Fried Artichokes

4 fresh artichokes
2 quarts water
3 Tablespoons lemon juice
4 eggs
1 cup milk
2 cups flour
Corn oil
Salt

Peel off tough leaves. Peel stems. Cut 1 inch off top of artichokes. Cut off thorny tips. Quarter lengthwise and cut out chokes. Combine water and lemon juice in large bowl. Soak quarters in lemon juice 10 minutes. Drain. Combine eggs and milk. Add flour and mix well. Cut artichoke quarters into ¼-inch slices. Pour oil ¾-inch deep in pan; heat to 350°F. Dip artichoke slices into batter; fry until golden. Drain on paper towels and salt to taste. Serve hot. Serves 8 to 10.

Dora Kemoll

Gougère aux Fines Herbes

½ cup butter
1 cup water
1 cup flour
4 eggs
2 Tablespoons chopped parsley
1 teaspoon dry mustard
1 teaspoon chervil
1 teaspoon salt
½ teaspoon thyme
½ teaspoon oregano
½ teaspoon basil
¼ teaspoon cayenne
1½ cups grated Swiss cheese

Cut butter into pieces, put in saucepan with water and bring to a boil. When butter is melted, remove pan from heat; add flour and beat vigorously until smooth paste forms. Return pan to medium heat and beat until paste is shiny, about 1 minute. Remove from heat. Add eggs, one at a time, beating well after each until thoroughly blended. Beat in parsley, mustard, chervil, salt, thyme, oregano, basil and cayenne. Fold in cheese. Lightly grease and flour large baking sheet. Trace 2 7-inch circles in flour with finger. Drop mixture by tablespoons to form 2 rings. Smooth rings with rubber spatula. Bake at 450°F for 12 minutes, reduce heat to 325°F and bake for 30 minutes. Serve hot or cold. Slice or break apart. Makes 2 rings.

Jane Holtzer

Italian Cheese Balls

1½ cups fresh bread crumbs
½ pound freshly grated Parmesan cheese
3 eggs, lightly beaten
½ Tablespoon chopped fresh parlsey
¼ teaspoon salt
Freshly ground pepper
Dash nutmeg
Flour
1 egg, beaten

Combine bread crumbs, cheese, eggs, parsley, salt, pepper and nutmeg; mix well. Shape into small balls, roll in flour and dip in beaten egg. Fry in hot oil until golden. Makes 24.

Sally Randolf

Stuffed Mushrooms

1 pound frozen chopped spinach
½ cup butter
2 cloves garlic
½ teaspoon fresh lemon juice
Salt and white pepper to taste
24 large fresh mushrooms
6 slices Mozzarella cheese
½ cup white wine (optional)

Thaw spinach, squeeze out any excess water. Let butter soften but do not allow to become oily. Mash garlic finely and mix thoroughly with butter and lemon juice. Melt half the butter in sauté pan. Add spinach; cook until any liquid is evaporated. Cool. Add salt and pepper to taste. Remove stems from mushrooms. Wash thoroughly. Fill each cap with a portion of spinach mixture. Cut cheese into 1½-inch square pieces. Put 1 square cheese on each mushroom. Dot mushrooms with remaining garlic butter. Place on lightly greased flat serving plates. Let stand for 10 minutes before baking. Bake at 375°F for 10 to 15 minutes or until cheese is melted. If desired, just prior to serving pour wine into saucepan and cook for 3 to 4 minutes. Drizzle reduced liquid over each portion. Serves 4.

Massucci's

Swiss Canapé Broils

4 slices day-old bread
1 cup grated Swiss cheese
1 (2½ ounce) jar sliced mushrooms, drained
⅓ cup chopped pepperoni
⅓ cup mayonnaise
¼ cup chopped onion
2 Tablespoons chopped black olives

Trim crusts from bread. Cut each slice into 4 squares and lightly toast. Combine cheese, mushrooms, pepperoni, mayonnaise, onion and olives in bowl and mix well. Spread mixture on toasted bread squares, spreading out to edges. Broil 3 inches from heat until cheese melts. Makes 16.

Pam Cole

Burgundy Beef Balls

Meatballs:

1 pound lean ground beef
1½ cups red Burgundy wine, divided
1 cup bread crumbs
3 Tablespoons minced onion
1 egg
1 teaspoon dry mustard
1 teaspoon salt
½ teaspoon thyme
¼ teaspoon freshly ground pepper
12 strips thin-sliced bacon

Mustard Mayonnaise:

¼ cup Dijon mustard
¼ cup mayonnaise
1 teaspoon Worcestershire sauce

Meatballs:

Combine ground beef, 1 cup wine, bread crumbs, onion, egg, mustard, salt, thyme and pepper in large bowl, and mix well. Shape into 24 small balls. Cut bacon strips in half crosswise; wrap strips around meatballs, and secure with toothpick. Bake in jelly roll pan at 375°F for 20 to 25 minutes. Drain on paper towels. Serve in chafing dish; add ½ cup wine to prevent drying. Serve with mustard mayonnaise. Makes 24 meatballs.

Mustard Mayonnaise:

Combine mustard, mayonnaise and Worcestershire sauce. Mix well. Makes ½ cup.

Frances Benton

Meat Balls

Meat Balls:

2 pounds ground chuck
1 cup corn flake crumbs
⅓ cup ketchup
⅓ cup minced parsley
2 eggs
2 Tablespoons minced onion
2 Tablespoons Kikkoman soy sauce
½ teaspoon garlic powder
¼ teaspoon freshly ground pepper

Meat Balls:

Combine ground chuck, cornflake crumbs, ketchup, parsley, eggs, onion, soy sauce, garlic powder and pepper in large bowl. Shape into 48 meatballs. Place in single layer in jelly roll pan and bake at 350°F for 30 minutes. While meat balls are cooking make sauce.

Sauce:

1 (1 pound) can whole cranberry sauce
1 (12 ounce) bottle chili sauce
2 Tablespoons brown sugar
1 Tablespoon lemon juice

Sauce:

Combine cranberry sauce, chili sauce, brown sugar and lemon juice in saucepan. Melt over low heat. Pour over meatballs and bake at 350°F for another 30 minutes. Makes 48.

Mrs. Kevin Price

Toasted Ravioli

½ cup milk
2 eggs, beaten
24 frozen bite size ravioli
½ cup seasoned bread crumbs
Oil
½ cup freshly grated Parmesan cheese

Combine milk and eggs. Dip ravioli into egg mixture and dredge in bread crumbs. Deep fry in 350°F oil until they are brown and rise to top, about 3 to 4 minutes. Remove from oil and sprinkle liberally with cheese. Serve immediately. Makes 24.

Al's Restaurant

Pâté

2 pounds pork or chicken livers
1⅓ cups heavy cream
½ cup cognac
3 eggs
⅔ cup pork or chicken fat, diced
1 onion, chopped
½ cup flour
3 teaspoons salt
1½ teaspoons white pepper
1 teaspoon MSG
1 teaspoon ground ginger
1 teaspoon allspice
1 Tablespoon rendered pork or chicken fat

Purée livers, cream, cognac and eggs in food processor or blender. Gradually add fat, chopped onion and flour; blend until finely puréed. Add salt, pepper, MSG, ginger and allspice; blend until mixed. Pour mixture into 3-quart mold or several smaller molds which have been greased with rendered pork or chicken fat; lay a piece of greased aluminum foil over top. Place mold in pan of water; bake at 325°F for 2 to 2½ hours. Makes 2 quarts.

Lynn Springer

Sukiyaki Skewers

⅓ cup Kikkoman soy sauce
¼ cup sugar
1 teaspoon freshly grated ginger or ¼ teaspoon powdered ginger
1 pound sirloin tip roast, cut in thin strips
½ pound fresh green beans
4 large carrots, cut into 3-inch sticks
Melted butter

Combine soy sauce, sugar and ginger in baking dish. Add meat and let stand 2 hours. Cook beans and carrots until barely tender. Wrap half the meat strips around bundles of 3 or 4 beans; wrap other half around bundles of 3 or 4 carrot sticks. Thread on 2 parallel skewers, ladder fashion. Brush with melted butter. Broil for 5 minutes, turning once. Makes 20.

Pam Cole

Diablotins

½ pound bleu cheese
½ cup butter
1 cup chopped pecans
1 loaf small diameter French bread

Mix bleu cheese and butter together until smooth. Stir in pecans. Slice bread into thin slices and toast on one side. Spread bleu cheese mixture on untoasted sides. Broil until mixture melts and browns lightly.

William G. Zibart

Pot Stickers

Filling:
1¾ pounds lean ground beef
1½ cups water
¼ cup Kikkoman soy sauce
2 Tablespoons sesame oil
½ teaspoon salt
7 green onions, minced
2 Tablespoons very finely chopped fresh ginger
½ pound fresh mushrooms, chopped
½ pound bamboo shoots, chopped
Finely chopped celery and/or finely chopped onions (amount optional)

Filling:
Put beef in large bowl and stir in water until well combined. Add soy sauce, sesame oil and salt; mix well. Add green onions and ginger, mixing lightly. Fold in mushrooms, bamboo shoots and celery or onions.

Dough:
3 cups flour
1 cup water

Dough:
Combine flour and water in bowl and work together with hands. Dough will be very stiff. Cover and set in warm, draft-free place for 1 hour. Work ¼ of dough at a time. Keep rest covered with a damp towel. Roll into sausage-like stick. Cut off pieces about 1½ inches long, dust with flour and shape into balls. Flatten, then roll into thin circles about 4 inches in diameter. Place circle in palm of hand and spread 2 teaspoons filling in center. Fold over to form semi-circle; pinch edges together with thumb and forefinger.

Pot Stickers

Frying:

Vegetable oil
1 cup water
Kikkoman soy sauce (optional)
White vinegar (optional)

Frying:
Heat wok. Add just enough oil to cover bottom. Place pot stickers along sides of bottom. Add water, cover wok and steam for about 7 minutes. The water will disappear after 5 minutes; reduce heat to prevent bottom from burning. Remove pot stickers from pan with spatula. Sprinkle with mixture of soy sauce and vinegar, if desired. Makes about 40.

John Pei
Yen Ching Restaurant

Cantonese Chicken Wings

1 cup sugar
1 cup water
1 cup Kikkoman soy sauce
½ cup pineapple juice
¼ cup vegetable oil
1 teaspoon ginger
1 teaspoon garlic powder
4 pounds chicken wings, tips removed

Combine sugar, water, soy sauce, pineapple juice, oil, ginger and garlic powder and stir until sugar is dissolved. Put chicken wings in large bowl, pour marinade over, cover and marinate 24 hours, basting occasionally. Bake at 350°F for 45 minutes or until brown. Makes 36 to 40.

Patti Lewis

Bouillabaisse Bites

24 medium shrimp, peeled and deveined
24 medium sea scallops
2 cups tomato sauce
1 (6½ ounce) can minced clams
1 Tablespoon Pernod
2 cloves garlic, minced
1 bay leaf
1 teaspoon basil
1 teaspoon salt
½ teaspoon freshly ground pepper
Pinch saffron

Skewer shrimp and scallops on 8-inch bamboo skewers, using 1 shrimp and 1 scallop per skewer; wrap tail of shrimp around scallop. Mix tomato sauce, clams, Pernod, garlic, bay leaf, basil, salt, pepper and saffron together in sauce pan. Bring mixture to gentle simmer and cook 20 minutes. Arrange skewered fish in shallow baking dish. Drizzle sauce over skewers. Bake, uncovered, at 350°F for 25 minutes. Makes 24.

Lawrence Fulton

Clam Dip

½ cup butter
1 medium onion, minced
1 clove garlic, minced
1 teaspoon chopped parsley
1 teaspoon oregano
½ cup Italian bread crumbs
2 (6½ ounce) cans minced clams, drained
Juice from one can of clams
1 teaspoon lemon juice
Dash Tabasco
¼ pound Mozzarella cheese, grated
2 Tablespoons Parmesan cheese

Melt butter in deep skillet and sauté onion and garlic for a few minutes. Add parsley and oregano. Slowly stir in bread crumbs, clams, clam juice, lemon juice and Tabasco. Pour mixture into 1½-quart greased baking dish. Fold in Mozzarella cheese and sprinkle with Parmesan cheese. Bake at 350°F for 20 to 25 minutes. Makes 4 cups.

Lynn Hill

Clams Dimaggio

4 slices bacon
½ cup Italian bread crumbs
¼ cup freshly grated Parmesan cheese
¼ cup butter, melted
¼ cup Vermouth
2 Tablespoons heavy cream
1 Tablespoon chopped onion
1 Tablespoon chopped green pepper
2 teaspoons lemon juice
1 clove garlic, minced
½ teaspoon oregano
¼ teaspoon salt
⅛ teaspoon freshly ground pepper
2 dashes Tabasco
1 (8 ounce) can minced clams, drained
1 (6 ounce) can crabmeat, drained

Cut each bacon slice in 4 pieces; cook until half done. Mix bread crumbs, cheese, butter, Vermouth, cream, onion, green pepper, lemon juice, garlic, oregano, salt, pepper and Tabasco in large saucepan. Blend in clams and crabmeat. Cook 5 minutes. Spoon mixture into 2-inch scallop shells. Place a piece of bacon on top of each. Set on baking sheet and broil 2 minutes until hot and bacon is crisp. Makes 16.

Pat Schoeffel

Mushroom and Crab Eleganté

1 pound fresh mushrooms, sliced
Butter
1 (8 ounce) package cream cheese
1 (6 ounce) can Alaskan king crab
3 chopped green onions
1 teaspoon Kikkoman soy sauce
½ teaspoon lemon juice

Sauté mushrooms in butter. Heat sautéed mushrooms, cream cheese, crab, onions, soy sauce and lemon juice together in top of double boiler. Serve in chafing dish with crackers. Serves 6 to 8.

Sarah Duncan

Crab Rangoon

½ cup chopped green onions
3 Tablespoons butter
2 (8 ounce) packages cream cheese
2 (6 ounce) cans crabmeat
¼ cup light cream
½ teaspoon Chinese five spice powder
⅛ teaspoon garlic powder
1 (1 pound) package won ton skins
2 cups vegetable oil
Bottled sweet and sour sauce

Sauté green onions in butter. Stir in cream cheese, crabmeat and cream. Cook until cheese is melted. Add five spice powder and garlic powder. Place 1 Tablespoon crab mixture in center of won ton skin. With a drop of water on fingertip, pinch together east and west corners. Bring southern tip up to meet east and west corners in center. Heat 1 inch oil in skillet to 375°F. Pick up won ton skin by northern tip and drop into oil. Turn over in about 1 minute. Fry until golden. Remove with a slotted spoon and drain on paper towels. Serve at room temperature with sweet and sour sauce. Makes about 6 dozen.

Mrs. W. Lynton Edwards III

Curried Shrimp and Cheese Canapés

4 ounces shrimp, cooked, peeled deveined and chopped
1 (3 ounce) package cream cheese, softened
½ cup grated Cheddar cheese
½ cup freshly grated Parmesan cheese
½ cup mayonnaise
2 Tablespoons grated onion
2 Tablespoons snipped chives
1 teaspoon curry powder
1 loaf narrow French bread
Minced fresh parsley

Combine shrimp, cream cheese, Cheddar cheese, Parmesan cheese, mayonnaise, onion, chives and curry powder and mix well. Cut bread into ½-inch slices and toast on one side. Spread shrimp mixture on untoasted side of slices, put on large cookie sheet and broil until shrimp mixture is heated through. Spirnkle with parsley. Makes 48.

Anne Leopold

Deviled Stuffed Mushrooms

1 pound large fresh mushrooms
1 (4½ ounce) can deviled ham
¾ cup grated Swiss cheese
1 Tablespoon mayonnaise
1 Tablespoon onion soup mix
1 teaspoon prepared mustard
Splash white wine
Minced parsley

Remove stems from mushrooms. Chop stems and combine with deviled ham, cheese, mayonnaise, onion soup mix, mustard and wine. Spoon mixture into mushroom caps, filling until rounded. Sprinkle with parsley. Broil 5 minutes or until tops are bubbly. Makes about 25.

Mrs. W. Lynton Edwards III

Shrimp Appetizer Quiches

1 (8 ounce) package extra light flaky buttermilk biscuits
1 cup small cooked shrimp
1 egg
½ cup heavy cream
2 Tablespoons minced green onion
½ teaspoon salt
¼ teaspoon dill weed
⅛ teaspoon cayenne
½ cup grated Swiss cheese

Separate biscuits into 24 equal pieces. Press into generously greased 1¾-inch muffin tins. Divide shrimp equally into tins. Beat egg, cream, onion, salt, dill and cayenne together until well blended. Pour 2 teaspoons mixture over each tin. Sprinkle cheese over tops. Bake at 375°F for 20 minutes or until edges are brown and centers appear set. Cool 5 minutes. Serve warm. Makes 24.

Gwen Rosenfeld

Deep-fried Asparagus

2 cups sifted flour
Salt
¼ teaspoon freshly ground pepper
⅓ cup olive oil
1½ cups lukewarm water
5 dozen fresh asparagus spears
3 egg whites
Shortening for deep frying

Sift flour and 1 teaspoon salt into large mixing bowl. Add pepper. Gradually beat in oil and water with wire whisk. Beat until mixture is smooth and as thick as heavy cream. Set mixture aside at room temperature for 2 hours. Peel and trim asparagus spears. Boil asparagus in large amount of rapidly boiling water for 2 minutes. Drain immediately and rinse with cold water. Drain very well; pat asparagus dry with paper towels. Set aside until completely cool. After 2 hours, beat egg whites with a pinch of salt until stiff. Fold whites into batter. Heat shortening in deep fryer to 370°F on a frying thermometer. Dip asparagus spears into batter and fry, a few at a time, until golden brown. Turn asparagus to brown on all sides. Drain asparagus on paper towels. Cool completely. Wrap asparagus, in one layer, in foil. Refrigerate until 15 minutes before serving. Place asparagus on jelly roll pan. Bake at 400°F until asparagus is hot and crisp, about 10 minutes. Sprinkle with salt and serve immediately. Makes 5 dozen.

Susan Katzman

Salmon Snappers

10 1-inch slices day-old French bread
1 (6½ ounce) can salmon, drained
3 Tablespoons minced onion
1 egg yolk
½ teaspoon salt
¼ teaspoon freshly ground pepper
Oil

Remove crusts from bread, and cut each slice into 4 squares. With a sharp knife, cut a pocket in each. Mix salmon, onion, egg yolk, salt and pepper until well blended. Place a scant teaspoon of salmon mixture inside each square; secure with toothpick. Fry in deep hot oil until golden brown. Drain. Makes 40.

Lucyanne Mueller Boston

Mushroom Turnovers

Dough:

1 (8 ounce) package cream cheese, softened

½ cup butter

1½ cups flour

1 teaspoon salt

Dough:

Cream butter and cream cheese. Blend in flour and salt. Wrap in wax paper. Chill at least 1 hour. Roll dough ⅛ inch thick and cut into 3-inch rounds. Put ½ teaspoon filling on each round and fold in half. Brush edge of dough with water and seal with a fork. Prick top of crust. Place on lightly greased cookie sheet and bake at 400°F for 20 minutes. Makes 36.

Filling:

¼ pound fresh mushrooms, finely chopped

2 Tablespoons finely chopped onion

Butter

1½ Tablespoons flour

¼ teaspoon salt

⅛ teaspoon freshly ground pepper

⅛ teaspoon thyme

½ cup sour cream

Filling:

Sauté mushrooms and onion in butter for 5 minutes. Add flour, salt, pepper and thyme; blend well. Stir in sour cream. Chill at least 1 hour.

Carolyn Grand

Spiedini

1 loaf French bread, trimmed and sliced into 16 ¾-inch slices

12 ½-inch thick squares of Mozzarella cheese, same size as bread

½ cup unsalted butter

1 (2 ounce) can anchovy fillets

Skewer bread and cheese alternately on wooden skewers beginning and ending with bread, using 4 slices of bread and 3 slices of cheese per skewer. Place on cookie sheet and bake at 350°F for 15 minutes or until bread is toasty and cheese begins to melt. Meanwhile, melt butter in small saucepan. Mash the anchovies and add to butter. Simmer a few minutes. Pour mixture over skewers and serve immediately. Serves 4.

Paula Norris

Ratatouille in Raw Mushroom Caps

1 unpeeled medium eggplant, coarsely chopped
1 pound zucchini, coarsely chopped
1 Tablespoon salt
6 Tablespoons oil, divided
1 teaspoon thyme
½ teaspoon ground coriander
Pinch cumin
2 cups finely minced onion
¾ cup peeled, seeded and chopped tomatoes
¾ cup seeded and chopped green or red peppers
2 cloves garlic, minced
Pinch sugar
⅓ cup minced parsley, divided
½ teaspoon basil
Salt and freshly ground pepper to taste
50 large firm fresh mushrooms, stems removed

Place eggplant and zucchini in colander and sprinkle with salt; let stand 30 minutes to drain. Rinse and pat dry with paper towels. Heat 3 tablespoons oil in large skillet over high heat. Add eggplant and zucchini and sauté 1 minute. Cover and cook for 3 minutes, shaking pan several times until vegetables are steamed through. Add thyme, coriander and cumin and blend well. Remove from skillet and set aside. Heat 3 Tablespoons oil in skillet. Add onion and sauté until soft. Add tomatoes, peppers, garlic and sugar. Cover and cook 5 minutes, shaking pan frequently. Remove lid and cook until liquid has evaporated. Return eggplant and zucchini to skillet with 2 Tablespoons parsley, basil, salt and pepper. Put in greased 1½-quart baking dish. Bake at 350°F for 40 minutes. Pour off any excess liquid. Fill each mushroom cap with 1½ Tablespoons of ratatouille. Sprinkle with remaining parsley. Serve warm or at room temperature. Makes 50.

Ann Garrett

Cheese Wafers

3 cups grated Cheddar cheese
1½ cups butter
3 cups flour
1½ teaspoons salt
1 teaspoon cayenne
2 cups Rice Krispies

Blend cheese and butter. Combine flour, salt and cayenne. Slowly add to cheese mixture. Blend in Rice Krispies. Roll into nickel-sized balls; flatten to ¼-inch. Bake on ungreased cookie sheet at 350°F for 15 minutes. Cool on wire rack. Makes 4 dozen.

Maureen Cobb

Soups

Chilled Strawberry Soup

1 quart fresh strawberries, washed and hulled
1 cup orange juice
1¼ teaspoons instant tapioca
⅛ teaspoon allspice
⅛ teaspoon cinnamon
1 cup buttermilk
½ cup sugar
1 Tablespoon fresh lemon juice
1 teaspoon grated fresh lemon rind

Set aside 6 strawberries. Purée remaining strawberries in food processor or blender; strain into large saucepan. Add orange juice. Mix tapioca with ¼ cup strawberry mixture. Add to saucepan with allspice and cinnamon. Heat, stirring constantly, until mixture comes to a boil. Cook 1 minute, or until thickened. Pour soup into a large bowl. Add buttermilk, sugar, lemon juice and lemon rind and blend well. Slice reserved strawberries and fold into soup. Cover and chill at least 8 hours. Serves 4.

Janet Zimmerman

Southern Style Corn Chowder

2 ounces lean salt pork, diced
½ cup unsalted butter, divided
3 large onions, chopped
1 large green pepper, seeded and diced
8 medium potatoes, peeled and diced
4 cups milk
2 cups heavy cream
5 cups fresh corn kernels, or frozen kernels, cooked until tender
¼ cup minced fresh parsley
Salt and freshly ground pepper to taste
Freshly grated nutmeg
Crisp-cooked bacon, crumbled (garnish)

Cook salt pork in large skillet over low heat until 2 Tablespoons fat have been rendered. Remove any remaining solid pork. Add 2 Tablespoons butter to skillet and melt. Increase heat to medium, add onion and sauté until golden. Add green pepper and sauté briefly until just tender. Remove from heat. Cook potatoes in boiling salted water to cover until potatoes are tender but still hold their shape. Drain well. Combine milk and cream in large saucepan and heat slowly. Add onions, green pepper, potatoes, corn, parsley, salt, pepper and nutmeg. Bring just to simmer, then remove from heat and let stand at least 3 hours to cool and thicken. Just before serving, reheat soup slowly. Carefully stir in remaining butter. Pass bacon separately to garnish. Serves 8 to 12.

Jean McDermott

Hearty Clam Chowder

4 slices bacon, cut in small pieces
3 green onions and tops, chopped
1 carrot, finely chopped
1 stalk celery, thinly sliced
2 Tablespoons chopped green pepper
1 clove garlic, minced
5 medium potatoes, peeled and cut in ½-inch cubes
2 cups water
1 teaspoon Worcestershire sauce
1 teaspoon salt
½ teaspoon freshly ground pepper
½ teaspoon thyme
4 drops Tabasco
2 (8 ounce) cans minced clams, undrained
2 cups light cream

Sauté bacon until crisp in large soup pot. Drain bacon; pour off all but 1 Tablespoon fat. Add green onions and tops, carrot, celery, green pepper and garlic. Sauté briefly until soft. Add potatoes, pour in water and season with Worcestershire sauce, salt, pepper, thyme and Tabasco. Cover pan and simmer 15 minutes, or until potatoes are tender. Mash mixture slightly with a potato masher. Add clams and cream. Stir well. Heat until piping hot, but do not boil. Serves 4 to 6.

Carlin Sachar

Blender Cream of Avocado Soup

1 ripe avocado
1½ cups chicken broth
1½ Tablespoons lemon juice
1 cup light cream
Salt and freshly ground pepper to taste
1 or 2 dashes cayenne
Lemon slices (garnish)

Put pulp of avocado in blender container. Add broth and lemon juice. Blend until puréed. Add cream, salt, pepper and cayenne. Mix well. Chill. Garnish with lemon slices. Serves 4.

Betty Fendel

Mushroom Soup

1 pound fresh mushrooms, cleaned and sliced
3 Tablespoons butter
2 Tablespoons flour
4 cups chicken stock
¼ cup dry sherry

Place mushrooms in soup pot without water or oil. Cover and cook over very low heat about 15 minutes until only a small amount of mushroom liquid remains. Add butter, and when melted, sprinkle with flour. Cook, stirring, for a few minutes longer. Slowly add chicken stock, stirring constantly. Simmer 10 minutes. Remove mushrooms with slotted spoon. Reserve ½ cup of the cooked mushrooms and put rest in a blender or food processor. Add sherry, blending until smooth. If needed, add ¼ cup of soup liquid to achieve a smooth purée. Stir puréed mushrooms into soup and return reserved sliced mushrooms to pot. Reheat. Serves 6.

Fran DeGere

Cold Mint-Cucumber Soup

3 Tablespoons butter
1 medium onion, chopped
1 clove garlic, minced
3 medium cucumbers, peeled, seeded and thinly sliced
3 Tablespoons flour
2 cups chicken broth
2 Tablespoons finely chopped fresh mint
1 cup half and half
1 cup yogurt
Salt and freshly ground white pepper to taste
Thin cucumber slices (garnish)

Melt butter in large skillet over medium heat. Add onion and garlic and sauté until limp but not brown. Add sliced cucumbers and cook slowly until soft. Remove from heat. Stir in flour, then broth, blending well. Place over medium high heat and bring to a boil. Reduce heat and simmer 5 minutes. Add mint. Transfer to processor or blender in batches and purée. Pour in bowl, cover and chill well. Just before serving, combine half and half and yogurt and stir into soup, mixing well. Add salt and pepper. Garnish with sliced cucumber. Serves 4 to 6.

Randolf-Skage Caterers

Curried Asparagus Soup

1 pound fresh asparagus
6 cups chicken stock
¼ cup butter
3 Tablespoons flour
3 egg yolks
1 cup heavy cream
1 teaspoon curry powder
Salt and freshly ground white pepper to taste

Remove and discard woody ends from asparagus stalks. Scrape spears with vegetable peeler. Cut off tips and reserve. Dice stalks and combine with stock in 4-quart saucepan. Bring to boil and cook, uncovered, 10 minutes or until very tender. Cool, then purée in blender or food processor. Set aside. Melt butter over low heat in 4-quart saucepan. Add flour and cook, stirring constantly, 2 to 3 minutes. Stir in purée and bring to boil over medium heat. Add asparagus tips. Cover and simmer 10 minutes or until tips are tender. Combine yolks, cream and curry thoroughly with whisk. Add to soup and heat through, but do not boil. Add salt and pepper. Serves 6 to 8.

Ally D'Arly

Carrot-Yogurt Soup

1 pound carrots, peeled
3 to 4 cups chicken broth
Salt to taste
1 onion, minced
2 Tablespoons butter
1½ Tablespoons curry powder
1½ cups yogurt or sour cream
Freshly ground pepper to taste
Minced parsley (garnish)

Cut carrots into 1-inch pieces and put into saucepan with 3 cups chicken broth. Add salt and cook over moderate heat until tender. Drain carrots and reserve broth. Sauté onion in butter until soft. Stir in curry powder and cook for 2 minutes. Purée carrots and onion mixture in blender. Put purée and reserved chicken broth in saucepan. Add more broth if necessary to make 3 cups. Simmer for 5 minutes. Add yogurt or sour cream gradually while stirrring. Do not let soup boil. Season with pepper. Sprinkle with parsley. Can be served hot or cold. Serves 6.

Priscilla Allen

Zucchini Soup

1 Tablespoon butter
1 Tablespoon vegetable oil
1 small onion, chopped
6 cups chicken stock or broth
6 medium zucchini, sliced
1 sprig fresh basil or thyme
White pepper to taste
Lemon wedges and/or yogurt (garnish)

Heat butter and oil in medium skillet. Add onion and sauté until soft. Add chicken stock, zucchini and basil or thyme; simmer 10 minutes, stirring occasionally. Transfer to blender in batches and purée. Season with pepper and reheat or chill. Garnish with lemon wedges and/or yogurt. Serves 6.

Iris Terrace

Broiled Tomato Soup

½ cup butter
2 Tablespoons olive oil
1 large onion, thinly sliced
1 teaspoon fresh dill
1 teaspoon fresh thyme
1 teaspoon fresh basil
8 medium tomatoes, peeled and cut into chunks
3 Tablespoons tomato paste
3¾ cups chicken broth, divided
¼ cup flour
2 teaspoons sugar
1½ teaspoons salt
¼ teaspoon freshly ground pepper
1 cup heavy cream
½ cup freshly grated Parmesan cheese
Freshly grated Parmesan cheese

Combine butter, oil, onion, dill, thyme and basil in 5-quart saucepan over medium-low heat. Cook, stirring occasionally, until onion is softened and golden. Add tomatoes and tomato paste and simmer 10 minutes, stirring occasionally. Blend flour and ½ cup chicken broth in small bowl; stir until flour dissolves. Add to tomato mixture with remaining broth. Increase heat to high and bring mixture to just below boiling point; reduce heat and simmer 25 minutes, stirring frequently. Remove soup in batches to blender or food processor and purée. Return soup to saucepan and reheat slowly. Whip cream until stiff and fold in ½ cup Parmesan cheese. Ladle hot soup into individual bowls or large broilerproof casserole and dollop whipped cream over top. Sprinkle with additional cheese and broil 6 inches from preheated broiler for 30 to 60 seconds. Watch carefully to make sure cream does not burn. Serve immediately. Serves 6.

Susan Gardner

Hot Scallop Kettle Soup

1 pound fresh bay scallops
¼ cup butter
¼ pound fresh mushrooms, sliced
1 small onion, chopped
1 large stalk celery, chopped
½ large carrot, chopped
2 Tablespoons minced parsley
½ cup red wine
¼ to ½ cup brandy
1 (8 ounce) can tomatoes, undrained, chopped
2 Tablespoons dry bread crumbs
Salt and freshly ground pepper to taste
Pinch cayenne
French bread
Butter

Wash scallops in cold water and dry completely. Melt butter in large saucepan over medium heat and add mushrooms, onion, celery, carrot and parsley. Sauté, stirring frequently, until onions are yellow. Add scallops, wine and heated brandy. Set ablaze. When flames subside, add tomatoes. Cover and simmer slowly for 5 to 7 minutes. Stir in bread crumbs. Add salt, pepper and cayenne. Serve with, or on, slices of French bread sautéed in butter. Serves 4.

Suzy Wahl

Beef Gulyas Soup

4 slices bacon
1 cup chopped onions
2 cloves garlic, minced
1½ Tablespoons paprika
2 teaspoons salt
1 (2 pound) boneless beef pot roast, cut into 1-inch cubes
2 cups water
1 (6 ounce) can tomato paste
3 medium potatoes, peeled and finely chopped
Sour cream and chopped green onion (garnish)

Cook bacon until crisp in 4-quart Dutch oven. Drain and crumble bacon, reserving drippings. Cook onion and garlic in drippings until onion is tender but not brown. Stir in paprika and salt. Add meat and bacon; cook, stirring over low heat 2 to 3 minutes. Add water and tomato paste. Cover and simmer over low heat 1½ hours. Add potatoes. Continue cooking slowly about 20 minutes or until potatoes are tender. Skim off excess fat. Serve hot topped with sour cream and green onions. Serves 6.

Marilyn Steinbrecher

Blender Tomato Soup

2 (1 pound) cans plum tomatoes
1 strip orange peel
½ small dried hot chili pepper
⅛ teaspoon ground cumin
Salt and freshly ground pepper to taste
Chopped green onions or chives (garnish)

Put tomatoes, orange peel, chili pepper, cumin, salt and pepper in blender. Blend until puréed. Chill. Garnish with green onions or chives. Serves 4.

Beth Standish

Black Bean Soup

Soup:

1 pound black beans
8 cups water
1½ Tablespoons salt
5 cloves garlic, crushed
2 Tablespoons vinegar
1½ teaspoons cumin
1½ teaspoons oregano
Vegetable oil
1 large onion, chopped
1 large green pepper, chopped

Marinade:

1 cup cooked rice
2 Tablespoons finely chopped onion
2 Tablespoons vinegar
1 Tablespoon olive oil

Soup:

In 5-quart saucepan, soak beans in water overnight. Drain and rinse. Add 2 quarts water to beans with salt. Bring to a boil, cover and simmer until soft, about 1½ hours. Combine garlic, vinegar, cumin and oregano in small bowl. Heat oil in skillet and sauté onion and pepper until onions are lightly browned. Stir in garlic mixture and sauté 1 to 2 minutes more. Add to beans, cover and simmer about 1 hour. Transfer about half the soup to blender; purée and return to pot. Serves 6 to 8.

Marinade:

Combine rice, onion, vinegar and oil in small bowl. Cover and marinate 2 to 3 hours at room temperature. Add a generous tablespoon rice mixture to each serving.

Kathi Cywinski

Snappy Tomato Consommé

3 cups tomato juice
1½ cups beef bouillon
2 Tablespoons lemon juice
2 (5-inch) pieces celery
1 bay leaf
1 teaspoon Worcestershire sauce
½ teaspoon sugar
½ teaspoon grated fresh lemon rind
¼ teaspoon fresh thyme
Tabasco to taste
Lemon slices (garnish)

Combine tomato juice, bouillon, lemon juice, celery, bay leaf, Worcestershire sauce, sugar, lemon rind, thyme and Tabasco and bring to a boil. Reduce heat and simmer 2 to 3 minutes. Remove celery and bay leaf. Garnish with lemon slices. Serves 4.

Virginia Pepper

Cold Artichoke Soup

1 (10½ ounce) can water packed artichoke hearts, drained
1½ cups chicken stock
¼ to ½ teaspoon oregano
2 Tablespoons fresh lemon juice
½ teaspoon salt
½ teaspoon chicken stock base
½ cup half and half
½ cup heavy cream
Thinly sliced lemons and/or chives (garnish)

Purée artichoke hearts, chicken stock and oregano in blender. Pour into saucepan; heat slowly. Add lemon juice, salt and chicken stock base. Stir in half and half and cream. Cool and chill. Garnish with lemons and/or chives. Serves 4.

Mrs. Richard D. Davis

Mulligatawney Soup

1 (2 to 3 pound) chicken
10 cups water
1 carrot
1 onion, chopped
1 stalk celery
1 Tablespoon salt
4 peppercorns
1 (1 pound) can tomatoes, undrained, cut up
2 carrots, finely chopped
1 onion, finely chopped
3 stalks celery, finely chopped
5 sprigs parsley, minced
½ cup uncooked rice
2 Tablespoons tomato paste
1 Tablespoon flour
1 Tablespoon curry powder
2 cloves garlic, minced
1 bay leaf
Salt and freshly ground pepper to taste
1 apple, peeled, finely chopped

Cook chicken with water, 1 carrot, 1 onion, 1 stalk celery, 1 Tablespoon salt and 4 peppercorns in soup pot until tender, about 1 hour. Remove chicken and reserve stock. Shred cooled chicken from bones. Put 2 quarts broth, tomatoes, chopped carrots, chopped onion, chopped celery and parsley in soup pot; bring to boil. Add rice, tomato paste, flour, curry powder, garlic, bay leaf, salt and pepper. Cook about 15 minutes. Add chicken and apple and cook 15 minutes. Remove bay leaf and adjust seasonings. Serves 8.

Phyl Maxwell

Cold Almond Soup

4 cups chicken broth
2 cups heavy cream
8 ounces blanched almonds, ground
Salt and pepper to taste
1 cup sour cream

Combine broth and cream in a saucepan and heat to not quite a boil. Whisk in almonds and heat to a simmer. Simmer 5 minutes. Remove from heat, add salt and pepper and cool to room temperature. Whisk in sour cream and refrigerate. Serves 6.

Diane Thomson

Mushroom Soup with Parmesan Cheese

1 Tablespoon butter
1 Tablespoon olive oil
1 medium onion, grated
1 clove garlic, minced
1 pound fresh mushroom caps, thinly sliced
3 Tablespoons tomato paste
3 cups chicken stock
2 Tablespoons sweet vermouth
½ teaspoon salt
Dash freshly ground pepper
4 (1-inch thick) slices Italian bread
Butter
4 egg yolks
2½ Tablespoons freshly grated Parmesan cheese
2 Tablespoons finely chopped parsley

Melt butter and olive oil in a large saucepan. Sauté onion and garlic. Stir in mushrooms; sauté 5 minutes and add tomato paste. Mix well and add chicken stock. Stir and add vermouth. Add salt and pepper. Simmer for 10 minutes. Butter bread slices and toast on one side under broiler. Beat together egg yolks, cheese and parsley. Beat egg mixture into boiling soup. Place a slice of bread in each bowl and add soup. Serves 4.

Pam Cole

Spinach Soup

6 cups chicken broth
2 cups cooked fresh spinach or 3 (10 ounce) packages frozen spinach, cooked
2 Tablespoons butter, softened
2 Tablespoons flour
½ teaspoon nutmeg
½ teaspoon salt
¼ teaspoon freshly ground pepper
¼ teaspoon garlic powder
Sour cream or yogurt (garnish)

Purée 2 cups broth and all the spinach in a blender or food processor. Put in a 4-quart saucepan. Purée remaining broth, butter, flour and nutmeg. Add to spinach mixture and bring to a boil, stirring constantly. Add salt, pepper and garlic powder. Simmer for 10 minutes. Serve hot, topped with small dollop of sour cream or yogurt. Serves 8.

Ann McReynolds Edwards

Cream of Broccoli Soup

⅓ cup butter
1 cup wine
2 cups chopped broccoli
⅔ cup chopped onion
⅔ cup chopped celery
⅓ cup flour
6 cups chicken broth
½ teaspoon salt
½ teaspoon freshly ground pepper
¼ teaspoon crushed thyme
2 cups light cream

Melt butter in 4-quart saucepan. Add wine, broccoli, onion and celery. Cook for 5 minutes over low heat. Blend in flour and chicken broth. Bring to a boil. Add salt, pepper and thyme. Simmer about 5 minutes until vegetables are tender. Remove 2 cups at a time and blend in a blender. Add cream and reheat until hot. Serves 12.

Nan Blandin Fisher

Portuguese Soup

2 cups chopped onions
6 cloves garlic, chopped
6 Tablespoons vegetable oil
1 pound garlic flavored, smoked pork sausage, cut into bite-sized pieces
10 cups beef stock
1 head green cabbage, cored and chopped into medium pieces
12 small new potatoes, scrubbed and quartered
1 (1 pound) can kidney beans, undrained
1 (1 pound) bottle ketchup
½ cup vinegar
Salt and freshly ground pepper to taste

Sauté onions and garlic in oil until transparent. Add sausage slices and brown lightly. Add stock, cabbage, potatoes, kidney beans, ketchup, vinegar, salt and pepper. Bring soup to boil, stirring frequently. Reduce heat; simmer for 35 to 45 minutes, stirring occasionally. Serves 8 to 10.

Marilyn Steinbrecher

Velvet Corn Soup

¼ cup butter
¼ cup finely chopped onion
3 cups fresh or frozen corn
4 cups half and half
1 egg, beaten
1¼ teaspoons salt
½ teaspoon white pepper

Melt butter, add onion and sauté until soft but not brown. Add corn and cook for 5 minutes; do not brown. Add half and half and egg. Cook, stirring constantly, until mixture begins to boil, about 3 minutes. Add salt and pepper. Cool slightly, put in a blender and blend until creamy. Strain and reheat. May also be served cold. Serves 8.

Helen Herber

Cream of Cauliflower Soup

2 Tablespoons vegetable oil
½ cup chopped onion
1 small carrot, peeled and grated
1 cup chopped celery
1 (1 pound) head cauliflower, cut into florets
2 Tablespoons chopped parsley, divided
8 cups chicken stock
Bouquet garni (1 teaspoon tarragon, ½ teaspoon pepper corns, ½ bay leaf tied in cheesecloth)
¼ cup butter
¾ cup flour
2 cups milk
1 cup half and half
1 Tablespoon salt
1 cup sour cream

Heat oil in 8-quart stock pot over medium heat. Add onion and sauté until transparent, stirring frequently. Add carrot and celery and cook 2 minutes, stirring frequently. Add cauliflower and 1 Tablespoon parsley. Cover, reduce heat to low and cook 15 minutes, stirring occasionally. Add chicken stock and bouquet garni and bring to boil over medium heat. Reduce heat and simmer 5 minutes. Melt butter in 2-quart saucepan. Stir in flour to make a roux. Slowly add milk, whisking constantly to blend. Bring mixture to boil over medium heat, stirring frequently, until mixture is thick and smooth. Remove from heat and stir in half and half. Stir into simmering soup. Add salt and simmer gently for 15 to 20 minutes. Just before serving, remove bouquet garni; mix a few Tablespoons soup with sour cream. Stir sour cream mixture into soup. Add remaining parsley. Reheat and serve. Serves 8 to 10.

Dot McCleary

German Potato Soup

7 slices lean bacon, diced
3 large onions, finely chopped
6 fresh mushrooms, finely chopped
4½ Tablespoons flour
9 cups beef bouillon
6 large potatoes, peeled and sliced very thin
3 egg yolks
1½ cups sour cream
2 Tablespoons minced parsley

Sauté bacon in deep kettle until crisp. Stir in onions and mushrooms, and sauté until vegetables are soft, about 5 minutes. Blend in flour and gradually add bouillon, stirring constantly. Add potatoes and simmer for 1 hour. Beat egg yolks and mix with sour cream. Stir ½ cup of the hot soup slowly into egg yolk mixture. Add this mixture to the soup and simmer for 10 minutes, stirring constantly. Serve immediately, sprinkled with parsley. Serves 8.

Bernard Watson Gerdelman

Chicken Chowder

5 whole chicken breasts, halved and skinned
1 medium onion, quartered
1 bay leaf
1 teaspoon salt
Water
10 medium potatoes, peeled and cut into ½-inch cubes
2 (2x4-inch) thin slices salt pork
6 medium onions, chopped
Salt and freshly ground pepper to taste
6 cups scalded milk
½ cup butter
Scant Tablespoon arrowroot flour

Cover chicken breasts, quartered onion, bay leaf and salt with cold water in large skillet. Cover and bring to boil. Lower heat and simmer until chicken is tender. Parboil potato cubes for 5 minutes. Cut salt pork into ¼-inch cubes. Sauté salt pork in large kettle until golden; remove with slotted spoon and drain. Add chopped onions to kettle and sauté until transparent, adding more bacon fat if necessary. When chicken is tender, remove from skillet. Let broth simmer for 15 minutes. Remove meat from bones and cut into cubes. Strain chicken broth and add 1½ cups to kettle with chicken, drained potatoes, onion and salt pork. Add salt and pepper. Add milk and butter. Simmer until flavors blend. Cool and refrigerate overnight. If desired, thicken with arrowroot flour. Reheat slowly. Serves 10.

Cynthia Allen

Cheese Soup

1 small onion, coarsely chopped
1 small green pepper, coarsely chopped
2 celery stalks, cut into small pieces
2 carrots, cut into small pieces
¼ cup butter
¼ cup flour
3½ cups chicken broth
3 cups grated Cheddar cheese
1½ cups milk
2 Tablespoons sherry (optional)
Salt and freshly ground pepper to taste
Minced fresh parsley (garnish)

Combine onion, green pepper, celery and carrots in blender and finely chop. Melt butter in 3-quart saucepan over medium heat. Add vegetables and cook 8 to 10 minutes, stirring occasionally. Add flour and stir until well blended. Pour in chicken broth and bring to boil, stirring constantly, until soup is slightly thickened. Remove from heat. Add cheese and allow to melt. Add milk, sherry, salt and pepper and mix thoroughly. Sprinkle each serving with parsley. Serves 6.

Dot McCleary

Summer Garden Soup

¼ cup butter
½ pound carrots, finely shredded
8 green onions, minced
2 small zucchini, finely shredded
1 Tablespoon minced fresh tarragon
1½ teaspoons minced fresh basil
½ clove garlic, minced
1 cup frozen tiny peas, thawed
4 cups chicken stock
1 cup yogurt
Salt and freshly ground pepper to taste

Melt butter in 4-quart saucepan over medium heat. Add carrots, onions, zucchini, tarragon, basil and garlic. Cover and cook until vegetables are slightly softened, about 5 minutes, shaking pan often. Add peas and stock, increase heat to high and bring to boil. Transfer to bowl and cool completely. Stir in yogurt, cover and chill. Season with salt and pepper just before serving. Serves 6.

Diane Thomson

Gazpacho

1½ cups chilled tomato juice, divided
1 small onion, sliced
½ green pepper, seeded and sliced
1 clove garlic, sliced
2 medium tomatoes, peeled, seeded and quartered
½ medium cucumber, peeled and sliced
1 teaspoon salt
¼ teaspoon freshly ground pepper
½ cup chilled chicken broth
3 Tablespoons wine vinegar
2 Tablespoons olive oil
½ Tablespoon Worcestershire sauce
2 drops Tabasco
Cucumber, diced green pepper, chopped onion, chopped tomatoes, croutons (garnish)

Put ½ cup tomato juice, onion, green pepper and garlic in blender and blend 30 seconds. Add tomatoes, cucumber, salt and pepper. Blend 20 seconds or until ingredients are chopped, but not smooth. Pour into bowl. Stir in remaining tomato juice, broth, vinegar, olive oil, Worcestershire sauce and Tabasco. Cover and chill well. Garnish as desired. Serves 4.

Janet Zanni

Steak Soup

¼ cup butter
1 cup flour
8 cups water
1 pound ground beef
1 (28 ounce) can tomatoes
1 pound frozen mixed vegetables
1 cup chopped onions
1 cup coarsely chopped carrots
1 cup coarsely chopped celery
2 Tablespoons powdered beef bouillon
1 Tablespoon MSG
1 teaspoon freshly ground pepper

Melt butter in soup pot. Stir in flour to make a smooth paste. Add water slowly. Sauté ground beef in a skillet. Drain fat. Add meat to soup pot. Add tomatoes, mixed vegetables, onions, carrots, celery, bouillon, MSG and pepper and bring to a boil. Reduce heat and simmer until vegetables are tender, about 1 hour. Do not salt. Serves 8.

Donna Nussbaum

Famous's Onion Soup

2 pounds yellow onions
¾ cup butter, divided
1 Tablespoon sweet Hungarian paprika
1 teaspoon freshly ground pepper
1 bay leaf
8 cups rich beef stock
½ cup flour
½ cup Chablis
1 teaspoon salt, or to taste
Kitchen Bouquet
French bread
2 cups grated imported Swiss or Gruyère cheese, divided

Peel onions, cut in half and slice ⅛-inch thick. You should have 1½ pounds trimmed onions. Melt ¼ cup butter in Dutch oven and add onions. Sauté slowly for 1 to 1½ hours, stirring frequently. Add paprika, pepper and bay leaf and sauté. Add beef stock and bring to a boil. Blend flour and ½ cup butter together and add, piece by piece, to liquid, stirring vigorously until completely combined. Simmer for 1 hour. Add wine. Adjust color to rich brown with Kitchen Bouquet. Remove bay leaf. Add salt to taste. Refrigerate at least 8 hours. To serve, heat soup slowly. Fill warmed fireproof individual casseroles with about 1 cup warmed soup each. Top each with ¼-inch thick slice French bread. Top each with ¼ cup grated cheese and put under preheated broiler or middle rack for 5 minutes. Serve immediately. Serves 8.

Manfred Zettl

Spicy Tomato Soup

1 quart canned tomatoes
1 (12 ounce) can tomato juice
1 cup sour cream
4 green onions including 2 inches of green tops, chopped
2 Tablespoons tomato paste
1 Tablespoon fresh lemon juice
2 teaspoons grated fresh lemon rind
1 teaspoon curry powder
¼ teaspoon powdered thyme
Freshly ground pepper to taste
4 jiggers vodka

Boil tomatoes for 20 minutes. Strain and cool. Add tomato juice, sour cream, green onions, tomato paste, lemon juice, lemon rind, curry powder, thyme and pepper; mix well. Cover and refrigerate until thoroughly chilled. Serve with jigger of vodka. Serves 4.

Parties & More

Salads and Dressings

Crab Salade N'Orleans

1 pound crab meat
2 cups cooked macaroni shells
1 cup chopped celery
½ cup chopped green pepper
1 cup mayonnaise
¼ cup flat beer
1 teaspoon lemon juice
1 teaspoon minced onion
1 teaspoon salt
½ teaspoon curry powder
¼ teaspoon dry mustard
Dash freshly ground pepper
Lettuce

Combine crab, macaroni, celery and green pepper in glass bowl. Combine mayonnaise, beer, lemon juice, onion, salt, curry powder, mustard and pepper and mix well. Toss crab mixture and dressing together gently. Refrigerate for 3 to 4 hours. Arrange on beds of lettuce. Serves 8.

Starr Themasen

Yogurt Cauliflower Salad

1 (2½ pound) cauliflower, trimmed and separated into florets
3 Tablespoons white vinegar
3 hard-boiled eggs
2 cups yogurt
⅓ cup olive oil
¼ cup minced capers
2 Tablespoons minced green onions
2 Tablespoons lemon juice
4 teaspoons Dijon mustard
Salt and freshly ground pepper to taste

Cook cauliflower in 6 cups boiling salted water with white vinegar in covered pan for 5 minutes. Drain cauliflower in colander and refresh under cold running water. Drain well; put in salad bowl to cool. Halve eggs and remove yolks, reserving whites. Force yolks through sieve into bowl, gradually stir in yogurt and beat in oil, drop by drop. Stir in capers, green onions, lemon juice, mustard, salt and pepper. Pour over cauliflower; toss salad carefully. Cover and chill for 4 hours. Garnish with chopped egg whites. Serves 6.

Priscilla Hunter

Greek Salad

Salad:

2 small unpeeled zucchini
1 small unpeeled cucumber
3 small tomatoes
1 small red onion, peeled
1 cup large radishes

Salad:

Thinly slice zucchini, cucumber, tomatoes, onion and radishes. Combine in large bowl.

Dressing:

¼ cup vegetable oil
2 Tablespoons fresh lemon juice
½ teaspoon oregano leaves
Salt and freshly ground black pepper to taste

Dressing:

Mix oil, lemon juice, oregano, salt and pepper together until well combined. Pour dressing over vegetables, toss gently, but do not overmix.

Garnish:

¾ cup minced parsley
1 Tablespoon dill weed
4 ounces Feta cheese
2 medium heads Bibb lettuce
24 Greek olives

Garnish:

Combine parsley and dill weed in small bowl. Stir in cheese. Line individual bowls with lettuce leaves. Spoon salad carefully into each bowl. Sprinkle with herb-cheese mixture and garnish with 4 olives per salad. Serves 6.

Susan Christensen

Curry Rice Salad

1½ cups cooked rice
½ cup minced onion
2 Tablespoons vegetable oil
1 Tablespoon cider vinegar
2 teaspoons salt
½ teaspoon curry powder
1 (10 ounce) package frozen peas, thawed
1 cup diced celery
¾ cup mayonnaise

Combine rice, onion, oil, vinegar, salt and curry powder in large bowl. Cover and refrigerate for 3 hours. Add peas, celery and mayonnaise and mix well. Cover and refrigerate at least 3 hours. Serves 6.

Barbara Ferrenbach

Green Bean Salad

3 (10 ounce) packages frozen cut green beans, slightly cooked
2 (13 ounce) cans hearts of palm, drained
1 (14 ounce) can artichoke hearts, drained
1 (6 ounce) can pitted black olives
1 (3¾ ounce) jar marinated mushrooms, drained
1 (4 ounce) jar sliced pimientos, drained
1 (8 ounce) bottle vinegar and oil dressing

Combine green beans, hearts of palm, artichoke hearts, olives, mushrooms and pimientos in large bowl. Toss with dressing, cover and refrigerate at least 8 hours. Serves 10.

Evelyn Dressel

Garbanzo Salad

½ cup olive oil
3 Tablespoons minced onion
2 Tablespoons wine vinegar
1 teaspoon Dijon mustard
1 clove garlic, crushed
¾ teaspoon basil
¾ teaspoon oregano
¾ teaspoon salt
½ teaspoon freshly ground pepper
2 (15 ounce) cans garbanzo beans, drained
3 green onions, minced
3 Tablespoons minced fresh parsley
2 Tablespoons mayonnaise

Combine oil, onion, vinegar, mustard, garlic, basil, oregano, salt and pepper. Pour over garbanzo beans and marinate at least 8 hours in refrigerator. Just before serving, stir in green onions, parsley and mayonnaise. Serves 8 to 10.

Hannah Langsam

Cold Wild Rice Salad

1 pound wild rice, cooked
2 pints cherry tomatoes, halved
2 (6 ounce) jars marinated artichokes, undrained
1 (10 ounce) package frozen peas, slightly cooked
1 green pepper, sliced
1 bunch green onions, sliced
½ cup slivered almonds
1 (16 ounce) bottle Italian dressing

Combine wild rice, tomatoes, artichokes, peas, green pepper, green onions and almonds in large bowl and mix well. Stir in dressing. Refrigerate at least 8 hours. Serves 8.

Susan Wisely

Apricot Salad Supreme

Salad:

2 (3 ounce) packages lemon gelatin
2½ cups hot water
1 (17 ounce) can apricots, drained (reserving juice) and diced
1 (20 ounce) can crushed pineapple
1 cup miniature marshmallows

Dressing:

1 cup reserved apricot juice
¾ cup sugar
2 egg yolks, beaten
3 Tablespoons flour
½ cup heavy cream, whipped
½ cup grated Cheddar cheese

Salad:

Dissolve gelatin in hot water. Cool and add apricots, pineapple and marshmallows. Pour into 7 or 8-cup mold. Refrigerate until set. Remove from mold onto serving dish. Top with cooked dressing. Serves 8 to 10.

Dressing:

Cook apricot juice, sugar, egg yolks and flour until thick. Cool and add whipped cream. Spread on gelatin and sprinkle with grated cheese.

Mrs. Joneal Joplin

Caesar Salad in the Bowl

3 cloves garlic, chopped
7 anchovies, drained and chopped
Pinch salt
2 dashes Worcestershire sauce
2 Tablespoons lemon juice
⅔ cup vegetable oil
⅓ cup red wine vinegar
¼ teaspoon dry mustard
2 eggs at room temperature
⅜ teaspoon freshly ground pepper, divided
3 heads Romaine lettuce, washed and dried well
6 Tablespoons freshly grated Parmesan cheese
Freshly grated Parmesan cheese (garnish)

Mash garlic into large wooden bowl until it disappears. Add anchovies and small pinch of salt; mash into bowl and remove any excess that does not rub in. Sprinkle Worcestershire sauce around bowl. Mash lemon juice into bowl. Add oil and vinegar; mash and stir to get as smooth as possible. Mash in mustard. Add eggs and mix. Add ⅛ teaspoon pepper. Tear lettuce into bowl. Sprinkle with Parmesan cheese. Toss well. Add croutons and remaining pepper. Dust individual servings with Parmesan cheese. Serves 8.

Croutons:
8 slices bread
Butter, softened
6 Tablespoons freshly grated Parmesan cheese

Croutons:
Trim crusts from bread. Spread both sides with butter and cut in cubes. Put on baking sheet. Bake at 350°F for 10 minutes or until golden brown. Put Parmesan cheese in paper bag. Add croutons. Shake.

Port St. Louis

Olive Salad

1 pound large green olives, cracked
1 cup diced celery
6 Tablespoons wine vinegar
¼ cup diced or crushed garlic
3 Tablespoons olive oil
1 Tablespoon oregano
1 Tablespoon freshly ground pepper

Place olives, celery, vinegar, garlic, olive oil, oregano and pepper in large bowl. Mix together well. Let stand at least 1 hour before serving. Do not refrigerate unless room is very hot. Serves 4 to 6.

J. Viviano and Sons

Cranberry Salad

1 (6 ounce) package lemon gelatin
1¼ cups boiling water
1 quart cranberries, ground
2 cups sugar
1 cup ground celery
1 unpeeled orange, ground
1 unpeeled apple, ground
½ cup pecans, ground

Dissolve gelatin in water in large bowl. Add cranberries, sugar, celery, orange, apple and pecans. Stir well. Pour into 9 x 13-inch baking dish. Refrigerate until set, about 3 hours. Serves 12.

Tina Rush

Apple Cider Salad

Salad:
1 quart apple cider, divided
2 (3 ounce) packages lemon gelatin
2 cups unpeeled chopped apples
½ cup diced celery
½ cup chopped walnuts

Fruit Mayonnaise:
2 Tablespoons confectioners' sugar
1¼ Tablespoons cream cheese, softened
1 cup mayonnaise
½ cup sour cream
3 Tablespoons orange juice
1½ teaspoons grated orange rind

Salad:
Heat 2 cups cider with gelatin over low heat until gelatin is dissolved. Chill until partially set. Add remaining cider, apples, celery and walnuts. Pour into a 2-quart mold or 10 individual molds. Refrigerate at least 8 hours. Remove from mold onto serving dish. Top with fruit mayonnaise. Serves 10.

Fruit Mayonnaise:
Cream sugar and cream cheese. Blend in mayonnaise, sour cream, orange juice and orange rind. Makes 1¾ cups sauce.

Joyce Patterson

Crown Salad

¼ cup cold water
1 Tablespoon unflavored gelatin
1 clove garlic, halved
3 (3 ounce) packages cream cheese
2 cups ground Kosher pickles, drained
1 cup mayonnaise
¼ cup minced parsley
½ teaspoon salt
Lettuce
2 hard-boiled egg yolks (garnish)

Soften gelatin in cold water; set over hot water to dissolve. Cool to lukewarm. Rub salad bowl with garlic. Add cream cheese, pickles, mayonnaise, parsley and salt and mix well. Add gelatin mixture and beat thoroughly. Pour into 6-cup mold; chill until firm. Remove from mold onto lettuce and garnish with sieved egg yolks. Serves 8 to 10.

Winifred Jeep

Horseradish Salad

2 cups boiling water
1 (3 ounce) package lime gelatin
1 (3 ounce) package lemon gelatin
1 (20 ounce) can crushed pineapple, undrained
1 pound small curd cottage cheese
1 (14 ounce) can sweetened condensed milk
½ cup mayonnaise
½ cup chopped pecans
2 teaspoons horseradish

Dissolve lime and lemon gelatins in boiling water in large bowl. Cool and add pineapple, cottage cheese, condensed milk, mayonnaise, pecans and horseradish. Pour into greased 9 x 13-inch pan. Chill until set. Serves 12 to 15.

Joyce Patterson

Hot Chicken Salad

4 cups cubed cooked chicken
4 cups chopped celery
¼ cup grated onion
2 teaspoons salt
½ teaspoon tarragon
2 cups mayonnaise
¼ cup dry vermouth
1 Tablespoon lemon juice
1 cup sliced toasted blanched almonds
1 cup corn flakes
½ cup freshly grated Parmesan cheese

Combine chicken, celery, onion, salt and tarragon in large bowl. Combine mayonnaise, vermouth and lemon juice and mix with chicken mixture. Let stand for 1 hour. Spoon into 2-quart baking dish. Top with corn flakes and Parmesan cheese. Bake at 350°F for 25 minutes. Serves 12 to 15.

Mrs. William Haack

Oriental Spinach Salad

Salad:

1½ pounds spinach, washed, dried and deveined
10 green onions, cut into ½-inch pieces
1 (11 ounce) can mandarin oranges, drained
1 (4 ounce) jar sliced pimientos, drained
10 slices bacon, cooked crisp and drained

Dressing:

1 teaspoon sugar
1 teaspoon dry mustard
1 teaspoon paprika
⅓ cup lemon juice
⅓ cup Kikkoman soy sauce
⅓ cup olive oil

Salad:

Tear spinach into bite-sized pieces. Combine in large bowl with green onions, mandarin oranges and pimientos. Add bacon and toss with dressing just before serving. Serves 8 to 10.

Dressing:

Put sugar, dry mustard and paprika in jar. Add lemon juice, soy sauce and oil. Shake well.

Rella W. Hawkins

Molded Asparagus Salad

1 cup water
¾ cup sugar
½ cup vinegar
1 Tablespoon lemon juice
½ teaspoon salt
½ cup cold water
1 Tablespoon unflavored gelatin
1 (10½ ounce) can cut asparagus, drained
1 cup chopped celery
½ cup chopped pecans
½ cup stuffed olives, chopped
2 whole pimientos, chopped
2 teaspoons grated onion
Mayonnaise (garnish)

Combine 1 cup water, sugar, vinegar, lemon juice and salt in saucepan and bring to a boil. Boil 2 minutes. Soften gelatin in ½ cup cold water and add to vinegar mixture, stirring until dissolved. Chill until consistency of unbeaten egg whites. Fold in asparagus, celery, pecans, olives, pimientos and onions. Spoon into 1½-quart mold. Chill until firm. Remove from mold onto serving dish. Serve with mayonnaise. Serves 6 to 8.

Esther Goff

Hot Rice Salad

1 cup Italian salad dressing
1 cup water
1 cup rice
1 (5 ounce) can water chestnuts, drained and cut up
½ (10 ounce) package frozen tiny green peas
1 small cucumber, seeded and diced
3 green onions, thinly sliced
6 stuffed olives, sliced

Bring salad dressing and water to boil in large saucepan. Add rice, cover tightly, lower heat and cook until rice is done. Add water chestnuts, peas, cucumber, onion and olives; mix well. Serve warm. Serves 6.

Judy Talbot

Potato Salad Bleu Cheese

8 large potatoes
½ cup diced celery
½ cup chopped toasted blanched almonds
½ cup chopped green onions, including tops
3 Tablespoons minced fresh parsley
2 teaspoons salt
½ teaspoon celery seed
¼ teaspoon freshly ground black pepper
2 cups sour cream
4 ounces bleu cheese, crumbled
6 Tablespoons tarragon white wine vinegar
Salt and freshly ground pepper to taste
Minced parsley (garnish)
Sliced radishes (garnish)
Sieved hard-boiled egg (garnish)

Boil potatoes, peel and cut into ½-inch cubes. Combine potatoes, celery, almonds, green onions, parsley, salt, celery seed and pepper in large bowl. Combine sour cream, bleu cheese and vinegar. Toss potato mixture with dressing, adding milk if necessary. Add salt and pepper to taste. Cover and chill for several hours. Garnish as desired. Serves 8.

Madeline Stribling

Zucchini Salad

1 pound firm zucchini
1 Tablespoon imported sesame oil
2 Tablespoons plus 2 teaspoons rice vinegar
4 teaspoons Kikkoman soy sauce
2 teaspoons sugar

Scrub and trim zucchini. Halve zucchini lengthwise and scoop out seeds. Halve zucchini crosswise and shred lengthwise with vegetable peeler. Toss shreds with sesame oil in serving bowl. Combine vinegar, soy sauce and sugar in small bowl and stir until sugar is dissolved. Pour over zucchini and toss. Cover and refrigerate for at least 2 hours, but not overnight. Serves 4 to 6.

Judy Richards

Fettuccine Salad

½ pound fettuccine noodles
½ cup heavy cream
½ cup minced fresh parsley
½ cup freshly grated Parmesan cheese
2 Tablespoons olive oil
2 Tablespoons white wine vinegar
8 fresh mushrooms, thinly sliced
2 green onions, thinly sliced
Salt and freshly ground white pepper to taste

Cook noodles in rapidly boiling salted water until al dente. Drain well. Combine cream, parsley, cheese, oil, vinegar, mushrooms, onions, salt and pepper in large bowl and blend well. Add noodles, but do not toss. Cover and chill. Bring to room temperature and toss just before serving. Serves 4.

Marilyn G. Fuller

Chicken Party-Pie Salad

2 cups diced cooked chicken
1 (9 ounce) can pineapple tidbits, drained
1 cup walnuts or pecans, chopped
½ cup chopped celery
Salt to taste
1 cup sour cream
⅔ cup mayonnaise
1 baked 8-inch cheese pastry shell
3 Tablespoons grated sharp Cheddar cheese
Sliced olives (garnish)

Cheese Pastry:
Add ½ cup grated sharp Cheddar cheese to flour mixture in single crust pie shell recipe.

Combine chicken, pineapple, nuts and celery. Combine sour cream and mayonnaise. Add ⅔ cup sour cream mixture to chicken mixture and mix well. Spoon chicken mixture into pastry shell. Top with remaining sour cream mixture. Sprinkle with cheese. Chill. Garnish with sliced olives. Serves 6.

Mrs. Carl J. Dreyer

Paella Salad

1 (6 ounce) package yellow rice
⅓ cup vegetable oil
2 Tablespoons tarragon vinegar
1⅛ teaspoons salt, divided
½ teaspoon curry powder
¼ teaspoon MSG
⅛ teaspoon dry mustard
⅛ teaspoon white pepper
2 cups diced cooked chicken
1 cup peeled and deveined boiled shrimp
1 tomato, peeled and chopped
½ cup cooked peas
⅓ cup finely chopped celery
¼ cup minced onion
1 Tablespoon chopped pimiento

Cook rice according to package directions. Combine oil, vinegar, ⅛ teaspoon salt, curry powder, MSG, mustard and pepper. Pour over hot rice. Cool to room temperature. Add chicken, shrimp, tomato, peas, celery, onion, pimiento and 1 teaspoon salt. Toss lightly to mix well. Refrigerate at least 3 hours. Serves 6 to 8.

Kathryn Allison

Marinated Salad

1 bunch fresh broccoli
1 head cauliflower
1 pound fresh mushrooms, sliced or 2 (8 ounce) cans sliced mushrooms, drained
1 pint cherry tomatoes, halved
2 (6 ounce) cans pitted black olives, drained and sliced
2 (8 ounce) cans water chestnuts, drained and sliced
1 red onion, thinly sliced
2 (0.7 ounce) packages dry Italian dressing mix
½ cup red wine vinegar
¼ cup water
1⅓ cups vegetable oil

Separate broccoli and cauliflower into florets. Combine with mushrooms, tomatoes, olives, water chestnuts and onion in large bowl. Prepare dressing according to package directions using vinegar, water and oil. Pour over vegetables; cover and marinate at least 8 hours. Toss well before serving. Serves 16.

Lois Bredin

White Bean Sausage Salad

12 ounces small dry white navy beans
1 medium onion, halved
1 clove garlic, halved
1 Tablespoon salt
Freshly ground pepper to taste
1 pound Italian sausage
5 Tablespoons olive oil
1 clove garlic, minced
1 large onion, minced
1 pound unpeeled zucchini, thinly sliced
1 (4 ounce) jar whole pimientos, drained, cut into ¼-inch squares
3 stalks celery, minced
⅓ cup red wine vinegar
1 Tablespoon fresh lemon juice
1 teaspoon basil
1 teaspoon thyme
1 teaspoon ground coriander
1 teaspoon salt
½ teaspoon oregano leaves
Freshly ground pepper to taste
Pinch cayenne
Boston lettuce
16 Greek olives, drained
1 cup parsley, minced
1 small lemon, scored and thinly sliced

Soak beans in cold water overnight. Drain. Place beans in saucepan with water to cover by 1 inch. Add medium onion, halved garlic clove, salt and pepper. Bring to boil over medium heat; cover and simmer for 1 hour or until tender. Do not overcook. Drain, discarding onion and garlic. Cook sausage in ½ inch water in large skillet over medium-high heat. Turn sausage after 8 minutes. After water evaporates, brown sausage on all sides; slice thinly. Heat oil in large skillet; add minced garlic and onion and sauté for 10 minutes, stirring frequently. Add zucchini. Cover and steam over high heat for 3 minutes, shaking pan. Add beans, sausage, pimientos, celery, vinegar, lemon juice, basil, thyme, coriander, salt, oregano, pepper and cayenne. Heat for 5 minutes. Line a salad bowl with lettuce leaves. Spoon in salad and arrange olives on top. Garnish with parsley. Arrange lemon slices around edge of salad. Serves 6 as main course, 12 as salad.

Nancy Phillips

Lotus Bean Salad

1 (16 ounce) can bean sprouts, drained and coarsely chopped
1 (16 ounce) can kidney beans, drained
1 (8 ounce) can baby lima beans, drained
1 Tablespoon finely chopped onion
1 Tablespoon finely chopped green pepper
¼ cup vegetable oil
1 Tablespoon Kikkoman soy sauce
½ teaspoon oregano
½ cup cider vinegar
¼ cup sugar

Combine bean sprouts, kidney beans, lima beans, onion and green pepper. Combine oil, soy sauce and oregano; toss with vegetables. Bring vinegar and sugar to boil and cook until sugar dissolves. Pour over vegetable mixture and mix well. Refrigerate at least 8 hours. Serves 6 to 8.

Warren Grauel

24-Hour Slaw

Slaw:
1 medium head cabbage
¾ cup sugar
2 medium onions

Dressing:
1 cup cider vinegar
1½ teaspoons salt
1 teaspoon prepared mustard
1 teaspoon celery salt
1 teaspoon sugar
1 cup vegetable oil

Slaw:
Slice cabbage; stir in sugar. Slice onions and separate into rings. Place half of cabbage in crock or glass bowl; cover with onion rings. Add rest of cabbage. Pour hot dressing slowly over cabbage mixture. Do not stir. Cover and refrigerate at least 24 hours. Serves 8 to 10.

Dressing:
Combine vinegar, salt, mustard, celery salt and sugar in large saucepan. Bring to a rolling boil. Stir in oil and bring to boil again.

Jean Lange

The Pasta House Company Salad

1 head iceberg lettuce
1/3 head romaine lettuce
1 cup canned artichoke hearts
1 cup thinly sliced peeled Italian red onions
1 cup pimientos, well drained and diced
2/3 cup 5% olive oil, 1st press
1/3 cup Regina red wine vinegar (not garlic)
1 heaping teaspoon salt
1/4 heaping teaspoon freshly ground pepper
2/3 cup freshly grated Parmigiano cheese
Hearts of Palm (optional)

Clean and wash lettuce, and let it drain completely. Place in refrigerator to chill. Remove when well chilled. Split head of iceberg in half, pulling the heart of lettuce out of both halves and breaking in pieces. Do not use knife on lettuce. Only separate rest of lettuce as it will break up when tossed. Tear each romaine leaf into 3 sections. Place all lettuce in large bowl. Crush well-drained artichoke hearts in hand and add to bowl. Do not use marinated artichoke hearts. Add Italian red onions and pimientos. Drain pimientos completely or salad will turn red. Measure and pour onto salad: olive oil, vinegar, salt and pepper. Sprinkle with Parmigiano cheese. Toss until well mixed. Serves 4.

The Pasta House Company

Raspberry-Rhubarb Salad

1 (16 ounce) package frozen rhubarb
3/4 cup water
2 cups unsweetened pineapple juice
3 Tablespoons sugar
1 (6 ounce) package raspberry gelatin
2 cups chopped unpeeled tart apples
1 cup chopped pecans

Cook rhubarb in water until almost tender; drain. Add pineapple juice and sugar. Add gelatin; stir until dissolved. Chill until partially set. Add apples and nuts; fold in well. Pour into a 6-cup mold. Refrigerate until set. Serves 12.

Lynn Hill

Scandinavian Fruit Salad

4 medium oranges, peeled
Water
2 Tablespoons honey
2 Tablespoons lemon juice
½ teaspoon anise seed, crushed
½ teaspoon dry mustard
4 medium apples, cored and sliced
1 cup red grapes, halved and seeded
½ cup dried figs, sliced
Bibb lettuce leaves

Section oranges over small bowl to catch juice. Measure juice and add water to make ½ cup liquid. Combine orange juice, honey, lemon juice, anise seed and mustard in small saucepan; bring to a boil. Cool. Combine oranges, apples, grapes and figs with dressing and toss well. Cover and chill at least 8 hours. Serve in lettuce-lined bowl. Serves 10.

Etta Taylor

Seafood Salad

1 pound shrimp, cooked in spices, peeled and deveined
1 (14 ounce) can artichoke hearts, drained
Bibb lettuce leaves
2 pounds crabmeat
8 hard-boiled eggs, sliced
1 (6 ounce) can pitted black olives, drained
1 bunch green onions, chopped
1 green pepper, thinly sliced
1 tomato, cut into 8 wedges

Marinate shrimp and artichoke hearts in dressing at least 8 hours. Spread lettuce leaves on plate. Arrange beds of shrimp, crabmeat, eggs, olives, onions, green pepper, artichoke hearts and tomatoes. Pour dressing over top. Serves 8.

Dressing:
1 cup mayonnaise
¾ cup cocktail sauce
½ cup yogurt
3 Tablespoons vanilla ice cream

Dressing:
Combine mayonnaise, cocktail sauce, yogurt and ice cream and blend well. Chill.

Tricia Reay

Salmon Salad Supreme

Mold:

½ cup water
2 Tablespoons unflavored gelatin
½ cup vinegar
2 egg yolks, beaten
3 Tablespoons sugar
2 Tablespoons horseradish
2½ teaspoons salt
2 teaspoons dry mustard
1 (15½ ounce) can red salmon, drained
2 cups chopped celery
1 cup heavy cream, whipped

Topping:

1 cup mayonnaise
1 cucumber, chopped
1 teaspoon prepared mustard
1 teaspoon lemon juice
2 or 3 drops green food coloring

Mold:

Dissolve gelatin in water. Combine vinegar, egg yolks, sugar, horseradish, salt and mustard in top of double boiler. Add dissolved gelatin. Cook, stirring frequently, over hot water for 15 minutes. Cool. Add salmon, celery and whipped cream. Pour into 2-quart mold and refrigerate until set. Unmold and cover with topping. Serves 8.

Topping:

Combine mayonnaise, cucumber, mustard, lemon juice and green food coloring. Mix well. Refrigerate.

Mrs. Wayne E. Babler

Special Tuna Salad

2 (6½ ounce) cans white albacore tuna, drained
1 (11 ounce) can mandarin oranges, well drained
2 hard-boiled eggs, chopped
1 green pepper, slivered
½ cup mayonnaise
Boston or bibb lettuce cups
¾ cup English walnuts (garnish)

Break tuna into chunks in bowl. Add mandarin oranges, eggs and green pepper. Add mayonnaise and toss lightly so mandarin oranges remain intact. Chill for several hours. Serve in lettuce cups and garnish with walnuts. Serves 6.

Mrs. John P. Baird

Mexican Taco Salad

1 pound ground beef
1 (1¼ ounce) package taco seasoning mix
1 head iceberg lettuce, finely chopped
1 bunch red leaf lettuce, finely chopped
1 (15 ounce) can kidney beans, drained
½ pound grated Cheddar cheese
2 tomatoes, chopped
1 red onion, finely chopped
1 green pepper, finely chopped
1 avocado, finely chopped
1 (7 ounce) bag taco chips, crushed
Italian salad dressing
Salt and freshly ground pepper to taste

Brown ground beef with taco seasoning mix according to directions on package. Cool. Put iceberg and leaf lettuce in large bowl. Top with kidney beans, cheese, tomatoes, onion, green pepper, avocado and taco chips. Toss gently. Add meat mixture, enough dressing to lightly glaze ingredients, salt and pepper and toss again. Make just before serving. Serves 6 to 8.

Phyl Maxwell

Chicken Salad Deluxe

3 cups diced cooked chicken
1 cup artichoke hearts, quartered
1 teaspoon grated onion
¾ teaspoon salt
Freshly ground pepper to taste
¾ cup mayonnaise
2 Tablespoons vegetable oil
1 Tablespoon lemon juice
Lettuce leaves
¼ cup almonds, toasted (garnish)

Combine chicken, artichoke hearts, onion, salt and pepper in large bowl. Combine mayonnaise, oil and lemon juice and mix thoroughly with chicken mixture. Refrigerate for at least 1 hour. Serve on lettuce leaves with almonds sprinkled on top. Serves 4.

Donna Nussbaum

Hot Potato, Pepper and Sausage Salad

4 cups sliced onions
½ cup olive oil, divided
2 cups julienne green pepper
1 pound Polish sausage, thinly sliced
2 cloves garlic, minced
1 teaspoon oregano
1½ cups dry white wine
2 Tablespoons red wine vinegar
2 pounds small new potatoes
2 Tablespoons minced fresh parsley

Cook and stir onion in ¼ cup olive oil in large skillet, over moderate heat, for 5 minutes. Add green pepper, Polish sausage, garlic and oregano and cook for 10 minutes. Transfer to large bowl, cover and keep warm. Add wine and vinegar to same skillet and cook over moderate heat until liquid is reduced to about ¾ cup. Cut potatoes in ½-inch slices, put in saucepan, add water to cover and cook until tender. Drain well. Add ¼ cup olive oil in a stream to liquid in skillet; heat over moderate heat until hot and well combined. Add potatoes and toss gently. Add potato mixture to sausage mixture and combine gently. Sprinkle salad with parsley before serving. Serves 6.

Nancy Monson

Green Bean and Mushroom Salad

1 pound green beans, trimmed
¼ pound fresh mushrooms, thinly sliced
3 Tablespoons vegetable oil
1½ Tablespoons red wine vinegar
1½ Tablespoons lemon juice
1½ Tablespoons minced onion
1 Tablespoon minced fresh parsley
½ teaspoon sugar
Salt and freshly ground pepper to taste

Cook green beans in boiling salted water for 8 minutes, or until tender crisp. Drain beans and refresh under cold running water; drain well. Chill. Wrap mushrooms in plastic wrap and chill. Combine oil, vinegar, lemon juice, onion, parsley, sugar, salt and pepper in bowl; mix well. Cover and let stand for 1 hour. Cut beans into 2-inch pieces and toss with mushrooms and dressing. Serves 4 to 6.

Rosemary Green

Salade Niçoise

1 clove garlic, cut
2 (6½ ounce) cans tuna, drained and flaked
2 anchovies, chopped
2 Tablespoons capers
1 sprig parsley, chopped
Pinch basil
1 cup olive oil
¼ cup wine vinegar
Salt and freshly ground pepper to taste
½ pound fresh green beans
½ head lettuce, thinly sliced
2 hard-boiled eggs, thinly sliced
1 medium tomato, thinly sliced
½ medium green pepper, thinly sliced
½ medium onion, thinly sliced
8 radishes, thinly sliced
6 pitted black olives, thinly sliced
3 pitted green olives, thinly sliced
3 fresh mushrooms, thinly sliced
Hard-boiled egg, tomato, anchovies and olives (garnish)

Rub inside of salad bowl thoroughly with cut garlic. Discard garlic. Combine tuna, anchovies, capers, parsley and basil in the bowl. Pour olive oil and vinegar over mixture, sprinkle with salt and pepper. Let mixture stand for 30 minutes. Cook green beans until tender crisp, drain and refresh under cold running water. Cut beans into thin slices. Add sliced beans, lettuce, eggs, tomato, green pepper, onion, radishes, olives and mushrooms to bowl and toss salad thoroughly. Garnish with slices of hard-boiled egg, tomato, anchovies and olives. Serves 4.

Nancy Monson

Potato Salad

9 large new potatoes, washed
6 eggs
1 medium sweet onion
1 teaspoon sugar
1 teaspoon celery seed
Salt and freshly ground pepper to taste
¼ cup mayonnaise
1 teaspoon mustard

Place potatoes in heavy pan, cover with water and cook for 40 minutes. Hard boil eggs. Refrigerate potatoes and eggs overnight. Peel and cube potatoes and eggs; place in large bowl. Dice onion and add to potatoes; mix lightly. Sprinkle with sugar, celery seed, salt and pepper; toss lightly. Add mayonnaise and mustard; mix with fork until well combined. Add additional mayonnaise if needed. Serves 8.

Mrs. Gene McNary

Home Valley Ranch Salad Dressing

2 cups buttermilk
2 cups mayonnaise
2½ Tablespoons parsley flakes
1 teaspoon onion salt
1 teaspoon garlic powder
½ teaspoon MSG
½ teaspoon freshly ground pepper

Beat buttermilk and mayonnaise until smooth. Add parsley flakes, onion salt, garlic powder, MSG and pepper. Stir well. Let stand, uncovered, in refrigerator for 24 hours. Transfer to jar and keep refrigerated. Makes 4 cups.

Dorothy Reay

Garlic Cream Dressing

½ cup sour cream
⅓ cup mayonnaise
¼ cup half and half
2 Tablespoons white wine vinegar
2 Tablespoons vegetable oil
3 large cloves garlic, chopped
1½ teaspoons sugar
½ teaspoon salt
Freshly ground pepper to taste

Combine sour cream, mayonnaise, half and half, vinegar, oil, garlic, sugar, salt and pepper in blender or food processor. Blend for 15 seconds. Put dressing in bowl, cover and refrigerate for at least 1 hour. Makes 1 cup.

Roberta May

Bleu Cheese Dressing with Chives

1 cup buttermilk
½ cup olive oil
⅓ cup crumbled bleu cheese
⅓ cup snipped fresh chives

Combine buttermilk, oil, bleu cheese and chives in blender or food processor. Blend for 30 seconds. Makes 2 cups.

Lucy Mayer

Centralia House Salad Dressing

½ cup olive oil
2 ounces dark wine vinegar
2 ounces bleu cheese
2 ounces feta cheese
6 anchovies
½ small white onion, sliced
1 small clove garlic, minced
1½ cups mayonnaise
¾ teaspoon salt
½ teaspoon white pepper
½ teaspoon sugar
1 cup sour cream
Bibb lettuce
Romaine lettuce
Iceberg lettuce
Escarole lettuce
Freshly ground pepper to taste

Put oil, vinegar, bleu cheese, feta cheese and anchovies in blender; blend until smooth. Pour most of mixture into large mixing bowl. Add onion and garlic to remaining mixture in blender and liquefy. Add mayonnaise, salt, white pepper and sugar and blend again. Pour into mixing bowl. Add sour cream and whip with electric mixer about 15 minutes. Combine equal parts bibb, romaine, iceberg and escarole lettuce. Toss with just enough dressing to coat the leaves. Serve with freshly ground black pepper. Dressing does not keep well. Makes 3 cups.

Centralia House

Salad Bowl Dressing

¼ cup olive oil
1 clove garlic
½ cup vegetable oil
½ cup freshly grated Parmesan cheese
¼ cup crumbled bleu cheese
⅓ cup fresh lemon juice
1 Tablespoon Worcestershire sauce
½ teaspoon dry mustard
Salt and freshly ground pepper to taste
1 egg

Put olive oil in blender, press in garlic and blend to combine. Add vegetable oil, Parmesan cheese, bleu cheese, lemon juice, Worcestershire sauce, mustard, salt and pepper. Blend to combine. Add egg and mix well. Makes 1½ cups.

Mary Ellen Dixon

Roquefort French Dressing

¼ cup wine vinegar
¼ teaspoon salt
Freshly ground pepper to taste
½ cup olive oil
2 Tablespoons heavy cream
¼ cup crumbled Roquefort cheese
Few drops lemon juice

Combine vinegar, salt and pepper in small bowl. Add olive oil and cream in a stream; beat until well blended. Stir in cheese and lemon juice. Makes 1 cup.

Allane Herter

Anchovy French Dressing

2 anchovies
1 Tablespoon wine vinegar
½ teaspoon Dijon mustard
Freshly ground pepper to taste
¼ cup olive oil

Chop and mash anchovies to a paste. Combine with vinegar, mustard and pepper in small bowl. Add olive oil in a stream, beating until the dressing is well blended. Makes ⅓ cup.

Gerry Housh

Mayonnaise

1 large egg
1 teaspoon fresh lemon juice
1 teaspoon red wine vinegar
1 teaspoon Dijon mustard
1 teaspoon salt
Freshly ground white pepper to taste
1½ cups peanut oil

Combine egg, lemon juice, vinegar, mustard, salt, pepper and 3 Tablespoons oil in blender. Turn machine on/off to blend and slightly thicken mixture. With the machine running, add remaining oil in slow steady stream. Allow mixture to thicken as oil is added. Taste and adjust seasoning as needed. Makes 1¾ cups.

Marshall Kramer

Sandwiches and Relishes

Italian Cheese Crostini

4 ounces sliced Provolone cheese
3 ounces sliced Bel Paese cheese
⅔ cup ricotta cheese
8 slices large round Italian bread
4 eggs, beaten
½ cup light cream
½ cup olive oil
4 large cloves garlic, crushed

Cut Provolone and Bel Paese into ¼-inch squares. Add ricotta and mix well. Spread cheese mixture evenly on 4 slices of bread. Top each with slice of bread and cut in half crosswise. Combine eggs and cream in bowl and beat well. Heat olive oil and garlic in skillet at 325°F. Remove browned garlic from pan. Dip each sandwich in egg mixture, coating it completely. Place in skillet and sauté on each side until golden brown. Serves 4.

Helen Drier

Eggplant Supreme Sandwich

1 (1 pound) eggplant, unpeeled
1 cup parsley sprigs, firmly packed
½ small onion
1 clove garlic, or to taste
½ cup homemade mayonnaise
2 teaspoons fresh lemon juice
1 teaspoon salt
½ teaspoon basil
½ teaspoon oregano
½ teaspoon dill
½ teaspoon Dijon mustard
Freshly ground pepper to taste
Pita bread
Crudites
Lettuce
Baby shrimp

Place eggplant in shallow baking dish and bake at 350°F for 50 to 60 minutes, or until completely softened, turning once to cook evenly. Allow to cool, then cut into 6 to 8 pieces. Place parsley in food processor and mince. With machine running, add onion and garlic, and mince. Add eggplant pieces to purée, stopping once or twice to scrape down sides of bowl with spatula. Add mayonnaise, lemon juice, salt, basil, oregano, dill, mustard and pepper; let machine run 5 seconds, if necessary. Spoon into crock or bowl; cover and refrigerate. Serve in pita bread with crudites and lettuce and baby shrimp. Makes 2 cups.

Marshall Kramer

English Puffed Crab Sandwiches

1 (6 ounce) can Alaskan crabmeat or ½ pound frozen crabmeat, thawed
1 Tablespoon fresh lemon juice
3 eggs, separated
2 Tablespoons mayonnaise
1 Tablespoon chopped ripe olives
1 Tablespoon chopped parsley
1 Tablespoon prepared mustard
¼ teaspoon salt
Dash cayenne
8 English muffins, split and lightly toasted

Drain crabmeat, slice finely and pat dry. Sprinkle with lemon juice. Beat egg yolks until thick and lemon-colored. Blend in mayonnaise, olives, parsley, mustard, salt and cayenne. Beat egg whites until stiff but not dry. Fold into egg yolk mixture. Fold in crabmeat. Spread mixture on English muffins. Bake at 350°F for 15 to 20 minutes until lightly browned and puffy. Serve immediately. Makes 16.

Mrs. Ethan A. H. Shepley, Jr.

Clubhouse Burgers

3 pounds lean ground beef
1 teaspoon salt
½ teaspoon freshly ground pepper
2 (3 ounce) packages cream cheese, softened
2 Tablespoons crumbled bleu cheese
2 Tablespoons minced onion
1 Tablespoon milk
2 teaspoons creamy horseradish
2 teaspoons prepared mustard
6 large fresh mushrooms
Butter
Chutney (optional)

Combine beef, salt and pepper in large bowl and mix gently with hands. Shape into 12 4-inch patties. Combine cream cheese, bleu cheese, onion, milk, horseradish and mustard and mix until smooth. Divide filling over top of 6 patties, spreading to within ½-inch of edge. Top with remaining patties and press edges together gently to seal. Broil in preheated broiler to desired doneness. Sauté mushrooms in butter and top each patty with a mushroom. Serve with chutney if desired. Serves 6.

Wallace K. Leopold

Hot Corned Beef Sandwiches

1 (12 ounce) can corned beef, broken up
1 cup grated Cheddar cheese
½ cup pickle relish
½ cup ketchup
2 Tablespoons Worcestershire sauce
8 to 10 hamburger buns, split

Combine corned beef, cheese, relish, ketchup and Worcestershire sauce in bowl. Spread on bottom of hamburger buns. Cover with top of buns. Wrap in foil. Bake at 375°F for 20 minutes. Makes 8 to 10.

Peg Wells

Picadillo Tacos

1 onion, chopped
2 Tablespoons vegetable oil
½ cup chopped green pepper
3 large cloves garlic, minced
1 pound lean ground beef
1 (1 pound) can plum tomatoes, chopped, undrained
⅔ cup chopped pimiento-stuffed green olives
½ cup corn
⅓ cup raisins
2 Tablespoons brown sugar
1½ Tablespoons vinegar
⅛ teaspoon cinnamon
Pinch cloves
Salt and freshly ground pepper to taste
12 taco shells, heated
3 cups shredded iceberg lettuce
½ cup grated Monterey Jack cheese

Cook onion in oil in large skillet over moderate heat until softened, stirring occasionally. Add green pepper and garlic and cook, stirring, for 3 minutes. Add ground beef and cook, stirring, until brown. Add tomatoes, olives, corn, raisins, sugar, vinegar, cinnamon, cloves, salt and pepper. Cook for 5 to 10 minutes, stirring occasionally, until excess liquid is evaporated. Spoon ⅓ cup mixture into each taco shell. Top with lettuce and cheese. Makes 12.

Ben K. Kelley

Spicy Felafel

1 (16 ounce) can garbanzo beans, drained
1 medium onion, coarsely diced
1 firm tomato, cut up
1 rib celery, scraped and sliced
2 large or 3 small eggs
¼ cup chopped fresh parsley
1 Tablespoon diced pimiento (reserve liquid)
2 medium cloves garlic, pressed
1 teaspoon salt
1 teaspoon coriander
1 teaspoon chili powder
1½ to 1¾ cups dry bread crumbs
Vegetable oil
Pita bread
Salad Filler
T'hini Sauce

Grind garbanzo beans, onion, tomato and celery together. Add eggs, parsley, pimiento, garlic, salt, coriander and chili powder; mix well. Add 1½ cups bread crumbs. Mix well. Mixture should just bind together; it will be loose. Add up to ¼ cup additional bread crumbs if needed. Refrigerate for 1 or 2 days or freeze. Shape mixture into little balls no larger than 1 to 1½-inch in diameter. Pour oil in skillet to equal ¼-inch depth; heat to 360° to 380°F. Fry balls in oil, turning carefully when brown on bottom. Browning takes 2 to 3 minutes on each side. Best fried in afternoon; do not drain; do not refrigerate. Rewarm in same skillet to serve. Cut pitas in half. Each half pita will form a pocket. Place salad filler in each pocket. Put 4 or 5 felafels on top. Spoon T'hini sauce over felafels. Makes 60 felafels or about 12 sandwiches.

Salad Filler:

½ small head lettuce, finely chopped
1 small cucumber, finely chopped
1 tomato, finely chopped
1 small onion or 1 green onion, finely chopped
½ green pepper, finely chopped
1 Tablespoon minced fresh parsley

Salad Filler:

Mix lettuce, cucumber, tomato, onion, green pepper and parsley together. Refrigerate in airtight container until 2 hours before serving. Serve at room temperature. Can be made a day or two in advance.

Spicy Felafel

T'hini Sauce:

1 (16 ounce) can T'hini (ground sesame seeds)
1¼ cups water
¾ cup fresh lemon juice
3 Tablespoons finely diced fresh parsley
2 large cloves garlic, pressed
1 teaspoon paprika
1 teaspoon salt
½ teaspoon freshly ground pepper
Liquid from pimientos used in felafels

T'hini Sauce:
Combine T'hini, water, lemon juice, parsley, garlic, paprika, salt, pepper and pimiento liquid in blender or food processor. Blend until sauce is consistency of pourable salad dressing. Divide into 3 portions and freeze. Can be thawed and refrozen. One portion is sufficient for one recipe felafel. Makes 1 quart.

Sharon Winstein

Spiced Beef with Lettuce

¼ cup water
1½ pounds ground sirloin or chuck steak
3 Tablespoons fresh lime juice
3 Tablespoons finely chopped mint leaves
2 Tablespoons nam pla (fish sauce)
1 Tablespoon finely chopped green onions
1 Tablespoon finely chopped fresh coriander leaves
¼ teaspoon finely chopped red chile peppers or chili powder
¼ teaspoon garlic salt
Sprinkle MSG
Sprinkle sugar
Sprinkle freshly ground pepper
12 Romaine lettuce leaves

Heat water in skillet until hot. Put chopped beef in water and stir fry over medium heat until almost done. Pour beef and juice into large bowl; let cool for 10 minutes. Mix in lime juice, mint, nam pla, onions, coriander, chile peppers, garlic salt, MSG, sugar and pepper. Spoon mixture into lettuce leaves. Wrap lettuce around beef and eat with fingers. Serves 4 to 6.

Mrs. Wallace Chappell

Nutty Tuna Pockets

1 (6½ ounce) can tuna, drained
1 cup grated Cheddar cheese
½ cup chopped lettuce
⅓ cup chopped almonds, pecans or walnuts
¼ cup diced celery
¼ cup chopped green pepper
¼ cup mayonnaise
1 teaspoon dill
½ teaspoon garlic salt
3 medium pita rounds

Combine tuna, cheese, lettuce, nuts, celery, green pepper, mayonnaise, dill and garlic salt in large bowl. Cut pita round in half to make pockets. Fill pockets with tuna mixture. Makes 6.

Garie Perry

Cevapcici in Pita

3 pounds lean ground beef
1½ pounds lean ground lamb
¼ cup minced fresh parsley
2 cloves garlic, minced
1½ teaspoons salt
½ teaspoon freshly ground pepper
Pinch oregano
¼ cup vegetable oil
5 green peppers, seeded and cut into ¼-inch strips
5 onions, cut into ¼-inch slices
10 small pita rounds, warmed
5 tomatoes, seeded and slivered

Combine ground beef, ground lamb, parsley, garlic, salt, pepper and oregano and blend gently with hands. Moisten hands with warm water and roll mixture into sausages about 2-inches long and ¾-inch thick. Heat oil in large skillet. Add peppers and onions and sauté until onions are lightly browned. Keep warm. Grill meat on preheated charcoal grill, turning frequently. Place 3 or 4 sausages in each pita round, add some of the pepper and onion mixture and top with tomatoes. Makes 10.

Tom Reay

Croque Monsieur

8 slices day old firm white bread
6 Tablespoons butter, softened, divided
12 thin slices cooked ham
4 thin slices Swiss cheese
1 Tablespoon flour
½ teaspoon salt
⅛ teaspoon freshly ground pepper
Dash paprika
1 cup light cream
½ cup grated Swiss cheese
3 eggs
3 Tablespoons milk

Trim crusts from bread. Spread one side of 4 of the slices with 2 Tablespoons butter. Top each with 2 slices ham, 1 slice cheese then 1 slice ham. Cover with remaining bread slices. Melt 1 Tablespoon butter in medium saucepan; blend in flour, salt, pepper and paprika. Slowly stir in cream. Cook, stirring constantly, until thickened and bubbly. Add cheese and cook until melted. Keep warm. Blend eggs and milk in pie plate. Dip sandwiches on both sides. Melt 3 Tablespoons butter in large skillet. Sauté sandwiches, turning once, until golden brown. Add more butter if needed. Spoon cheese sauce over sandwiches. Serves 4.

Elizabeth Hunt

State Fair Corn Dogs

1 pound hot dogs
1 cup flour
2 Tablespoons cornmeal
1½ teaspoons baking powder
½ teaspoon salt
3 Tablespoons butter
¾ cup milk
1 egg, beaten
1 onion, grated
Vegetable oil

Dry hot dogs with paper towels. Mix flour, cornmeal, baking powder and salt. Cut in butter. Stir in milk, egg and onion. Dip hot dogs in batter, letting excess drip into bowl. Heat oil 3 to 4 inches deep in deep fryer or heavy skillet to 365°F. Fry hot dogs in hot oil for about 6 minutes, turning once, or until brown. Drain on paper towels. Stick wooden skewer in end of each hot dog. Makes 10.

Mrs. Jack Merritt

Mustard

1 pint cider vinegar
¼ cup sugar
1 small dried red pepper
12 black peppercorns
1 Tablespoon mustard seed
1 teaspoon Worcestershire sauce
½ teaspoon celery seed
½ teaspoon paprika
¼ teaspoon celery salt
¼ teaspoon garlic powder
¼ teaspoon salt
3 (2 ounce) cans Coleman's dry mustard
2 cups sugar
6 egg yolks

Combine vinegar, sugar, red pepper, peppercorns, mustard seed, Worcestershire sauce, celery seed, paprika, celery salt, garlic powder and salt in saucepan. Heat to a boil. Remove from heat and cool. Combine vinegar mixture and mustard in top of double boiler and let soak for 8 hours or overnight. Add sugar and egg yolks. Set over boiling water and beat with hand or electric beater for 12 to 15 minutes. Pour into hot sterile jars and seal immediately with hot lids. Store in refrigerator. Makes 5 6-ounce jars.

Barbara Ferrenbach

Sweet Mustard

1 (2 ounce) can Coleman's dry mustard
¾ cup sugar
3 eggs
⅔ cup wine vinegar

Combine mustard and sugar in top of double boiler. Beat in eggs; stir in vinegar. Place over boiling water. Cook, stirring constantly, for 5 to 8 minutes, until thickened. Pour into hot sterile containers; cool and refrigerate. Makes 2 cups.

Deni Whitworth

Mustard Butter

¼ cup tarragon wine vinegar
5 teaspoons dried green bell pepper, finely chopped
½ cup butter (do not substitute)
5 teaspoons dry mustard
4 teaspoons onion powder
½ teaspoon cayenne

Soak green pepper in vinegar until soft. Cream butter, mustard, onion powder and cayenne. Stir in vinegar and green pepper until well blended. Cover and store in refrigerator. Serve with steaks, ham or hamburgers. Makes 1 cup.

Dorothy Reay

Mustard Cream Sauce

1 hard-boiled egg, cooled
1 egg yolk
2 teaspoons dry mustard
2 teaspoons red wine vinegar
Salt and freshly ground pepper to taste
⅓ cup heavy cream

Force yolk of hard-boiled egg through sieve into a bowl. Add egg yolk and stir until mixture is a smooth paste. Stir in mustard and vinegar. Add salt and pepper. Beat cream until it holds stiff peaks and fold it into yolk mixture. Serve sauce with chilled poached salmon or seafood salad. Slice hard-boiled egg white into rings and use as garnish. Serves 4.

Margaret House

Herb Butter

½ cup unsalted butter, softened
1 Tablespoon minced fresh herb or 1 teaspoon dried herb of choice

Combine butter and herb. Let stand at room temperature for 1 hour before serving. Basil, chive, dill, oregano, rosemary and tarragon make excellent butters. Makes ½ cup.

Kogut's Curry Sauce

2 cups and 2 Tablespoons mayonnaise
¼ cup fresh lemon juice
3 Tablespoons curry powder
2 Tablespoons ginger
1 Tablespoon honey
1 teaspoon paprika
1 teaspoon Tabasco
1 teaspoon freshly ground pepper
½ teaspoon salt

Combine mayonnaise, lemon juice, curry powder, ginger, honey, paprika, Tabasco, pepper and salt; mix well. Serve with or vegetables. Makes 2½ cups.

Joyce Lee Kogut
The Ladle

Corn Relish

1 gallon or 36 ears white corn
1 large head cabbage
8 onions
6 green peppers
8 cups white vinegar
3 cups sugar
2 Tablespoons celery seed
2 Tablespoons mustard seed
2 Tablespoons salt

Cut corn off cob. Grind cabbage, onions and green peppers in grinder or food processor. Combine corn, cabbage mixture, vinegar, sugar, celery seed, mustard seed and salt in large kettle. Cook over medium heat for 30 minutes. Ladle into hot sterile jars and seal with hot lids. Makes about 12 pints.

Gwen Springett

Aunt Anna May's Chili Sauce

5 pounds ripe tomatoes
2 pounds onions
1 green pepper
5 pounds apples, quartered and cored
2 cups brown sugar
2½ teaspoons salt
2 teaspoons celery seed
1 teaspoon cinnamon
½ teaspoon cloves
½ teaspoon dry mustard
½ teaspoon black pepper
Paraffin

Grind tomatoes, onions and green pepper together through grinder or food processor. Combine apples and sugar in kettle; cook until hot. Add salt, celery seed, cinnamon, cloves, mustard and pepper. Stir in tomato mixture. Simmer, uncovered, until thick, 1 to 2 hours. Spoon hot chili sauce into hot sterile glass jars. Cool thoroughly. Melt paraffin in top of double boiler. Spoon liquid paraffin on top of cooled chili sauce to a depth of about ½ inch. Top with screw-on caps to insure freshness. Store at room temperature until seal is broken, then refrigerate. Makes 4 quarts.

Ann McReynolds Edwards

Pepper Jelly

¾ cup chopped green peppers
¼ cup chopped hot red peppers
6½ cups sugar
1½ cups apple cider vinegar
1 (6 ounce) bottle liquid pectin
Few drops red or green food coloring (optional)

Grind peppers together in grinder or food processor. Mix sugar, vinegar and peppers in large saucepan. Bring to a boil and boil for 2 minutes. Set off heat for 10 minutes, stirring occasionally. Add liquid pectin and let sit for 10 minutes. Add food coloring, if desired, skim and pour into hot sterile jars. Cover with hot lids. Makes 8 to 10 half pints.

Peggy Ezzell

Chris's Red Pepper Relish

24 red bell peppers
7 medium onions
3 cups cider vinegar
3 cups sugar
2 Tablespoons mustard seed
2 Tablespoons salt

Grind peppers and onions; reserve the juice. Combine peppers, onions, juice, vinegar, sugar, mustard seed and salt in kettle and boil for 30 minutes. Pack into hot sterile jars and seal at once with hot lids. Refrigerate after opening. Makes 4 pints.

Lynne Caldwell

Cinnamon Pickle Rings

Yellow cucumbers
2 cups lime juice
Water
3 cups cider vinegar, divided
1 (1 ounce) bottle red food color
1 teaspoon alum
10 cups sugar
1 (9½ ounce) package red hots
8 cinnamon sticks

Peel and slice enough large cucumbers ⅓-inch thick to fill a 2-gallon crock. Cut out seeds with spoon. Combine lime juice and 8½ quarts water; pour over cucumbers in crock. Let stand for 24 hours. Drain and wash. Soak cucumbers in clear cold water for 3 hours. Drain. Place cucumbers in large kettle. Mix 1 cup vinegar, food color, alum and enough water to cover cucumbers. Simmer for 2 hours. Drain. Combine sugar, 2 cups vinegar, 2 cups water, red hots and cinnamon sticks. Pour over cucumber slices and bring to a full boil. Fill hot sterile jars with pickles. Seal at once with hot lids. Makes 6 quarts.

Dorothy Crocker

Watermelon Pickles

Rind of 1 watermelon
Water
6 Tablespoons salt
12 cups sugar
4 cups white vinegar
2 slices lemon
2 teaspoons whole cloves
2 teaspoons whole allspice

Remove all traces of pink flesh and green outer peel of the melon. Cut pale green rind into small pieces. Soak rind in a brine of 8 cups water and salt. There should be enough brine to completely cover rind. Let stand overnight. Next morning, drain and rinse the rind. Put rind in saucepan with water and boil until tender. Drain well. Combine sugar and vinegar; bring to a boil. Add rind, bring back to a boil and boil for 3 minutes. Remove from heat, cover, and let stand overnight. Next day, bring to a boil, remove from heat, and let stand overnight. Repeat this process for 3 days. On the last day, add lemon, cloves and allspice; boil for 10 minutes. Remove rind with slotted spoon and place in hot sterile jars. Cook syrup for 10 to 15 minutes. Pour boiling hot syrup over rind until jars are filled. Seal with hot self-sealing lids. Let stand 6 weeks before using. Makes 12 pints.

Gwen Springett

Apricot Chutney

1 (29 ounce) can apricot halves
2 cups brown sugar
2 cups white vinegar
1 cup chopped onions
1 cup golden raisins
½ cup diced crystallized ginger
2 Tablespoons mustard seed
1 teaspoon chili powder
1 teaspoon ground cloves
1 teaspoon salt
1 clove garlic, minced

Drain apricots and reserve syrup. Dice apricots. Combine apricot syrup, sugar, vinegar, onions, raisins, ginger, mustard seeds, chili powder, cloves, salt and garlic in large saucepan. Bring to a boil, reduce heat, and simmer, uncovered, for 45 minutes. Stir in apricots and simmer, uncovered, for 45 minutes. Pour into hot sterile jars, leaving ½-inch headspace in jars. Seal with hot lids. Store in cool, dark, dry place. Makes 3 12 ounce jars.

Barbara Ferrenbach

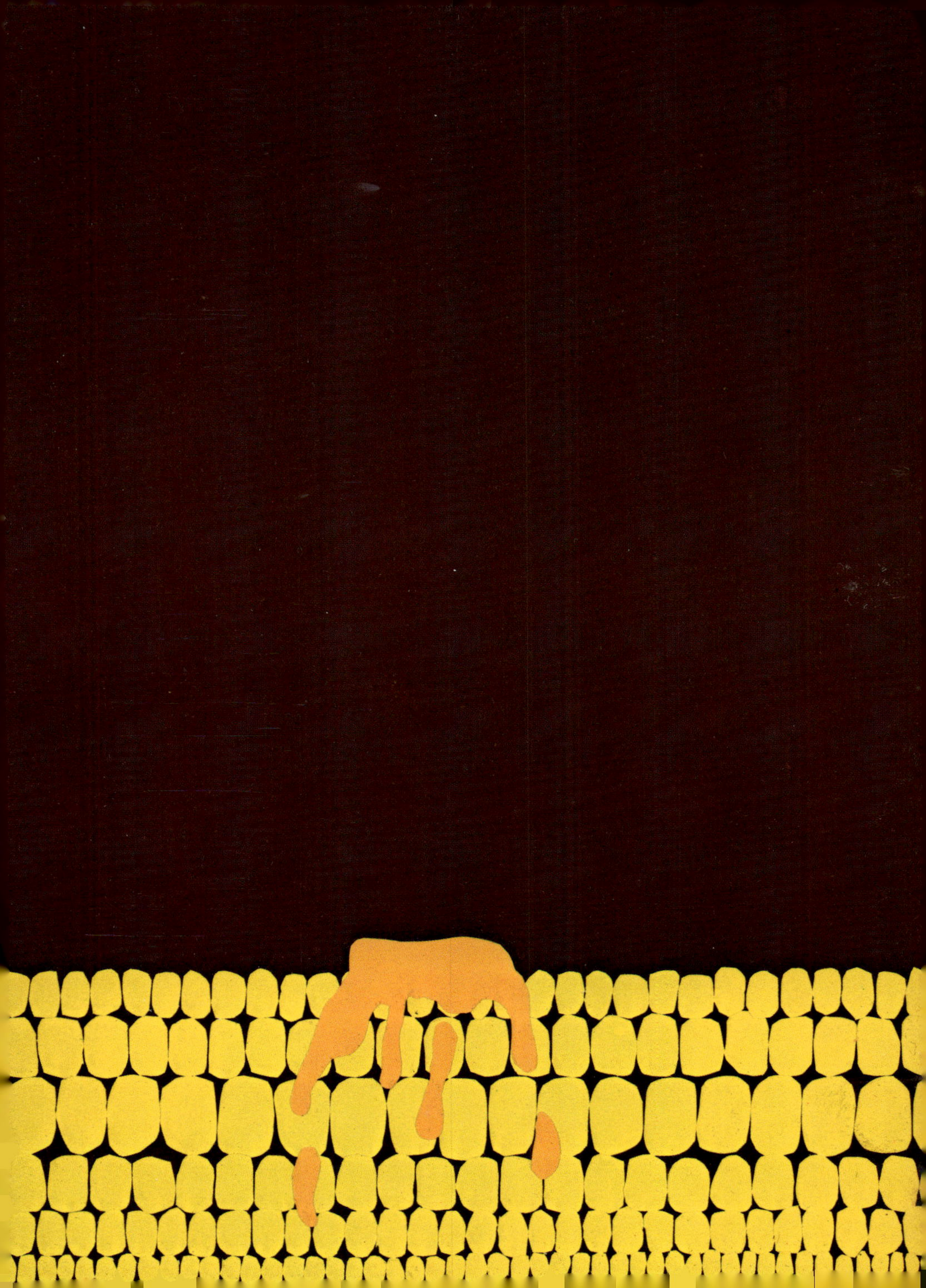

Vegetables

Artichoke Pie

Pastry for 2-crust pie
2 (14 ounce) cans artichoke hearts, drained
2 Tablespoons butter
4 eggs
¼ cup freshly grated Parmesan cheese
½ teaspoon salt
⅛ teaspoon pepper
8 ounces Mozzarella cheese, sliced

Prick bottom crust with fork. Slice artichokes; sauté in butter 2 or 3 minutes; put in pie shell. Combine eggs with Parmesan cheese, salt and pepper; mix well. Pour over artichokes. Top with Mozzerella cheese. Cover with top crust. Prick crust with fork. Bake at 375°F for 45 minutes. Serves 6.

Mrs. Arthur R. Bortnick

Baked Butter Beans

1 pound dry butter beans
1 large onion, halved
¼ cup brown sugar
1 Tablespoon salt
1½ teaspoons dry mustard
Boiling water
½ pound bacon or smoked ham hock

Wash beans and soak overnight. Parboil beans with onion. Cover and simmer for 1½ hours. Drain, reserving water. Wash beans, place in pot and cover with reserved water. Stir brown sugar, salt and mustard in ½ cup boiling water. Add to beans and mix thoroughly. Bury bacon or ham hock in beans. Bake at 325°F for 2 hours. Add boiling water, as needed, during first hour. Serves 6 to 8.

Hannah Amsden

Lima Beans in Tomato Sauce

3 slices bacon, chopped
4 cups cooked salted lima beans
1 (16 ounce) can tomatoes
¼ cup chopped onions
¼ cup brown sugar
¼ cup chili powder
1 Tablespoon vinegar

Fry chopped bacon in saucepan. Remove with slotted spoon and drain. Add beans, tomatoes, onions, sugar, chili powder and vinegar. Mix and simmer until thickened, about 25 minutes. Sprinkle beans with bacon. Serves 4 to 6.

Kathaleen Smith

Moros y Cristianos (Black Beans and Rice)

1 pound black turtle beans
1 ham hock
1 teaspoon salt or to taste
2 large Bermuda onions, finely chopped
2 large green peppers, finely chopped
6 cloves garlic, finely chopped
⅓ cup, or more, olive oil
3 cayenne peppers
1 teaspoon thyme
1 bay leaf
2 teaspoons tomato paste
Freshly ground black pepper to taste
1 teaspoon vinegar
Cooked rice
Sliced black olives (garnish)
Pimiento strips (garnish)

Wash beans, cover with cold water and soak overnight. The next morning, parboil ham for a few minutes, then bury in the beans. Add salt. Cook beans over high heat. Just before boiling, reduce heat to slow simmer. Cook for 1 hour or until done. Place onions, green peppers and garlic in heavy skillet; add oil, cayenne peppers, thyme and bay leaf. Simmer very gently until vegetables are translucent. Stir frequently. Do not let vegetables fry. Add tomato paste. When sauce thickens, remove the cayenne peppers and grind in generous amount of pepper. Pour sauce into beans and let simmer until deep mahogany color. Add vinegar near end of cooking time. Serve with rice and garnish with olives and pimiento. Serves 6 to 10.

Dulcia Serinus

Broccoli and Corn Casserole

1 (10 ounce) package cut broccoli, slightly thawed
1 (1 pound) can cream style corn
1 egg, beaten
2 Tablespoons butter, melted
1 Tablespoon minced onion, or 1 Tablespoon onion juice
Salt and freshly ground pepper to taste
¾ cup flavored croutons

Combine broccoli, corn, egg, butter, onion or onion juice, salt and pepper. Pour into buttered 1½-quart casserole. Cover with croutons. Bake at 325°F for 1 hour. Serves 6 to 8.

Garie Perry

Red Cabbage with Cranberries

2 to 3 pounds red cabbage, sliced
1 cup fresh cranberries
¼ cup dark brown sugar
¼ cup cider vinegar
3 Tablespoons butter
Salt to taste

Combine cabbage, cranberries, sugar, vinegar, butter and salt in 6-quart kettle. Cover and steam until juice develops, stirring occasionally. Lower heat and simmer until cabbage is tender, 45 minutes to an hour. Add more sugar or vinegar to taste. Serves 4 to 6.

Kathaleen Smith

Suzanne's Red Cabbage

1 very small head red cabbage, very thinly sliced
¼ cup unsalted butter
1 medium Jonathan apple, thinly sliced
¼ cup apple cider
2 Tablespoons white raisins
1 Tablespoon red wine vinegar
2 teaspoons brown sugar

Sauté cabbage in butter in covered pan until cabbage is limp. Add apple, apple cider, raisins, vinegar and sugar; cover tightly and simmer over low heat for 45 minutes to 1 hour. Serves 2.

Mrs. Frederick M. Switzer III

Gingered Carrots

5 medium carrots, sliced
2 Tablespoons butter
2 Tablespoons honey
½ teaspoon salt
¼ teaspoon ground ginger
⅛ teaspoon cinnamon

Combine carrots, butter, honey, salt, ginger and cinnamon in saucepan. Cover and cook over medium heat, stirring occasionally, 20 to 30 minutes until carrots are tender.

Gloria D. Clement

Orange Glazed Carrots

2 pounds carrots, peeled
1 to $1\frac{1}{2}$ cups water
1 teaspoon salt
¼ cup butter
¼ cup brown sugar
1 teaspoon grated fresh orange rind
¼ teaspoon ground cardamom

Cut carrots into lengthwise quarters, then halve. Bring water and salt to boil, add carrots, cover and simmer until tender. Drain. Add butter, brown sugar, orange rind and cardamom and stir until glazed. Serves 8.

Joyce Driemeyer

Special Carrots

2 pounds carrots, peeled and sliced
3 ribs celery with leaves, diced
½ large onion, diced
¾ cup dry white wine
¼ to ⅓ cup sugar
¼ cup butter
½ teaspoon dill weed

Combine carrots, celery and onion in large saucepan. Add wine, sugar, butter and dillweed. Cover and cook over low heat until carrots are tender but still firm. Serves 6 to 8.

Mrs. Carl J. Heifetz

Sautéed Eggplant

1 large eggplant, peeled and diced
3 Tablespoons vegetable oil
1 green pepper, diced
½ pound fresh mushrooms, sliced
½ cup tomato sauce
⅛ teaspoon oregano
Salt and freshly ground pepper to taste

Soak eggplant one hour in salted water. Drain. Sauté eggplant in oil in skillet until soft. Add green pepper and continue cooking until very soft. Add mushrooms and cook a few minutes longer. Add tomato sauce, oregano, salt and pepper. Heat thoroughly. Can be served hot or cold. Serves 4 to 6.

Joan Katz

Greek Style Cauliflower

1 large head fresh cauliflower
2 cups beef broth
½ cup dry white wine
¼ cup vegetable oil
3 Tablespoons fresh lemon juice
2 shallots, finely chopped
1 small clove garlic
1 bouquet garni
1 teaspoon fennel seed
1 teaspoon basil
1 teaspoon coriander
¼ teaspoon celery seed
Salt and freshly ground pepper to taste

Wash cauliflower and break into florets. Set aside. Combine broth, wine, oil, lemon juice, shallots, garlic, bouquet garni, fennel seed, basil, coriander, celery seed, salt and pepper in saucepan. Cover and simmer for 10 minutes. Add cauliflower and bring to a simmer. Remove from heat. Cool cauliflower in liquid. Cover and chill at least 4 hours. Serves 4 to 6.

Joyce Driemeyer

Grilled Mushrooms with Minced Clams

1½ (3 ounce) packages cream cheese, softened
1 (6½ ounce) can minced clams, drained
1 small onion, minced
Salt and freshly ground pepper to taste
1 egg, beaten
40 large fresh mushroom caps
½ cup bread crumbs
½ cup butter, divided

Combine cream cheese, clams, onion, salt and pepper. Add egg. Spoon into mushroom caps, sprinkle with bread crumbs and dot with butter. Heat remaining butter in broiler-proof pan and arrange mushrooms in it. Simmer over medium heat for 4 minutes. Broil 4 inches from heat until golden brown. Serves 8 to 10.

Pat Keith

Mushrooms à la Russe

½ cup butter
2 pounds fresh mushrooms, sliced
2 medium onions, finely diced
3 cups sour cream
2 teaspoons fresh lemon juice
2 teaspoons paprika
Salt and freshly ground pepper to taste

Melt butter in large skillet, add mushrooms and onions and sauté until tender. Add sour cream, lemon juice, paprika, salt and pepper and cook thoroughly over low heat. Serve over ham slices on toasted English muffins, or as appetizer with toast points. Serves 10 to 12.

Garie Perry

Onions Agrodolce

25 pearl onions, peeled
3 Tablespoons olive oil
¼ cup port wine
¼ cup red wine vinegar
¼ cup raisins or currants
2 Tablespoons brown sugar
Salt to taste
Cayenne to taste

Brown onions in olive oil in heavy saucepan. Add port, vinegar, raisins, brown sugar, salt and cayenne. Simmer slowly until onions are very soft and liquid has turned to syrup. Serves 4.

Barat K. Sparks

Five-Minute Okra

1 pound fresh tender okra
1 cup cornmeal
2 teaspoons seasoned salt
Freshly ground pepper to taste
¼ cup butter

Rinse okra and pat dry. Cut off stems and cut okra into ½-inch slices. Combine cornmeal, salt and pepper and roll okra in mixture. Melt butter in large skillet. Add okra and stir-fry a few minutes. Cover skillet and cook a few minutes. Remove lid and stir-fry a few minutes until okra is tender crisp. Serves 4.

Joyce Driemeyer

Northumberland Style Peas

¼ cup butter
3 pounds fresh green peas, shelled or 2 (10 ounce) packages frozen peas, thawed
2 ounces ham, minced
1 crisp lettuce heart, finely chopped
1 medium onion, minced
2 sprigs mint, finely chopped
2 Tablespoons water
Salt and freshly ground pepper to taste
1 teaspoon sugar
½ cup cream (optional)

Melt butter in saucepan; add peas, ham, lettuce heart, onion, mint, water, salt and pepper. Cook 15 minutes, shaking pan frequently. Add sugar and cream and cook 5 minutes. Serves 4 to 6.

Dulcia Serinus

Brandied Sweet Potatoes

6 large sweet potatoes, unpeeled
½ cup sugar
2½ teaspoons cornstarch
1½ teaspoons salt
½ teaspoon nutmeg
1 cup water
½ cup brandy
1 Tablespoon fresh lemon juice
¼ cup miniature marshmallows

Scrub sweet potatoes and cook in boiling water to cover in covered pan about 25 minutes or until barely tender. Drain and cool. Combine sugar, cornstarch, salt and nutmeg in 1-quart saucepan; gradually stir in water and cook over low heat, stirring constantly, until it becomes a clear sauce. Stir in brandy and lemon juice. Peel potatoes; cut into ½ to ¾-inch thick slices. Place in buttered 9 x 13-inch dish. Pour on sauce, cover and bake at 375°F for 30 minutes or until glazed, basting occasionally. Sprinkle marshmallows over potatoes; broil just until golden. Serves 8 to 10.

Pat Campos

Potato Dumplings

9 medium Idaho potatoes, unpeeled

3 eggs, well beaten

1 cup sifted flour

1⅓ cup bread crumbs, divided

1 teaspoon salt

½ teaspoon nutmeg

1 cup butter

2 Tablespoons chopped onions or mushrooms

2 Tablespoons fresh chives, dill or parsley (optional)

Boil potatoes until tender, remove skins and put through a ricer. Add eggs, flour, ⅔ cup bread crumbs, salt and nutmeg and mix thoroughly. Form mixture into dry walnut-sized balls. If mixture is too moist add more bread crumbs. Drop balls into boiling salted water or chicken broth. Boil for 3 minutes more after they rise to surface. Remove one and cut open; if center is dry, they are done. Remove balls with slotted spoon and put on heated platter. Heat butter in skillet, add ½ cup bread crumbs and onions or mushrooms. Cook for several minutes. Herbs may be added to dressing or used as garnish. Pour over dumplings. Serves 12.

Hannah Amsden

Pommes de Terre Fourées

3 large Idaho potatoes

2 eggs, separated

3 Tablespoons butter

2 Tablespoons cream

½ teaspoon salt

⅛ teaspoon freshly ground pepper

½ onion, minced

¼ cup slivered almonds

¼ cup freshly grated Parmesan cheese

1 pimiento, diced

¼ cup buttered bread crumbs

Bake potatoes at 400°F for 1 hour or until tender. Halve potatoes lengthwise and scoop out pulp, leaving shells intact. Mash pulp with egg yolks, mix in butter, cream, salt and pepper and whip until smooth. Add onion, almonds, cheese and pimiento. Beat egg whites until stiff and fold in. Pile mixture into potato shells using pastry tube to make attractive pattern. Sprinkle lightly with bread crumbs. Bake at 350°F until brown, about 20 minutes. Serves 6.

Maria Schweizer

Spinach-Ricotta Dumplings

1 (10 ounce) package frozen chopped spinach, thawed and squeezed dry
1½ cups ricotta cheese
1 cup fine dry bread crumbs
2 eggs, lightly beaten
¼ cup finely grated Parmesan cheese
¼ cup finely chopped green onions, white part only
1 teaspoon basil
½ teaspoon salt
¼ teaspoon nutmeg
1 clove garlic, crushed
Flour

Combine spinach, ricotta cheeese, bread crumbs, eggs, Parmesan cheese, onion, basil, salt, nutmeg and garlic in large bowl and mix well. Form mixture into walnut-sized balls. Roll lightly in flour. Place in layers on large platter with wax paper between layers and cover with wax paper. Chill well or freeze. Boil 2 inches water with 1 teaspoon salt. Reduce to simmer. Drop in half the dumplings. They will sink to the bottom. Cook until they float to surface, about 3 or 4 minutes. Remove with slotted spoon and poach remaining dumplings. Serve with tomato sauce or grated Parmesan cheese. Serves 6.

Corrine Schmidt

Spano Tyropita

1 to 1½ pounds filo dough
2 pounds cottage cheese
1 pound feta cheese
2 (10 ounce) packages frozen chopped spinach, thawed, drained and pressed dry
5 eggs, beaten
2 bunches green onions, including tops, minced
1 teaspoon dill weed
Salt to taste
2 to 2½ cups butter, melted and kept warm

Keep filo wrapped until ready to use. Combine cottage cheese, feta cheese, spinach, eggs, green onions, dill weed and salt in large bowl and mix well. Butter a 9 x 13-inch baking dish. Brush 10 layers of filo well with butter; cut and piece to fit pan. Cover with 1 inch of filling. Cover with another 10 or 12 filo layers which have been brushed with butter. Rewrap remaining dough. Brush top with butter. Refrigerate 10 minutes. Deeply score top layers into squares or diamond-shaped pieces. Makes about 30 pieces. Bake at 325°F for 30 minutes. Finish cuts through to bottom. Serve hot. Serves 12.

Garie Perry

Spinach Crêpes

Filling:

3 pounds fresh spinach or 2 (10 ounce) packages frozen chopped spinach

1 teaspoon salt

½ teaspoon nutmeg

½ cup finely chopped fresh mushrooms

⅓ cup butter, melted

3 Tablespoons flour

¼ cup freshly grated Parmesan cheese

2 Tablespoons heavy cream

Filling:

Cook fresh spinach until limp, drain and chop very fine, or thaw frozen spinach and drain well. Season with salt and nutmeg. Sauté mushrooms in butter briefly. Stir in flour. Add cheese and cream and cook until bubbly. Stir in spinach. Cook until mixture is heated through. Set aside.

Crêpes:

2 eggs

¾ cup flour

1 teaspoon grated fresh lemon rind

½ teaspoon salt

1¼ cups milk

2 Tablespoons butter, melted

1 Tablespoon brandy

Melted butter

¼ cup butter, melted

Freshly grated Parmesan cheese

5 fresh mushrooms, sliced and sautéed (garnish)

Chopped fresh parsley (garnish)

Crêpes:

Whisk eggs slightly. Add flour, lemon rind and salt. Mix in milk, butter, brandy and stir until smooth. Heat a 6 to 8-inch skillet. Brush with melted butter. Pour in 2½ Tablespoons batter and tip skillet until an even layer covers bottom. Cook until light brown, then flip and cook other side. Brush skillet with butter before cooking each crêpe. Spread several Tablespoons filling over each crêpe, roll up and arrange on heat proof platter or in shallow baking dish. Brush crêpes with melted butter and sprinkle generously with Parmesan cheese. Bake at 350°F for 15 minutes. Garnish with mushrooms and parsley. Makes 12.

Etta Taylor

Crustless Spinach Quiche

2 (10 ounce) packages frozen chopped spinach
8 eggs, beaten
4 cups grated Cheddar cheese
1 cup milk
1 medium onion, chopped
1 teaspoon basil
1 teaspoon oregano
⅛ teaspoon freshly ground pepper
3 (3 ounce) packages chipped beef, cut up

Cook spinach according to package directions. Drain well and squeeeze dry. Combine eggs, cheese, milk, onion, basil, oregano and pepper in large bowl. Add chipped beef and spinach and mix well. Pour into greased 9 x 13-inch pan. Bake at 325°F until set, about 30 minutes. Serves 12 to 14.

Mrs. James Shapleigh

Stewed Green Beans

1 small onion, finely chopped
¼ cup unsalted butter, melted
1 pound fresh green beans, cut into 2-inch lengths
½ cup tomato sauce
¼ cup water
1 Tablespoon minced fresh flat parsley
2 garlic cloves, minced
1 teaspoon minced fresh mint leaves
1 teaspoon fennel seeds
Salt and freshly ground pepper to taste

Sauté onion in butter until golden. Add beans and sauté, stirring constantly, until beans are bright green. Add tomato sauce, water, parsley, garlic, mint, fennel seeds, salt and pepper and simmer gently 30 minutes, or until beans are tender. Serves 4 to 6.

Barat K. Sparks

Squash and Swiss Cheese Casserole

3 to 4 pounds yellow squash, cut in $\frac{1}{3}$-inch slices
2 medium onions, minced
6 sprigs parsley
2 bay leaves
½ teaspoon leaf thyme
6 Tablespoons butter
6 Tablespoons flour
3 cups milk
Dash salt
1 teaspoon seasoned salt
⅛ teaspoon nutmeg
Dash Worcestershire sauce
4 egg yolks, beaten
1⅓ cups grated Swiss cheese
Dash cayenne
⅓ cup buttered bread crumbs

Place squash in saucepan with onion, parsley, bay leaves and thyme. Cover with boiling salted water and cook until squash is barely tender. Drain; remove parsley and bay leaves. While squash cooks, make cream sauce. Melt butter in saucepan, blend in flour, then gradually add milk and salt. Cook, stirring constantly, until thickened. Add seasoned salt, nutmeg and Worcestershire sauce. Remove from heat; blend in egg yolks gradually. Stir in 1 cup cheese and cayenne. Combine squash with sauce, stirring gently. Pour into buttered 9 x 13-inch baking dish. Combine remaining cheese with bread crumbs. Sprinkle over squash and bake at 350°F for 35 minutes. Serves 12.

Elizabeth Hunt

Janssen's Temptation

2 Tablespoons vegetable oil
4 large onions, chopped
12 medium potatoes, cut into shoestring strips
2 (10 ounce) packages frozen peas
2 (2 ounce) cans anchovies, minced
2 cups half and half

Heat oil over medium heat, add onion and cook until soft. Remove with slotted spoon. Add oil, if necessary, to equal 2 Tablespoons. Add potatoes and brown to medium brown. Drain. Put half the potatoes in greased 9 x 13-inch baking dish; cover with half onions, 1 package peas, and 1 can anchovies. Drizzle 1 cup half and half over vegetables. Repeat layers. Bake at 350°F for 1 hour. Let set for 10 minutes. Serves 12.

Vivian T. Kirk

Spinach and Artichokes

½ cup chopped green onions including tops
½ cup butter
2 (10 ounce) packages frozen chopped spinach, cooked and well drained
1 (14 ounce) can artichoke hearts
1 cup sour cream
½ cup freshly grated Parmesan cheese
Salt and freshly ground pepper to taste
¼ teaspoon nutmeg (optional)

Sauté onions in butter. Add spinach, artichokes, sour cream, salt, pepper and nutmeg, if desired. Combine well and spoon into 1½-quart casserole. Sprinkle with Parmesan cheese. Bake at 350°F for 20 to 30 minutes.

Helen S. Unterberger

Vegetable Medley

1 pound frozen French-style green beans
1 pound frozen broccoli spears, cut into 1-inch pieces
1 pound frozen baby lima beans
1 cup mayonnaise
2 hard-boiled eggs, chopped
3 slices bacon, cooked crisp and crumbled
3 Tablespoons fresh lemon juice
2 Tablespoons minced onion
1 teaspoon Worcestershire sauce
1 teaspoon prepared mustard
¼ teaspoon garlic salt
Dash Tabasco

Cook green beans, broccoli and lima beans according to package directions. Drain and combine. Make sauce while vegetables are cooking. Combine mayonnaise, eggs, bacon, lemon juice, onion, Worcestershire sauce, mustard, garlic salt and Tabasco in saucepan. Cook over low heat, stirring constantly, until heated through. Do not boil. Keep hot over hot water until ready to serve. Pour over vegetables and mix gently. Serves 8 to 10.

Marion Cairns

Herbed Tomato Pie

Crust:

2 cups flour
½ cup unsalted butter, chilled
3 Tablespoons shortening, chilled
⅓ cup ice water
1 egg
1 teaspoon salt
⅛ teaspoon sugar
1 egg white

Crust:

Put flour in large bowl. Cut butter and shortening into bits; cut into flour until texture of coarse meal. Beat ice water, egg, salt and sugar together. Combine liquid with flour mixture until dough clings together. Turn onto board, push dough away in 2 Tablespoon bits, using heel of hand in 6-inch smears. Gather dough, wrap in wax paper and cover with damp cloth. Refrigerate 2 hours or overnight. Butter outside of 9-inch pie pan. Roll dough to ¼ to ½-inch thickness; press tightly onto pan. Trim edges. Prick all over at ½-inch intervals with fork. Refrigerate for 1 hour. Bake on baking sheet in middle of oven at 425°F for 6 to 8 minutes or until dough pulls away from pan and begins to brown. Remove. Cool 5 minutes. Unmold and slip inside pie pan to support edges. Paint inside with egg white.

Fresh Tomato Purée:

4 large tomatoes, peeled, seeded, pressed dry and chopped
¾ cup minced onion
2 Tablespoons unsalted butter
½ teaspoon salt
¼ teaspoon freshly ground white pepper
⅛ teaspoon sugar
1 bouquet garni: 4 sprigs thyme, 4 sprigs flatleaf parsley and 1 bay leaf tied in cheesecloth

Fresh Tomato Purée:

Combine tomatoes, onion, butter, salt, pepper, sugar and bouquet garni in heavy sauce pan. Cover and simmer for 10 minutes. Remove cover, increase heat and cook until liquid has evaporated and mixture has reduced to a dry thick purée. Discard bouquet garni and let purée cool.

Herbed Tomato Pie

Custard Mixture:

1 cup heavy cream
½ cup light cream
2 eggs
2 egg yolks
2 cups fresh tomato purée
½ cup freshly grated Parmesan cheese
½ teaspoon salt
¼ teaspoon freshly ground white pepper

Custard Mixture:

Combine heavy cream, light cream, eggs and egg yolks. Stir in tomato purée, cheese, salt and pepper. Mix thoroughly.

2 tomatoes
Fresh thyme to taste
Salt and freshly ground pepper to taste
¼ cup freshly grated Parmesan cheese
Unsalted butter

Slice tomatoes into ½-inch thick slices, peel and pat dry. Fill crust with custard mixture. Cover top with tomato slices. Sprinkle with thyme, salt and pepper. Sprinkle top with Parmesan cheese and dot with butter. Bake on top rack of oven at 375°F for 25 to 30 minutes, or until knife inserted in center comes out clean. Makes 1 pie.

Madeline T. Stribling

Grecian Stuffed Tomatoes

12 large tomatoes
2 cups cooked rice
2 Tablespoons chopped onion
2 Tablespoons currants, plumped
3 cloves garlic, minced
½ teaspoon salt
Freshly ground pepper to taste
½ to ¾ cup olive oil
Chopped mint or basil (garnish)

Cut tops off tomatoes, scoop out flesh and combine with rice. Add onion, currants, garlic, salt and pepper. Stuff tomatoes with rice mixture and arrange in casserole. Pour olive oil over tomatoes. Cover and bake at 350°F for 25 to 30 minutes. Garnish. Serves 12.

Norma Pittman

Tomato with Pesto

Pesto:

1 cup fresh sweet basil leaves, lightly packed

1 cup fresh parsley sprigs, Italian flat leaf preferred

½ cup freshly grated Parmesan cheese

½ cup fruity olive oil

2 cloves garlic, crushed

Salt and freshly ground pepper to taste

¼ cup finely chopped pine nuts

Pesto:

Combine basil, parsley, cheese, oil and garlic in food processor or blender. Process or blend until smooth. Add salt and pepper. Stir in pine nuts. Cover and refrigerate for at least 1 hour.

Vinaigrette Dressing:

2 Tablespoons olive oil

1 clove garlic, crushed

1 teaspoon Dijon mustard

1 teaspon Kosher salt

½ teaspoon freshly ground pepper

½ teaspoon dry hot mustard

2 Tablespoons tarragon vinegar

1 teaspoon fresh lemon juice

¼ cup light vegetable oil

6 medium tomatoes

Vinaigrette Dressing:

Combine olive oil, garlic, Dijon mustard, salt, pepper and dry mustard. Combine vinegar and lemon juice; add to oil mixture. Add vegetable oil in a stream. Blend well.

Skin tomatoes and open top decoratively. Scoop out a little tomato flesh. Marinate tomatoes in vinaigrette dressing 30 minutes. Drain before serving and fill with pesto. Serves 6.

Madeline Stribling

New Potatoes and Scallions

12 small unpeeled new potatoes
2 teaspoons salt, divided
2 cups scallions, cut in 1½-inch pieces
1 Tablespoon butter
1 Tablespoon flour
⅛ teaspoon freshly ground pepper
1 cup milk
Chopped chives, mint or watercress (garnish)

Put potatoes in ½ inch boiling water with 1 teaspoon salt. Cover and cook for 10 minutes. Add scallions and cook until tender, about 4 minutes. Drain. While potatoes are cooking, melt butter in top of double boiler over boiling water. Stir in flour, 1 teaspoon salt and pepper. Whisk in milk gradually and cook until thickened. Place vegetables in serving dish and pour sauce over. Garnish. Serves 4.

Minou Martin

California Vegetable Quiche

1 pound yellow squash
2 cups grated Swiss cheese
4 eggs, well beaten
1½ teaspoons salt
½ teaspoon dill
½ teaspoon oregano
¼ cup freshly grated Parmesan cheese

Steam squash until tender; mash and drain well. Combine squash, Swiss cheese, eggs, salt, dill and oregano in large bowl. Pour into greased 8-inch square pan and top with Parmesan cheese. Bake at 350°F for 30 minutes. Serves 6 to 8.

Mrs. Paul S. Meyer

Turnip Puff

4 cups mashed cooked turnips
2 cups soft bread crumbs
4 eggs, slightly beaten
½ cup butter, melted
2 Tablespoons sugar
2 teaspoons salt
¼ teaspoon freshly ground pepper
2 Tablespoons butter, melted

Mix turnips, bread crumbs, eggs, ½ cup butter, sugar, salt and pepper together thoroughly. Spoon into buttered 1½-quart soufflé mold. Brush top with 2 Tablespoons melted butter. Bake at 375°F for 1 hour. Serves 6 to 8.

Barat K. Sparks

Zucchini Continental

8 to 10 medium zucchini
½ cup butter
1 cup grated mild Cheddar cheese
1 cup sour cream
¼ cup snipped chives
½ teaspoon salt
⅛ teaspoon paprika
1 cup bread crumbs
Butter
Freshly grated Parmesan cheese

Wash zucchini and boil until just done, about 10 minutes. Cut off ends and cut in half lengthwise. Arrange in buttered baking dish. Melt ½ cup butter and mix in Cheddar cheese and sour cream. Stir until well blended. Add chives, salt and paprika. Pour mixture over zucchini and sprinkle bread crumbs evenly on top. Dot with butter and sprinkle with Parmesan cheese. Bake at 350°F until bubbly, about 30 minutes. Serves 8 to 10.

Lynn Caldwell

Zucchini Pancakes

3 cups coarsely grated zucchini
1 egg
Salt and freshly ground pepper to taste
½ cup flour
1 teaspoon baking powder
¼ cup butter, melted
¼ cup freshly grated Parmesan cheese

Combine zucchini, egg, salt and pepper. Sift flour and baking powder together. Add to zucchini mixture. Drop by ¼ cupfuls onto lightly greased griddle. Cook until brown on both sides. Drizzle melted butter over pancakes and sprinkle with Parmesan cheese. Makes 12.

Sarasue Foster

Eggs and Cheese

Cheese Soufflé

Butter
Grated Parmesan cheese
3½ Tablespoons butter
4½ Tablespoons flour
1½ cups milk, scalded
6 egg yolks
1½ cups grated sharp Cheddar cheese
½ teaspoon salt
Dash white pepper
Dash cayenne or nutmeg
8 egg whites
Pinch salt
Pinch cream of tartar

Butter 1½-quart soufflé dish and sprinkle with grated Parmesan cheese. Set aside. Melt butter in medium saucepan, stir in flour and cook, stirring, for 2 minutes. Do not brown. Remove from heat and add milk. Beat until thick and smooth. Return to heat for 1 minute. Add egg yolks, one at a time, stirring briskly after each. Add cheese and stir until melted. Add salt, pepper and cayenne or nutmeg. Add pinch salt and cream of tartar to egg whites; beat until stiff. Stir large spoonful of egg whites into cheese mixture. Carefully fold in rest of whites. Pour into soufflé dish. Set in middle of 400°F oven. Turn heat down to 375°F. Bake for 25 minutes. Do not open door. Soufflé is done when it won't shake when touched lightly. Serves 4.

Mary Augustin

Quiche Jardine

½ cup chopped onion
½ cup chopped green pepper
¼ cup butter
2 (9-inch) pie crusts, unbaked
12 cherry tomatoes, sliced
1 Tablespoon thyme
2 cups grated Swiss cheese
1 cup heavy cream
2 eggs
2 dashes cayenne
Dash coarsely ground black pepper
Thin slices tomato and green pepper (garnish)

Sauté onion and green pepper in butter. Remove vegetables with slotted spoon and cover bottoms of pie crusts. Sauté tomatoes and thyme in butter remaining in skillet. Sprinkle tomatoes over other vegetables. Spread 1 cup cheese over each pie. Beat together cream, eggs, cayenne and black pepper. Pour half of mixture over each pie. Garnish tops with tomato and green pepper slices. Bake at 375°F for 20 to 25 minutes. Let pies set for a few minutes before serving. Serves 10 to 12.

Laurie Byrd

Garmish Kaiserschmarren

⅔ cup raisins
¼ cup brandy
4 large eggs, separated
½ cup sugar, divided
1 cup heavy cream
2 cups sifted flour
½ cup butter
½ cup confectioners' sugar
Tart berry syrup

Soak raisins in brandy. Beat egg yolks; stir in ¼ cup sugar and cream. Add flour slowly, stirring until smooth. Beat egg whites until stiff, fold into batter. Pour batter into 2 buttered 9-inch glass pie plates. Bake at 350°F until golden brown and puffed. Turn out on large cutting board and tear into pieces with 2 forks. Melt butter in skillet; add torn pieces, ¼ cup sugar and drained raisins. Sauté until all pieces are coated and golden brown. Put on warmed plates, dust with confectioners' sugar and serve with berry syrup. Serves 6.

Chez Rutz—Oberammergau

Cottage Cheese Pancakes

3 eggs
1 cup cottage cheese
¼ cup flour
2 Tablespoons vegetable oil
Salt to taste
Butter

Beat eggs. Blend in cottage cheese, flour, oil and salt. Melt butter on griddle and fry pancakes, turning when slightly brown. Makes 10.

Sharon Hamel

Savory Eggs

2 cups grated Cheddar cheese
¼ cup butter
1 cup light cream
2 Tablespoons Dijon mustard
½ teaspoon salt
¼ teaspoon freshly ground pepper
12 eggs, slightly beaten

Spread cheese in buttered 9 x 13-inch baking dish. Dot with butter. Combine cream, mustard, salt and pepper. Pour half cream mixture over cheese. Pour eggs into baking dish. Add rest of cream mixture. Bake at 325°F for 40 minutes, or until set. Serves 6 to 8.

Joyce Anicker

Cheese Blintzes

Blintzes:

2 eggs
1 cup milk
2 Tablespoons butter, melted
1 cup flour
½ teaspoon salt
Butter
Sour cream

Blintzes:

Beat eggs until foamy; add milk and melted butter. Add flour and salt; beat until smooth. Fry blintzes, one at a time, in hot, lightly buttered 8-inch skillet. Using 3 Tablespoons batter for each blintz, pour batter into skillet and tip to spread thinly. Fry over high heat for 2 minutes or until lightly browned on one side. Remove from pan and lay on towel to cool. Put 2 Tablespoons filling on browned side of each blintz and fold sides over to completely cover filling. Sauté blintzes in butter over medium heat for 5 minutes or until golden brown. Serve with sour cream. Makes 12 blintzes.

Filling:

1 pound small curd cottage cheese
½ cup sugar
1 teaspoon vanilla
1 teaspoon cinnamon

Filling:

Stir cottage cheese, sugar, vanilla and cinnamon together until well blended.

Sally Meyerson

Tomato Tart

2½ to 3 pounds ripe tomatoes
¼ cup olive oil
1 medium onion, chopped
3 to 4 large fresh basil leaves, chopped or ½ teaspoon dried basil
Salt and freshly ground pepper to taste
1 baked 10-inch pastry shell
6 to 10 2-inch tomatoes, peeled and sliced ¼-inch thick
1 round ricotta cheese, thinly sliced and cut into 2-inch pieces
Melted butter

Peel whole tomatoes and remove seeds; chop and drain in colander. Heat oil in large skillet. Add onion and cook slowly until soft and golden. Add tomatoes and cook slowly until almost all moisture has evaporated, 30 minutes to 1 hour. Stir in basil and season well with salt and pepper. Spread tomato mixture over bottom of pastry shell. Alternate sliced tomatoes and ricotta in rings until tart is covered. Brush with melted butter and sprinkle with salt and pepper. Broil for 5 minutes or until cheese softens and is slightly tan. Serve hot or at room temperature. Makes 1 tart.

Parties & More

Egg Brunch

½ pound fresh mushrooms
6 Tablespoons butter, divided
1 Tablespoon Worcestershire sauce
6 hard-boiled eggs
Salt and cayenne to taste
3 Tablespoons flour
1½ cups milk
½ cup grated Swiss cheese
1 cup fresh bread crumbs
1 Tablespoon butter

Wash mushrooms and grind coarsely through meat grinder or food processor. Sauté ground mushrooms in 3 Tablespoons butter; add Worcestershire sauce. Split eggs lengthwise; remove and mash yolks. Add mushrooms, salt and pepper; fill egg whites. Melt 3 Tablespoons butter in medium saucepan. Add flour and stir until smooth. Add milk gradually and cook, stirring, until thick and smooth. Add cheese and stir until melted. Arrange eggs in buttered 8 x 10-inch baking dish and pour cheese sauce over eggs. Sauté bread crumbs in butter and sprinkle over top. Bake at 350°F for 20 minutes or until bubbly. Serves 6 to 8.

Clay Hancock

Angel's Pancake

2 eggs, lightly beaten
½ cup flour
½ cup milk
Pinch nutmeg
¼ cup butter
2 Tablespoons confectioners' sugar
1 Tablespoon lemon juice

Combine eggs, flour, milk and nutmeg in mixing bowl. Mix until slightly lumpy. Melt butter in 12-inch iron skillet in 425°F oven. Pour in batter after butter melts. Bake 15 to 20 minutes until golden brown and puffy. Sprinkle with confectioners' sugar and return briefly to oven. Sprinkle with lemon juice. Serve plain or with honey, jam or syrup. Serves 4 to 6.

Dr. and Mrs. John E. Averett

Egg Foo-Yung

12 eggs
1 (1 pound) can bean sprouts, drained (save liquid)
1 (8 ounce) can water chestnuts, drained and chopped (save liquid)
1 (4½ ounce) can shrimp, drained
3 medium onions, thinly sliced
Salt and freshly ground pepper to taste
3 Tablespoons vegetable oil

Whip eggs with fork in medium bowl. Combine bean sprouts, water chestnuts, shrimp and onions in large bowl. Pour eggs over vegetables, add salt and pepper and mix well. Heat oil on griddle and fry mixture, pushing eggs over vegetables to make round cakes. Brown on both sides. Serve with sauce. Serves 8.

Egg Foo-Yung

Sauce:

½ cup cold water
3 Tablespoons cornstarch
½ cup boiling water
1 cube beef bouillon
1 Tablespoon brown sugar
2 Tablespoons Kikkoman soy sauce
2 Tablespoons dark molasses
1 Tablespoon Kitchen Bouquet
¼ teaspoon freshly ground pepper

Sauce:

Mix cold water and cornstarch. Dissolve bouillon cube and brown sugar in hot water. Combine mixtures in saucepan. Add soy sauce, molasses, Kitchen Bouquet, liquid from bean sprouts and water chestnuts and pepper. Add water if needed. Cook over medium heat until thick.

Dorothea Lowe

Sausage and Cheese Bake

1 (8 ounce) can refrigerated crescent rolls
10 ounces uncooked sausage, sliced
2 cups grated Swiss cheese
4 eggs, slightly beaten
¾ cup milk
2 Tablespoons chopped green pepper
½ teaspoon salt
¼ teaspoon freshly ground pepper
¼ teaspoon oregano

Separate dough into 2 large rectangles. Press over bottom and ½-inch up sides of 9 x 13-inch pan to form crust. Place sausage over crust and sprinkle with cheese. Combine eggs, milk, green pepper, salt, pepper and oregano and pour over cheese. Bake at 425°F for 20 to 25 minutes or until deep golden brown. Serves 6 to 8.

Mrs. Walter E. Clark, Jr.

Swiss Cheese Strata

1 pound pork sausage
1 teaspoon prepared mustard
6 slices bread
1 cup grated Swiss cheese
3 eggs, beaten
1¼ cups milk
¾ cup evaporated milk
1 teaspoon Worcestershire sauce
⅓ teaspoon salt
Dash freshly ground pepper
Dash nutmeg

Brown sausage, drain off grease and stir in mustard. Cut crusts from bread. Put 3 slices bread in bottom of buttered 8 x 10-inch baking dish. Cover with half the sausage and half the cheese. Repeat layers. Combine eggs, milk, evaporated milk, Worcestershire sauce, salt, pepper and nutmeg and pour over cheese. Bake at 350°F for 25 to 30 minutes. Serves 6.

Del Barger

Chile Rellenos

12 ounces Monterey Jack cheese
8 whole green chile peppers
Flour
4 eggs, separated
10 Tablespoons flour
Vegetable shortening
Hot tomato sauce

Cut cheese into 8 equal cubes of approximately ¾ x ¾ x 3-inches. Open chile peppers by holding at bottom and running hand up pepper to top, discarding seeds in the process. Wrap each cheese cube with a chile pepper and secure with a wooden toothpick. Dip each chile into flour and place on a tray. Place egg whites in a bowl and beat at medium high speed for 6 minutes or until fluffy. Add yolks and beat at medium speed for 2 minutes or until thoroughly blended. Put eggs in another bowl and blend in flour with wire whisk until completely absorbed with egg. Melt enough shortening in skillet to equal depth of 1½-inches. Dip each chile into batter and shake off excess. Place battered chiles into hot shortening and fry until golden brown. Turn and fry opposite side until golden brown. For best results, fry chile with any visible cheese up in skillet first so to not allow cheese to melt into oil. Drain excess oil from chiles. Serve with hot tomato sauce poured over the chile rellenos. Serves 4 to 8.

Casa Gallardo

Very French Toast

12 slices day old bread, buttered
¾ cup brown sugar
1¾ cups flour
1¼ teaspoons baking powder
½ teaspoon salt
2 eggs, separated
1 cup milk
3 Tablespoons butter, melted
Vegetable oil
Confectioners' sugar

Sprinkle 6 slices bread with brown sugar, using 2 Tablespoons per slice. Cover with remaining slices and cut each sandwich into quarters. Sift flour, baking powder and salt together. Add egg yolks, milk and butter and beat until smooth. Beat egg whites until stiff and fold into batter. Put oil in large skillet to ½-inch level. Place over medium heat. Dip each sandwich into batter and cook in oil until nicely browned. Turn once for even browning. When done, sprinkle with confectioners' sugar and serve promptly with tart jelly or warm syrup. Serves 4 to 8.

Max Deutch, M.D.

Pasta, Noodles and Rice

Pasta Scampi

3 Tablespoons butter
2 Tablespoons minced garlic
1½ pounds fresh shrimp, shelled and deveined
½ cup tomato sauce
¼ cup dry white wine
1¼ cups heavy cream, divided
½ teaspoon basil
½ teaspoon oregano
2 egg yolks
Salt and white pepper to taste
1 pound pasta
Butter
2 Tablespoons finely minced parsley

Melt butter in skillet. Add garlic and cook, stirring constantly, for 1 minute. Add shrimp and cook over medium-high heat, tossing until shrimp are bright pink on both sides. Add tomato sauce and wine and cook for 1 minute. Blend in 1 cup cream, basil and oregano. Beat egg yolks with remaining ¼ cup cream and add to sauce. Cook over medium heat, stirring constantly, until sauce thickens. Do not boil. Add salt and pepper. Cook pasta al dente and toss with butter. Spoon sauce over pasta and sprinkle with parsley. Serves 4 to 6.

Lee Leopold

Malfatti

1½ (10 ounce) packages frozen chopped spinach, cooked and well drained
1½ cups ricotta cheese
1 cup fine dry bread crumbs
2 eggs, beaten
¼ cup freshly grated Parmesan cheese
¼ cup minced green onions
1 teaspoon crumbled basil
1 clove garlic, crushed
¼ teaspoon salt
¼ teaspoon nutmeg
Flour
1 cup heavy cream
2 Tablespoons butter
2 Tablespoons freshly grated Parmesan cheese

Press all liquid from spinach. Combine spinach, ricotta cheese, eggs, Parmesan cheese, onion, basil, garlic, salt and nutmeg in large bowl. Cover and chill slightly. Form by rounded tablespoons into 3-inch fingers. Roll lightly in flour. Place in single layer in 9 x 13-inch baking dish. Cover loosely with plastic wrap and chill. Put 2 inches of hot water in large saucepan. Add salt and bring to a boil. Reduce heat to simmer and poach 6 to 8 Malfatti at a time in barely simmering water for 3 to 5 minutes. Malfatti will sink but will rise to top when cooked. Remove with slotted spoon and place in baking dish. Cover with cream, dot with butter and sprinkle with cheese. Cover and refrigerate until ready to serve. Bake at 350°F for 30 minutes or until bubbly. Serves 4 to 6.

Marianne Knaup

Fettuccine with Mushrooms and Salami

1 pound fresh mushrooms, thinly sliced
¾ cup butter
1½ cups chopped mild Italian salami
⅓ cup minced green onions
Freshly ground pepper to taste
1 cup heavy cream
4 egg yolks
½ cup freshly grated Parmesan cheese
1 pound fettuccine noodles

Cook mushrooms in butter in large skillet over moderate heat for 10 minutes or until liquid is evaporated and butter is golden. Stir in salami, green onions and pepper to taste. Cook for 3 minutes. Beat cream, egg yolks and Parmesan cheese together in large bowl. Cook noodles al dente, add to cream mixture and toss until well combined. Transfer to serving dish and spoon mushroom sauce over pasta. Serve immediately. Serves 4 to 6.

Judy Hocker

Spaghetti Soufflé

2 Tablespoons butter
2 Tablespoons flour
2 cups milk
½ cup freshly grated Parmesan cheese
1 teaspoon dry mustard
Cayenne to taste
Salt and freshly ground pepper to taste
¼ pound spaghetti
5 eggs, separated
Pinch salt
Tomato sauce

Melt butter in saucepan, stir in flour and cook for 1 minute. Add milk and cook, stirring constantly, until quite thick. Add cheese and stir until sauce is smooth and thick. Stir in mustard, cayenne, salt and pepper. Cook spaghetti al dente and drain well. Stir egg yolks into cheese sauce, one at a time, blending well after each addition. Add spaghetti and stir gently but well. Beat egg whites with pinch of salt until stiff, but not dry. Fold spaghetti mixture gently into beaten egg whites and spoon into buttered soufflé dish. Bake at 350°F for 25 minutes. Serve with flavorful tomato sauce. Serves 6.

Sybil Margulis

Pasta with Uncooked Tomato and Herb Sauce

1 pound very ripe tomatoes
4 cloves garlic, coarsely chopped
25 large leaves fresh basil
½ cup olive oil
Salt to taste
Generous amount of freshly ground pepper
1 pound pasta

Peel tomatoes, cut into small pieces and put in bowl. Add garlic. Tear basil leaves into thirds and add to bowl with oil, salt and pepper. Mix well, cover bowl and chill for at least 2 hours. Cook pasta al dente. Pour cold sauce over hot pasta. Toss very well and serve at once. Serves 4.

Joan Goodson

Lasagna

1 cup chopped onion
1 green pepper, chopped
3 cloves garlic, chopped
¼ cup vegetable oil
½ pound lean ground beef
3 links hot Italian sausage, removed from casings
1 (1 pound) can tomato purée
1 (1 pound) can peeled tomatoes
1 (4 ounce) can sliced button mushrooms
1 Tablespoon oregano
1 teaspoon salt
½ teaspoon fennel
½ teaspoon pepper
1 (8 ounce) package lasagna noodles
½ pound Mozzarella cheese, thinly sliced
½ pound ricotta cheese, crumbled
¼ pound freshly grated Parmesan cheese

Sauté onion, garlic and green pepper in oil until limp but not brown. Add ground beef and sausage and stir over medium heat, breaking up meat with spoon until it is crumbly and brown. Add tomato purée, tomatoes, mushrooms, oregano, salt, fennel and pepper. Cook slowly for 4 to 6 hours, stirring occasionally. Cook lasagna noodles according to package directions. Drain. Spread a ½-inch layer of sauce in 12x10x3-inch casserole. Cover with half the cooked noodles, half the Mozzarella cheese, half the crumbled ricotta cheese and half the Parmesan cheese. Repeat layers, saving 1 cup sauce to drizzle over top. Bake at 350°F for 1 hour. Serves 6 to 8.

Mary Tureen

Pasta Con Broccoli

½ pound shell noodles
¼ pound fresh mushrooms, sliced
½ cup butter
1 (10 ounce) package chopped broccoli, thawed
¼ cup cherry tomatoes, halved
½ cup freshly grated Parmesan cheese
½ cup heavy cream

Cook noodles in boiling water for 6 minutes; drain well. Sauté mushrooms in butter. Add noodles, broccoli and tomatoes and toss. Add grated cheese and cream and toss. Serve immediately. Serves 4 to 6.

Susan Gurock

Fettuccini Noodles

2 cups flour or more
2 eggs
Dash salt

Combine 2 cups flour, eggs and salt. Add flour as needed to make stiff dough. Roll out in oblong shape on floured surface. Let dry for 30 minutes. Cut into ⅓-inch wide noodles. Serves 4 to 6.

Kemoll's

Fettuccini Verdi

1 (10 ounce) package frozen spinach
1 cup flour or more
1 egg
1 teaspoon salt

Thaw spinach; squeeze until very dry. Place on tray and freeze again until hard. Put frozen spinach in grinder; grind twice. Combine spinach, 1 cup flour, egg and salt; knead. Add more flour as needed to make stiff dough. Roll out dough on floured surface into oblong shape. Let dry for 30 minutes. Cut into ⅓-inch wide noodles. Serves 2 to 3.

Kemoll's

Tortellini

Olive oil
½ pound chicken, cut up
½ pound pork, cut up
1 small onion, chopped
2 cloves garlic, minced
Beef stock
2 ounces prosciutto
2 ounces mortadella
1 egg
¼ cup ricotta cheese
¼ cup freshly grated Parmesan cheese
Pinch nutmeg
Fettuccini noodle dough

Cover bottom of saucepan with olive oil. Add chicken, pork, onion and garlic; sauté until lightly browned. Add beef stock to cover and cook for 45 minutes. Remove meat with a slotted spoon; reduce stock to about ½ cup. Add prosciutto and mortadella to meat mixture and put through meat grinder. Add egg, ricotta, Parmesan cheese, nutmeg and reduced beef stock. Roll out noodle dough evenly; cut into 2-inch circles. Wet edges of circles, place ¼ teaspoon filling in centers and fold over. Seal edges and form into doughnut shapes. Drop into boiling water. Check for doneness after 7 minutes. Drain. Serve with meat sauce or cream, butter and garlic sauce. Serves 4 to 6.

Kemoll's

Paglia e Fieno—Straw and Grass

3 Tablespoons butter
½ cup sliced fresh mushrooms
1 Tablespoon olive oil
1½ ounces prosciutto, cut into matchsticks
6 ounces homemade yellow noodles, cooked
3½ ounces homemade green noodles, cooked
1 cup heavy cream
½ cup frozen peas, cooked
Few grinds fresh black pepper
Salt and MSG to taste
¼ cup freshly grated Parmesan cheese

Melt butter in large skillet. Add mushrooms and lightly sauté. Put oil in another skillet, add prosciutto and sauté for 2 minutes. Combine mushrooms and prosciutto. Add noodles, cream, peas and pepper; toss gently. Add salt and MSG. Serve on plates and grate Parmesan on top. Makes 1 dinner serving or 4 appetizer servings.

Kemoll's

White Lasagna

1 pound sweet Italian sausage
½ pound lean ground beef
1 clove garlic, minced
½ teaspoon salt
½ pound (12 pieces) lasagna noodles
1 pint creamed cottage cheese or sour cream
2 eggs
Béchamel sauce
1 cup freshly grated Parmesan cheese
½ pound Mozzarella cheese, chopped
½ pound fresh mushrooms, sliced sautéed in butter, or 1 (4 ounce) can sliced mushrooms, drained
Paprika
Minced fresh or dried parsley

Boil sausages for a few minutes, cool, skin and grind. Sauté beef until lightly browned and mix with sausage, garlic and salt. Add few drops of oil to kettle of boiling salted water and cook lasagna noodles al dente. Run water in pan until noodles are cool enough to handle. Combine cottage cheese or sour cream with eggs. Arrange 3 noodles in buttered 9 x 13-inch pan. Cut noodles to fit or piece if necessary. Spoon some Béchamel sauce over noodles, sprinkle with part of the meat mixture, part of the Parmesan and Mozzarella cheese and spoon in part of the cottage cheese and egg mixture. Repeat layers until dish is full. Top with mushrooms, sprinkle with paprika and parsley. Cook at 375°F for 20 minutes. Allow to stand for 10 minutes before serving. Serves 8.

Béchamel Sauce:

3 Tablespoons butter, melted
½ cup water
1 yellow onion, coarsely chopped
3 Tablespoons flour
1½ teaspoons salt
½ teaspoon nutmeg
¼ teaspoon freshly ground white pepper
2 cups light cream, divided
1 cup milk
2 egg yolks

Béchamel Sauce:

Combine butter, water and onion in saucepan. Boil until water evaporates and onion is soft. Stir in flour and cook 3 minutes, stirring constantly; do not brown. Stir in salt, pepper and nutmeg. Add 1 cup cream and milk gradually. Stir constantly until sauce thickens. Beat 1 cup cream with egg yolks, stir into sauce and keep stirring until mixture almost boils. Do not boil.

Mrs. William J. Freschi

Bolognese Sauce

6 Tablespoons butter, divided
2½ Tablespoons olive oil
⅔ cup coarsely chopped bacon or prosciutto ham
1 large onion, sliced
1 carrot, finely grated
1 stalk celery, minced
¾ pound ground beef
¾ cup ground pork
¼ cup Italian sausage
2 or 3 chicken liver halves
⅔ cup red wine
1¼ cups rich beef bouillon
1 (12 ounce) can tomato paste
Salt and freshly ground pepper to taste
¼ cup light cream

Melt 3 Tablespoons butter in oil in large skillet. Add bacon or ham, onion, carrot and celery; sauté over low heat until vegetables are tender, about 8 to 10 minutes. Add beef, pork, sausage and livers and sauté until brown. Add wine and cook 5 minutes or until alcohol flavor evaporates. Stir in beef bouillon, tomato paste, salt and pepper. Cover and simmer for 1½ hours, stirring occasionally. Stir in cream. If thicker sauce is desired, cook, uncovered, to reduce. Correct seasonings. Stir 3 Tablespoons butter into hot sauce. Makes 4 cups.

JoAnn Kemoll Berger

Tomato Sauce for Pasta

3 Tablespoons olive oil
¼ pound beef, cut into 1-inch cubes
¼ pound pork, cut into 1-inch cubes
1 large onion, chopped
2 cloves garlic, minced
2 (28 ounce) cans imported Italian style tomatoes
1 (6 ounce) can tomato paste
¼ cup sugar
¼ cup minced fresh parsley
3 Tablespoons basil
2 bay leaves
Pinch baking soda

Heat olive oil in large skillet. Add beef, pork, onion and garlic and brown. Place in large heavy pot. Add tomatoes, tomato paste, sugar, parsley, basil and bay leaves. Cook for 3 hours and 45 minutes. Add baking soda and cook for 15 minutes. Serve over pasta. Makes 2 quarts.

Barbara Ferrenbach

Pasta Primavera

½ cup unsalted butter
1 medium onion, minced
1 large clove garlic, minced
1 pound thin asparagus, tough ends trimmed, cut into ¼-inch slices
½ pound mushrooms, thinly sliced
6 ounces cauliflower, broken into florets
1 medium zucchini, cut into ¼-inch slices
1 small carrot, halved lengthwise, cut into ⅛-inch diagonal slices
1 cup heavy cream
½ cup chicken broth
2 Tablespoons chopped fresh basil
1 cup frozen small peas, thawed
2 ounces prosciutto or cooked ham, chopped
5 green onions, chopped
Salt and freshly ground pepper to taste
1 pound fettucce or linguini cooked al dente, thoroughly drained.
1 cup freshly grated Parmesan cheese

Heat large skillet over medium high heat. Add butter, onion and garlic and sauté until onion is softened, about 2 minutes. Add asparagus, mushrooms, cauliflower, zucchini and carrot and stir fry for 2 minutes. Remove vegetables and set aside. Increase heat to high. Add cream, broth and basil and boil until liquid is reduced, about 3 minutes. Stir in peas, ham and green onion and cook 1 minute more. Season with salt and pepper to taste. Add pasta and cheese, tossing until thoroughly combined and pasta is heated through. Turn onto large platter and garnish with reserved vegetables. Serves 4 to 6.

Roxanne Fate

Charleston Steamed Rice

1½ cups rice
1¼ cups water
1 teaspoon salt

Place rice, water and salt in top of double-boiler. Cover and cook over boiling water for 30 minutes. Remove lid and fluff up rice with fork so that each grain stands up. Replace lid and cook for 10 minutes. Serves 4 to 6.

Peggy McClellan

Linguini with White Clam Sauce

½ cup olive oil
½ cup chopped fresh parsley
3 cloves garlic, minced
2 (6½ ounce) cans minced clams, drained (save liquid)
1 pound linguini

Heat olive oil in skillet. Add parsley and garlic and sauté for 5 minutes. Add clam liquid, bring to a boil and simmer over low heat for 5 minutes. Cook linguini al dente and drain well. Combine sauce, linguini and clams and heat through. Serves 4.

Jeanne Perabo

Almond Rice

¼ cup butter
1½ cups uncooked rice
¾ pound fresh mushrooms, sliced
1 onion, finely chopped
Freshly ground pepper to taste
3 cups beef consommé
½ cup chopped almonds
2 Tablespoons poppy seeds
Salt to taste

Melt butter in heavy saucepan. Add rice and brown. Add mushrooms, onions and pepper and sauté until onion is tender. Remove from heat. Add consommé, almonds, poppy seeds and salt; mix well. Spoon into buttered 2-quart casserole. Bake at 375°F for 1 hour. Serves 6 to 8.

Nancy Clifton

Baked Rice

¼ cup chopped onion
2 Tablespoons chopped green pepper
2 stalks celery, sliced diagonally
2 Tablespoons butter
1 cup uncooked regular rice
1½ cups water
½ cup white wine
1 chicken bouillon cube
Salt and freshly ground pepper to taste

Sauté onion, green pepper and celery in butter until tender; stir in rice and cook until lightly browned. Add water, wine, bouillon cube, salt and pepper; stir until bouillon cube is dissolved. Pour into lightly greased 2-quart casserole. Cover and bake at 350°F for 25 minutes, or until liquid is absorbed. Serves 6.

Mary Tureen

Mushroom and Pimiento Risotto

¾ pound fresh mushrooms
8 large shallots, peeled and minced
5 Tablespoons unsalted butter, divided
2½ cups chicken broth
1¼ cups long grain converted rice
½ teaspoon salt
1 Tablespoon fresh lemon juice
1 (4 ounce) jar sliced pimientos, drained
Freshly ground black pepper to taste

Trim stems from mushrooms. Mince stems. Melt 2 Tablespoons butter in 2-quart saucepan over medium-high heat. Sauté mushroom stems and shallots for 5 minutes until softened but not browned. Add broth, rice and salt and bring to a boil. Cover and simmer gently for 15 minutes or until liquid is absorbed. Remove from heat and set aside, covered, for 10 minutes. Slice mushroom caps. Melt 3 Tablespoons butter with lemon juice in large skillet over medium-high heat. Sauté mushrooms for 3 minutes. Combine mushrooms and their juices and pimientos with rice using a fork. Correct seasonings and add pepper. Serves 6.

Lee Heise

Green Chile Rice

¾ cup rice
2 cups sour cream
1 teaspoon salt
½ pound Monterey Jack cheese
1 (6 ounce) can whole green chiles, washed, seeds removed
¼ cup butter
½ pound grated Monterey Jack cheese
1 bunch green onions, chopped

Cook rice according to package directions. Combine with sour cream and salt. Arrange half of mixture in bottom of buttered 3-quart casserole. Cut ½ pound cheese into small squares and wrap in thin strips of green chiles. Put on rice. Top with remaining rice, dot with butter and sprinkle with grated cheese. Cover and refrigerate until ready to serve. Bake at 350°F for 30 minutes. Sprinkle green onions on top. Serves 6 to 8.

Shari Vagnino

Fish and Seafood

Holiday Seafood Sauterne in Vol au Vent

1½ pounds fresh cod fillets
2 cups water
Onion slice
Lemon slice
Celery leaves
Bay leaf
Salt and peppercorns
1 pound shrimp, peeled and deveined
¼ cup butter
1 cup finely chopped celery
½ cup finely chopped onion
5 Tablespoons flour
2 cups poaching liquid
½ cup sauterne
1 teaspoon instant chicken bouillon or 1 chicken bouillon cube
1 cup half and half or ½ cup milk and ½ cup mayonnaise
1 Tablespoon Worcestershire sauce
½ teaspoon dry mustard
3 or 4 drops Tabasco
1 pound scallops, halved or quartered
Vol au Vent or patty shells
Minced fresh parsley

Poach cod gently in water, onion slice, lemon slice, celery leaves, bay leaf, salt and peppercorns. Remove fish as soon as it becomes opaque. Reserve liquid. Cut up fish. Steam or boil shrimp until just pink. Cut up and add to fish. Melt butter in Dutch oven. Add celery and onions and sauté until onions are transparent. Remove vegetables with slotted spoon and add to seafood. Add flour to butter and blend for a few minutes. Add poaching liquid, sauterne and bouillon; stir until liquid begins to thicken. Add half and half and continue to cook until thickened. Blend in Worcestershire sauce, mustard and Tabasco. Add scallops and cook for a few minutes. Stir in fish mixture and heat until hot and bubbly. Do not boil. Spoon hot seafood mixture into preheated vol au vent and sprinkle with parsley. Include some of the pastry with each serving. Serves 10 to 12.

Joyce K. Driemeyer

Fresh Trout Baked in Foil

1 (¾ to 1 pound) trout per serving
Butter
Aluminum Foil
Salt and freshly ground pepper to taste
Paprika
Fresh lime juice
Fresh parsley or watercress, chopped

Arrange each trout on buttered 12-inch square of foil. Sprinkle both sides with salt, pepper, paprika and lime juice. Double fold edge of foil over fish making sealed packet. Bake at 350°F for 20 to 30 minutes, depending upon thickness of fish. Remove fish from packets and place on platter; pour juices from packets over fish and sprinkle with parsley or watercress.

Florence Wright

Baked Fish with Green Herbs

2 pounds fish fillets
¼ cup fine bread crumbs
3 Tablespoons minced parsley
2 teaspoons minced chives
Salt and freshly ground pepper to taste
6 Tablespoons olive oil
Lemon wedges (garnish)

Arrange fish in buttered 9 x 13-inch baking dish. Combine bread crumbs with parsley, chives, salt and pepper; sprinkle over fish. Sprinkle olive oil over bread crumbs. Bake at 375°F for 25 to 30 minutes or until fish flakes easily with fork. Serve with lemon wedges. Serves 4 to 5.

Pamela McGinniss

Baked Fish Fillets

2 pounds fresh fish fillets
2 teaspoons fresh lemon juice
Lemon pepper seasoning or freshly ground pepper
2 Tablespoons butter
1 medium onion, thinly sliced
6 slices cooked bacon, crumbled
½ cup soft bread crumbs
2 Tablespoons chopped fresh parsley

Put fillets, skin side down, in single layer in greased baking dish. Sprinkle fish with lemon juice and dash of lemon pepper seasoning or pepper. Melt butter, add onion and sauté until translucent; spread over fish. Combine bacon, bread crumbs and parsley, spread over fish. Bake at 350°F for 20 to 25 minutes or until fish flakes easily with a fork. Serves 6.

Grace McDermott

Marinated Fresh Halibut Steaks

2 pounds fresh halibut steaks, cut ½ to ¾-inch thick, center bone removed
½ cup olive oil
½ cup vegetable oil
1 small onion or 3 shallots, minced
¼ cup fresh lemon juice
¼ cup Dijon mustard
1 Tablespoon chopped fresh dill
1 large clove garlic, minced
Salt and freshly ground pepper to taste

Place fish in flat glass baking dish. Combine olive oil, vegetable oil, onion, lemon juice, mustard, dill, garlic, salt and pepper; pour over fish. Refrigerate for 3 hours. Drain fish and grill or broil, basting with marinade, about 8 to 10 minutes or until fish flakes easily with fork. Serves 4.

Gladys Waggoner

Fish Fillets in White Wine Sauce

2 pounds fish fillets
24 medium shrimp, peeled and deveined
½ pound small fresh mushrooms, quartered
4 Tablespoons butter, divided
2 Tablespoons finely chopped shallots
½ teaspoon salt, divided
¼ teaspoon freshly ground pepper, divided
½ cup dry white wine
¼ cup flour
1 teaspoon fresh lemon juice
Snipped fresh chives

Cut fish fillets into bite-sized pieces. Cut half the shrimp into ½-inch pieces. Butter bottom and sides of shallow flame proof dish or skillet with heat proof handle with 2 Tablespoons butter. Sprinkle shallots over bottom and sprinkle with ¼ teaspoon salt and ⅛ teaspoon pepper. Cover with fish and scatter shrimp pieces and mushrooms over fish. Top with whole shrimp. Add wine, ¼ teaspoon salt and ⅛ teaspoon pepper. Cover dish with wax paper and bring liquid to boil on top of stove. Place wax paper covered dish in 400°F oven and bake 10 minutes. Drain liquid into small saucepan, bring liquid to boil and reduce to about 1 cup. Melt 2 Tablespoons butter in saucepan and stir in flour. Add reduced fish stock gradually and cook until sauce is smooth and thick. Pour sauce over seafood; sprinkle with lemon juice and chives. Serves 8.

Ginger Nelson

Red Snapper Cendre

1 (3 pound) red snapper
9 slices firm white bread
¼ cup milk
2 Tablespoons unsalted butter
½ pound fresh mushrooms, minced
3 or 4 shallots, minced
3 Tablespoons minced parsley
1 teaspoon fennel seed
Salt and freshly ground pepper
¼ cup dry vermouth
3 sheets puff pastry
1 egg
1 Tablespoon water

Skin and bone fish, leaving head on and retaining original shape. Trim crusts from bread and dice bread. Soak bread in milk for 15 to 20 minutes. Melt butter in skillet. Add mushrooms, shallots and parsley; sauté for about 5 minutes. Add fennel seed, salt and pepper to taste. Stir in vermouth. Cook until fairly dry. Squeeze out bread slightly and add to mushroom mixture. Salt and pepper both sides of fish. Place dressing in cavity of fish. Lay 2 sheets pastry with long sides touching; roll thinly into 1 sheet. Place fish on pastry; trim edges, leaving 2 to 3 inches all around. Combine egg, water and pinch salt. Brush pastry with egg wash. Fold pastry up over fish, keeping fish shape. Place on jelly roll pan, seam side up, and brush with egg wash. Place last sheet of pastry on top and trim into fish shape. Chill for 1 hour. Slash pastry into mouth and fins. Do not cut too deep. Crimp edges of pastry. Brush with egg wash. Chill for 1 hour. Brush with egg wash. Place in 400°F oven, reduce heat to 375°F and bake for 45 to 50 minutes. Serves 4.

Andre Gotti
C. Exe. Chef
Old Warson Country Club

Sole Finocchio

2 (7 ounce) fillets of sole
1½ cups sliced fresh mushrooms
1 teaspoon minced shallots
2 to 3 Tablespoons clarified butter
½ cup dry vermouth
½ cup sweet vermouth
Pinch basil leaves
12 fennel seeds
4 to 6 Tablespoons tomato purée

Place sole on lightly buttered baking dish. Bake at 375°F for 7 minutes or until firm but flaky. Sauté mushrooms and shallots in clarified butter in large skillet until slightly tender. Add sweet and dry vermouth; ignite wine. Cook until reduced to half. Stir in basil and fennel and cook 1 minute. Lower heat to medium and add tomato purée. Stir until wine and purée are combined. Pour sauce over fish. Serves 2.

The Ladle

Salmon Mousse with Dill Sauce

Mousse:

1 (15½ ounce) can red salmon
1 (7½ ounce) can red salmon
½ cup boiling water
2 Tablespoons unflavored gelatin
1½ cups sour cream
½ cup mayonnaise
3 Tablespoons chopped onion
2 Tablespoons chopped capers
2 Tablespoons fresh lemon juice
1 teaspoon salt
1 teaspoon paprika
½ teaspoon Tabasco
Parsley (garnish)

Mousse:

Drain and bone salmon, reserving liquid. Mash salmon until smooth. Dissolve gelatin in boiling water, add liquid from salmon and let cool. Combine salmon, gelatin mixture, sour cream, mayonnaise, onion, capers, lemon juice, salt, paprika and Tabasco in large bowl. Mix well and pour into well greased 6-cup ring mold. Set in freezer for 10 minutes, then refrigerate. Unmold and garnish with parsley. Serves 6 to 8.

Dill Sauce:

1 egg
2 cups sour cream
3 Tablespoons fresh dill
2 Tablespoons chopped onion
1 Tablespoon chopped capers
Pinch sugar
Salt and freshly ground pepper to taste

Dill Sauce:

Beat egg. Add sour cream, dill, onion, capers, sugar, salt and pepper and mix well. Refrigerate.

Stella Pearlmutter

Sun Belt Snapper Fillets

2 pounds fresh red snapper fillets
1 teaspoon fresh lemon juice
¼ cup butter, melted
3 Tablespoons fresh orange juice
1 Tablespoon freshly grated orange rind
Salt and freshly ground pepper to taste
Dash nutmeg
1 Tablespoon chopped fresh parsley

Put fillets, skin side down, in single layer in buttered baking dish. Sprinkle with lemon juice. Set aside. Add orange juice and orange rind to melted butter and spread over fish. Sprinkle fish with salt, pepper and nutmeg. Bake at 350°F for 15 to 18 minutes or until fish flakes easily with fork. Do not overcook. Sprinkle with parsley. Serves 6.

Judy Hopper

Sautéed Lemon Sole with Julienne of Fresh Vegetable

¼ pound leeks, julienned
¼ pound carrots, julienned
1½ pounds lemon sole fillets
1 teaspoon fresh lemon juice
Salt and freshly ground pepper to taste
¼ cup butter
2 Tablespoons dry vermouth
¼ cup light cream
2 Tablespoons fresh chopped parsley

Cook leeks in boiling salted water until tender crisp, about 2 minutes. In another saucepan, cook carrots in boiling salted water until tender crisp, about 4 minutes. Drain vegetables and set aside. Sprinkle fillets with lemon juice, salt and pepper. Melt butter until bubbling in skillet and cook fillets in single layer a few minutes on each side until opaque. Remove fish to serving dish and artfully arrange vegetables over dish. Add vermouth to butter and juice remaining in skillet and cook for a few minutes. Stir in cream and cook until smooth. Pour sauce over fish and vegetables and sprinkle with parsley. Serves 4.

Joyce K. Driemeyer

Catfish Cooked in Beer Herb Batter

1½ cups flour
1 cup flat beer
2 teaspoons vegetable oil
Salt to taste
2 eggs, separated
¼ cup chopped fresh parsley
2 teaspoons finely chopped tarragon
2 teaspoons finely chopped marjoram
2 teaspoons chopped chives
3 to 4 pounds catfish
Oil for deep frying

Place flour in bowl; add beer, oil and salt. Blend roughly; it will be lumpy. Cover and let stand at room temperature for about 3 hours. When ready to cook, add egg yolks. Beat egg whites until stiff and fold in. Add parsley, tarragon, marjoram and chives. Dip cleaned and dried fish into batter. Heat oil for frying. Add fish and cook about 5 minutes on each side. Allow total of 10 minutes cooking per inch thickness of fish. Serves 4.

Marianne Collins

Fillets of Sole in Tomato, Garlic and Wine Sauce

1 onion, chopped
1 clove garlic, minced
1 Tablespoon butter
¼ cup dry white wine
1 (1 pound) can stewed tomatoes, drained and chopped
1 Tablespoon chopped fresh parsley
1 Tablespoon fresh lemon juice
⅛ teaspoon thyme
Salt and freshly ground pepper to taste
1 pound fillets of sole, cut into 4-inch pieces
Chopped fresh parsley (garnish)

Sauté onion and garlic in butter until onions are transparent. Add wine and continue cooking until wine is almost evaporated, about 3 minutes. Add tomatoes, parsley, lemon juice, thyme, salt and pepper and simmer for about 10 minutes. While sauce is simmering, bake fish. Place fillets in single layer in 9 x 13-inch baking dish. Bake at 350°F for 8 to 10 minutes or until fish flakes easily with fork. Remove fish to platter and spoon a little sauce over each fillet. Spoon remaining sauce around edges. Sprinkle with parsley. Serves 4.

Elaine Stephenson

Clish

¼ pound salt pork, cut into ⅛-inch cubes
2 medium onions, halved and thinly sliced
2 to 2½ cups diced potatoes
2 cups bottled clam juice
1 (6½ ounce) can chopped clams, undrained
1 pound cod, cut into ½-inch cubes, deboned
½ teaspoon salt
⅛ teaspoon freshly ground pepper
⅛ teaspoon mace
⅛ teaspoon thyme
4 drops Tabasco
5 cups whole milk
1 Tablespoon butter

Heat pork for 2 to 3 minutes in souppot over medium heat. Add onions and cook until slightly brown. Add potatoes, clam juice and clams; cook 15 minutes. Add cod and cook 5 minutes. Add salt, pepper, mace, thyme and Tabasco and mix well. Add milk and heat just to boiling. Add butter just before serving. Serve very hot with saltines or oyster crackers. Serves 4 to 5.

Lou Diane Perry

Portuguese Stew

1 bunch broccoli, broken into florets

1 head cauliflower, broken into florets

1 large red onion, sliced

2 zucchini, cut into long narrow strips

2 yellow squash, sliced

2 large tomatoes, quartered

1 pound fresh mushrooms, sliced

3 pounds jumbo shrimp, peeled and deveined

Minced parsley

Oregano

Thyme

Garlic powder

Onion salt

Freshly ground pepper

Butter

½ cup white wine

Line roaster with heavy-duty aluminum foil. Put in layer of broccoli and cauliflower. Sprinkle with parsley, oregano, thyme, garlic powder, onion salt and pepper. Top with small pieces of butter. Add layer of zucchini, squash, tomatoes and mushrooms. Sprinkle with seasonings and top with butter. Put shrimp on top. Sprinkle with seasonings and top with butter. Pour wine over shrimp. Close foil tightly. Bake at 375°F for 1 hour. Serves 6 to 8.

Tina M. Burke

Shrimp in Green Sauce

1 pound raw shrimp, peeled and deveined

2 Tablespoons flour

Salt and freshly ground pepper to taste

⅓ cup olive oil

4 teaspoons flour

¼ cup chopped green onions

1 clove garlic, finely minced

¾ cup chicken broth

½ cup white wine

¼ teaspoon Tabasco

½ cup frozen peas

½ cup chopped fresh parsley

Coat shrimp with 2 Tablespoons flour, salt and pepper. Heat oil in large skillet, add shrimp and cook 1½ to 2 minutes. Remove shrimp. Add 4 teaspoons flour to oil, stirring until smooth; add onions and garlic, while stirring. Add broth, wine and Tabasco. Cook over high heat until smooth and blended, about 2 minutes. Add shrimp, peas and parsley and simmer for a few minutes. Serve over rice. Serves 4.

Valerie Donovan

Sauté of Shrimp L'Antiboise

8 to 10 Italian plum tomatoes, peeled and seeded
5 Tablespoons olive oil, divided
1 medium zucchini, finely diced
Salt and freshly ground pepper to taste
1 red bell pepper, roasted, peeled, cored and finely sliced
1 small dried hot chile pepper, seeded and crumbled, or 1 fresh hot chile pepper, seeded and finely chopped
1 pound fresh shrimp, peeled and deveined
2 large cloves garlic, finely sliced
1 large sprig fresh thyme
3 Tablespoons finely minced fresh parsley
2 cloves garlic, finely minced
2 Tablespoons finely minced fresh thyme

Place tomatoes in colander, sprinkle with salt and let drain 30 to 60 minutes. Heat 2 Tablespoons oil in heavy skillet over medium high heat. Add zucchini, salt and pepper to taste and sauté until zucchini is soft. Add red pepper and cook 1 minute. Remove from heat. Heat 3 Tablespoons oil with chile pepper in large heavy skillet over high heat. When pepper has darkened, remove and discard. Add shrimp, sliced garlic and thyme sprig to skillet and stir-fry just until shrimp turn pink. Season with salt and pepper and discard garlic if it has burned. Add tomatoes and cook 2 to 3 minutes. Add zucchini mixture, parsley, minced garlic and thyme and mix well. Serves 4.

Mrs. Charles West

Shrimp Pie

1 (8 ounce) can refrigerated crescent rolls
2 cups (8 ounces) ½-inch cubes Monterey Jack cheese
1 (8 ounce) can stewed tomatoes, drained
6 ounces fresh shrimp, peeled and deveined
2 eggs, slightly beaten
1 Tablespoon freshly grated Parmesan cheese

Separate crescent dough into 8 triangles. Place 5 triangles in 9-inch pie plate, pressing together to form crust. Combine cheeses, tomatoes, shrimp and eggs in large bowl; pour into crust. Roll out remaining triangles so longest side is 9 inches. Cut into ½-inch strips. Twist strips, criss-cross over filling and tuck under edges to form lattice top. Press edge with fork to seal. Place pie pan on cookie sheet. Bake at 350°F for 50 to 60 minutes until crust is golden brown and filling has solidified. Makes 1 9-inch pie.

Christine Dawson

Shrimp with Apricots

½ cup chopped dried apricots
⅓ cup apricot flavored brandy
2 Tablespoons unsalted butter
1 Tablespoon vegetable oil
1 green pepper, cut lengthwise into ¼-inch strips
½ cup thinly sliced green onions including tops
1 clove garlic, minced
1 pound shrimp, peeled and deveined
2 teaspoons lemon juice
2 teaspoons cornstarch
1 teaspoon salt
3 drops Tabasco
¼ cup toasted slivered almonds

Combine apricots and brandy in small bowl; cover and let stand for 15 minutes. Heat butter and oil in 9-inch skillet, add green pepper, onions and garlic and sauté for a few minutes. Add shrimp and cook for 2 minutes. Add apricot mixture and cook for 2 minutes. Combine lemon juice, cornstarch, salt and Tabasco; stir into shrimp mixture. Cook, stirring, until thick. Sprinkle with almonds and serve over rice. Serves 4.

Josephine Howard

Shrimp and Scallop Gratin

1 pound shrimp, peeled and deveined
1 pound bay scallops
6 Tablespoons medium dry sherry
¾ cup French bread crumbs, lightly toasted
½ cup chopped fresh parsley
1 Tablespoon chopped green onion
2 cloves garlic, minced
½ teaspoon salt
¼ teaspoon oregano
Pinch cayenne
Freshly ground pepper to taste
½ cup unsalted butter, melted

Combine shrimp, scallops and sherry and place in buttered 8 x 10-inch baking or gratin dish. Combine bread crumbs, parsley, green onion, garlic, salt, oregano, cayenne and pepper and sprinkle over seafood. Drizzle butter over top of crumbs. Bake at 400°F for 10 to 12 minutes in upper third of oven. Serves 6.

Natalie Rothschild

Bar-B-Qued Shrimp

Jumbo shrimp, cleaned with shells on (12 per person)
3⅛ cups dry white wine
3 cups chili sauce
2½ cups olive oil
1½ cups unsalted butter
3 cups parsley tips
½ cup sweet basil
2 Tablespoons salt
1 Tablespoon fresh red pepper flakes
1 Tablespoon oregano
3 cloves garlic, pressed

Place wine, chili sauce, olive oil, butter, parsley tips, basil, salt, pepper flakes, oregano and garlic in large pot over high heat. Let it bubble, then reduce heat a little. Boil about 15 minutes until parsley breaks down. Stir before pouring over shrimp to prevent separating. Place shrimp in large baking dish in a flat layer. Pour sauce over shrimp and marinate for 1 hour. Bake at 400°F for 20 minutes total time, or just until they begin to curl. Do not cook longer. Turn and stir the shrimp after first 10 minutes and again after 10 minutes or just before serving. Serve with plenty of French bread for getting all the extra sauce. Makes sauce for 10 servings.

Centralia House

Scallops Dijonnaise

1 pound sea scallops, halved
1½ Tablespoons dry white wine
3 Tablespoons flour
1 teaspoon salt
Freshly ground pepper to taste
3 shallots, minced
1 clove garlic, minced
¼ cup clarified butter
½ cup dry white wine
½ cup heavy cream
2 Tablespoons Dijon mustard
Salt and freshly ground pepper to taste
Minced fresh parsley

Place scallops in medium bowl, add 1½ Tablespoons wine, cover and refrigerate for 1 hour. Combine flour, salt and pepper. Drain scallops and pat dry on paper towels. Dust scallops with flour mixture and shake off excess. Sauté shallots and garlic in butter until fragrant. Add scallops and sauté until golden. Transfer to serving dish. Deglaze skillet with ½ cup wine over high heat. Add cream and mustard and reduce sauce until thickened. Add salt and pepper. Pour over scallops and sprinkle with parsley. Serves 3 to 4.

Eleanor Brownfield

Gingered Scallops

1 Tablespoon butter
1 teaspoon peeled and finely minced fresh ginger
1 large clove garlic, minced
1 pound fresh scallops, halved (quartered if large)
1 teaspoon fresh lemon juice
Freshly ground black pepper to taste
4 green onions, sliced
Chopped fresh parsley or coriander (garnish)

Melt butter in skillet, add ginger and garlic and cook until fragrant. Add scallops, sprinkle with lemon juice and pepper, stir and cook about 2 minutes. Add onions and cook for 2 minutes. Sprinkle with parsley or coriander. Serves 4.

Claudia Moore

Crab Soufflé

¼ cup diced onion
2 Tablespoons butter
1 clove garlic, minced
2 Tablespoons flour
¾ cup milk
1 teaspoon finely chopped fresh chives
½ teaspoon marjoram
Dash nutmeg
2 eggs, separated
¾ cup grated mild Cheddar cheese
¼ cup chopped fresh parsley
1 (6¼ ounce) can lump crabmeat, drained and rinsed
⅛ teaspoon cream of tartar
Butter
2 Tablespoons grated Parmesan cheese

Sauté onion and garlic in butter until soft. Stir in flour; cook a few minutes. Add milk gradually and cook until mixture thickens. Stir in chives, marjoram and nutmeg. Beat egg yolks into mixture; stir in cheese and parsley, add crab and blend well. Beat egg whites until foamy, add cream of tartar and beat until stiff. Fold into crab mixture. Pour into a 1-quart soufflé dish which has been buttered and dusted with Parmesan cheese. Bake at 350°F for 25 to 30 minutes. Serve immediately. Serves 2 to 3.

Annette Mueller

Fisherman's Wharf Cioppino

½ cup olive oil
1¼ cups chopped onion
¾ cup chopped green onion
¾ cup chopped green pepper
3 or 4 cloves garlic, finely chopped
1 (11½ ounce) jar whole clams, undrained
1 (28 ounce) can tomatoes
1 (6 ounce) can tomato paste
1¾ cups Burgundy
¾ cup water
⅓ cup chopped fresh parsley
2 teaspoons salt
2 teaspoons oregano
½ teaspoon basil
¼ teaspoon freshly ground pepper
1½ pounds halibut steaks, or other firm white fish
3 (6½ ounce) cans king crab meat, drained and cartilage removed
½ pound raw shrimp, peeled and deveined

Heat oil in 6-quart kettle and sauté onions, green onions, green pepper and garlic until tender, about 10 minutes, stirring occasionally. Drain clams, reserving ¼ cup liquid. Set clams aside. Add clam liquid, tomatoes, tomato paste, Burgundy, water, parsley, salt, oregano, basil and pepper to sautéed vegetables and mix well. Bring to a boil, reduce heat, and simmer, uncovered, for 10 minutes, stirring frequently. Cut halibut in 1-inch pieces and discard skin and bones. Add fish, crab, shrimp and clams to tomato mixture. Cover and simmer 15 minutes. Uncover and simmer 15 minutes. Serves 8.

Suzy Wahl

Lobster Albanello

2 pounds fresh lobster meat
1 pound fresh mushrooms, sliced
6 Tablespoons butter
6 shallots
4 cups heavy cream
½ cup fish stock (if not available, substitute chicken broth)
1 cup dry white wine
Chopped fresh parsley (garnish)

Sauté in large skillet the lobster meat and mushrooms in butter with shallots. Add cream, fish stock and wine. Cook until sauce is well blended. Garnish with parsley. Serve with a chilled white wine and tossed green salad. Serves 4.

Tony's

Appetizer Oysters in Patty Shells

1 cup boiling water
1 chicken bouillon cube
6 Tablespoons butter, divided
3 Tablespoons flour
¼ cup coarsely chopped cooked country ham
1 (2 ounce) jar mushrooms, undrained
1 Tablespoon chopped fresh chives
1 teaspoon Kikkoman soy sauce
½ teaspoon lemon pepper seasoning
1 pint shucked fresh oysters with liquid or 2 (8 ounce) cans oysters with liquid
10 patty shells

Dissolve chicken bouillon cube in boiling water. Melt 4 Tablespoons butter in 2-quart saucepan, stir in flour, slowly add chicken stock and continue to stir until sauce is smooth. Continue to cook, stirring, until sauce thickens. Reduce heat; add ham, mushrooms, chives, soy sauce and lemon pepper seasoning. Simmer 2 to 3 minutes to blend. Melt 2 Tablespoons butter in another pan, add oysters and heat gently. Using slotted spoon, add oysters to sauce. If sauce is too thick, add oyster liquid to thin. Fill patty shells with oyster mixture. Place on cookie sheet and broil until hot, 1 to 2 minutes. Serves 10.

Nadine Briggs

Moules-Scallops-Marinière

5 pounds mussels, cleaned
1 pound bay scallops, cleaned
1 cup dry white wine
1 cup chopped fresh parsley
½ cup unsalted butter
3 Tablespoons chopped shallots
1 teaspoon salt
1 teaspoon freshly ground pepper
6 Tablespoons heavy cream
Chopped fresh parsley (garnish)

Combine mussels, scallops, wine, parsley, butter, shallots, salt and pepper in large souppot and simmer for 5 minutes. Remove mussels and scallops. Add cream and reduce sauce for about 5 minutes. Return mussels and scallops to pot to heat. Remove and serve at once. Garnish with chopped parsley. Serves 6.

Anthony's

Poultry

Crab-Stuffed Chicken Breasts

6 chicken breasts, skinned, boned and flattened
Salt and freshly ground pepper to taste
½ cup chopped onion
½ cup chopped celery
5 Tablespoons butter, divided
1 (6½ ounce) can crab meat, drained
½ cup herb seasoned stuffing mix
5 Tablespoons dry white wine, divided
2 Tablespoons flour
½ teaspoon paprika
¾ cup milk
1 (1¼ ounce) package Hollandaise sauce mix
½ cup shredded Swiss cheese
Finely minced parsley (garnish)

Sprinkle chicken breasts with salt and pepper. Sauté onion and celery in 3 Tablespoons butter until tender. Remove from heat; add crab, stuffing mix and 3 Tablespoons wine and toss lightly to blend. Place equal portion of mixture on each chicken breast, roll up and secure with skewers or tie with twine. Place in greased 12 x 8-inch baking dish. Melt 2 Tablespoons butter and drizzle over top. Bake at 375°F for 1 hour. Blend milk and Hollandaise sauce mix. Cook and stir over low heat until thickened. Add cheese and 2 Tablespoons wine; stir until cheese melts. Pour half the sauce over chicken breasts. Sprinkle with parsley. Pass remaining sauce at table. Serves 6.

Marion G. Cairns

Chicken Livers Marsala

1 pound chicken livers
Marsala wine
6 Tablespoons butter
6 green onions, minced
Flour
Salt and freshly ground pepper to taste
Paprika
⅔ cup Marsala wine
2 Tablespoons lemon juice
2 teaspoons sage
Minced parsley (garnish)

Marinate chicken livers in wine to cover for 1 hour. Drain and pat dry. Melt butter in large skillet. Add onions and sauté over medium heat until limp. Coat chicken livers with mixture of flour, salt, pepper and paprika. Shake off excess. Sauté with onions for 3 minutes or until firm but pink inside. Remove to serving plate and keep warm. Add ⅔ cup wine, lemon juice and sage to skillet and cook until slightly reduced. Pour over livers and garnish with parsley. Serves 4.

Nancy Garland

Chicken Tetrazzini

4 whole chicken breasts, skinned
1 onion, sliced
2 stalks celery, chopped
Salt
1 (10¾ ounce) can cream of chicken soup
8 ounces grated Cheddar cheese
1 cup sour cream
½ cup dry sherry
½ teaspoon freshly ground pepper
1 pint fresh mushrooms
½ pound spaghetti
½ cup freshly grated Parmesan cheese
½ cup herb seasoned bread crumbs

Cook chicken with onion and celery in salted water for 1 hour. Remove chicken and reserve broth. Combine soup, Cheddar cheese, sour cream, sherry and pepper in saucepan and heat, but do not boil. Cook mushrooms in chicken broth for a few minutes. Cook spaghetti in boiling salted water. Drain and rinse. Add mushrooms, onion, celery and 1 cup chicken broth to sauce. Cube chicken and add to sauce. Stir in spaghetti and blend well. Pour mixture into greased 9x13-inch baking dish. Sprinkle with Parmesan cheese and bread crumbs. Bake at 350°F for 30 minutes. Serves 8.

Ann O'Toole

Poulet Bastille

1 quart chicken stock
3 Tablespoons port wine
3 Tablespoons brandy
3 Tablespoons Grand Marnier
3 Tablespoons tomato paste
¼ teaspoon white pepper
2 cups peeled very ripe peaches, mashed
2 Tablespoons white vinegar
Sugar
¼ cup white wine
3 Tablespoons cornstarch
3 Tablespoons fresh lemon juice
8 chicken breasts, skinned, boned and sautéed
Melon balls, sliced fresh peaches, fresh berries (garnish)

Stir chicken stock, port, brandy, Grand Marnier, tomato paste and pepper together in heavy saucepan; reduce by ⅓ over low heat. Put peaches and vinegar in another heavy saucepan. Simmer until peaches are cooked smooth. Force through sieve and measure. Add equal amount of sugar. Boil until a drop of mixture forms a soft ball in ice water. Add stock mixture to peaches. Whisk until smooth. Add wine to cornstarch. Whisk into peach mixture. Simmer for 15 minutes. Skim any foam that rises. Add lemon juice. Mix well. Cool. Cover and refrigerate overnight. Reheat slowly. Serve over sautéed chicken breasts. Garnish with melon balls, peaches and berries. Serves 8.

Balaban's

Wild Duck

1 wild duck, cleaned
1 slice onion
1 slice unpared apple
1 stalk celery
6 ounces red wine

Place duck in center of piece of heavy duty aluminum foil. Place onion, apple and celery in cavity of duck. Pour wine over duck. Wrap tightly in foil; set in roasting pan. Bake at 350°F for 1½ hours. Uncover last few minutes for a crispy skin. If desired, more wine may be added to pan juices and poured over duck before serving. Serves 2.

Jean Lange

Chicken Legs with White Wine

4 large chicken leg and thigh joints
1½ slices bread
4 ounces chicken livers, chopped
4 ounces pork sausages, skinned and chopped
2 ounces button mushrooms, chopped
1 egg
6 Tablespoons cognac, divided
1½ Tablespoons chopped chives
1 Tablespoon chopped chervil
Salt and freshly ground pepper to taste
2 cups unsalted butter
½ cup chicken broth
4 strips fat salt pork
1 medium onion, finely chopped
1 shallot, chopped
1 or 2 sprigs parsley
1 bay leaf
½ clove garlic
¼ teaspoon thyme
1½ cups White Chablis
2 pounds spinach
4 paper frills

Bone thighs of chicken; leave drumsticks intact. Make bread crumbs from bread. Combine bread crumbs, livers, sausages, mushrooms, egg, 4 Tablespoons cognac, chives, chervil, salt and pepper. Melt ½ cup butter, cool and pour over mixture. Add chicken broth and mix well. Stuff thighs with mixture and shape them into little hams. Wrap each in a strip of salt pork and tie with string. Melt ½ cup butter in heavy skillet and sauté chicken legs until they are browned all over, about 15 minutes. Discard this butter as it will have discolored during cooking process. Add onion, shallot, parsley, bay leaf, garlic and thyme to skillet. Warm 2 Tablespoons cognac, pour over dish and flame. Add wine, cover and cook for 25 minutes. Sauté spinach in ½ cup butter. Season to taste with salt and pepper and make a bed of cooked spinach on a serving platter. Arrange chicken on top of spinach. Keep warm. Reduce sauce in which chicken was cooked by half. Remove from heat and beat in remaining ½ cup butter, cut into small pieces. When sauce is thick and creamy pour it over chicken legs. Decorate each one with a paper frill. Serve very hot. Serves 4.

Donna Arenson Orchard

Lemon Chicken with Mushrooms and Prosciutto

4½ chicken breasts, split, skinned and boned
5 Tablespoons Italian bread crumbs
1 Tablespoon flour
Oil and butter
2¼ cups chicken broth
2¼ cups fresh lemon juice
1 cup butter rolled and kneaded in equal amount of flour
2 cloves garlic, finely minced
½ pound fresh mushrooms, thinly sliced
¼ pound prosciutto or Canadian bacon, finely chopped
1½ cups white wine

Coat chicken breasts with combination of bread crumbs and flour. Heat equal parts of oil and butter to cover bottom of skillet and sauté chicken until lightly browned. Set aside on warm platter. Pour excess liquid from skillet. Heat broth and lemon juice until bubbly. Add butter-flour ball. As sauce thickens, add garlic; add mushrooms and prosciutto. Add wine and allow alcohol to cook off. Add chicken breasts to sauce and heat through. Serves 6.

Donna Herdbretter

Poulet Sauté à la Crème

1 (2½ to 3 pound) chicken, cut up
½ cup flour
4 Tablespoons butter, divided
1 Tablespoon vegetable oil
1½ cups sliced fresh mushrooms
½ ounce cognac
½ cup Chablis
1 cup chicken broth
Salt and freshly ground pepper to taste
1 cup heavy cream
1 Tablespoon chopped fresh parsley (garnish)

Dust chicken with flour very lightly. Melt 3 Tablespoons butter in oil in large skillet. Add chicken and sauté until brown. Add mushrooms and sauté for a few minutes. Pour in cognac and flambé. Remove mushrooms with slotted spoon. Pour in wine and cook for a few minutes. Add chicken broth, salt and pepper and cook for 30 minutes. When chicken is tender, place on platter with mushrooms. Combine remaining flour and butter in small bowl; stir in cream. Add to sauce in skillet very slowly, whisking, until sauce is smooth and thickened. Correct seasonings. Pour sauce over chicken and sprinkle with parsley. Serves 4.

L' Auberge Bretonne

Stuffed Cornish Game Hens

6 (1½ pound) Cornish game hens
1½ cups long grain rice
⅓ cup red wine
1½ teaspoons sugar
¾ teaspoon salt
⅛ teaspoon freshly ground pepper
⅛ teaspoon nutmeg
⅛ teaspoon allspice
⅓ cup toasted slivered almonds

Wash and dry game hens. Cook rice according to package. Add wine, sugar, salt, pepper, nutmeg and allspice to cooked rice; mix well. Stir in almonds. Stuff mixture lightly into cavities of hens. Place hens in shallow roasting pan; cover loosely with foil. Roast at 400°F for 30 minutes. Uncover and roast for 1 hour, basting occasionally with wine glaze. Serves 6.

Wine Glaze:
¼ cup red wine
3 Tablespoons butter, melted
1½ teaspoons fresh lemon juice

Wine Glaze:
Combine wine, butter and lemon juice. Stir well.

Marcia M. Bernstein

Turkey Delight

3 cups cooked turkey
2 cups French style green beans, drained
1 (10¾ ounce) can cream of celery soup
1 (8 ounce) can water chestnuts, diced
½ pound fresh mushrooms, sliced, sautéed in butter
1 cup mayonnaise
1 (6 ounce) package long grain and wild rice, cooked
1 (4 ounce) jar sliced pimientos, drained
1 medium onion, chopped
Salt and freshly ground pepper to taste

Combine turkey, green beans, soup, water chestnuts, mushrooms, mayonnaise, rice, pimientos, onion, salt and pepper and blend well. Pour into a 2½ or 3-quart casserole. Bake at 350°F for 25 to 30 minutes. Serves 8.

Betty Mathieu

African Spicy Chicken

½ cup fresh lemon juice
2 Tablespoons tomato paste
2 cloves garlic, mashed
1 Tablespoon salt
1 to 1½ teaspoons, cayenne
1 teaspoon hot dry mustard
½ cup vegetable oil
1 (4½ pound) chicken, cut up
1 cup roasted peanuts or peanuts and cashews
½ cup dried apple slices
Cooked rice

Combine lemon juice, tomato paste, garlic, salt, cayenne and mustard in large bowl. Add oil in a stream while beating. Continue beating until well combined. Chill overnight. Pat chicken dry. Add to marinade and toss well. Marinate for at least 4 hours. Drain chicken, reserving marinade. Broil chicken, skin side up, 6 inches from heat for 10 minutes. Turn and baste. Broil for 10 minutes or until juices run clear. Combine nuts and apple slices with remaining marinade in saucepan and heat. Put chicken on bed of rice and spoon sauce over chicken. Serves 4.

Suzy Wahl

Chicken Chinese

1 (2 to 2½ pound) chicken, cut up
1 cup sliced celery
½ cup sliced mushrooms
½ cup sliced onions
2 Tablespoons vegetable oil
2¼ cups chicken stock
⅓ cup Kikkoman soy sauce or to taste
¾ cup bean sprouts
¼ cup sliced bamboo shoots
¼ cup sliced water chestnuts
¼ cup cornstarch
Salt and pepper

Steam chicken until tender. Save stock. Remove meat from bones and julienne. Reserve ¼ cup white meat for garnish. Sauté celery, mushrooms and onions in oil for 5 minutes. Add stock and soy sauce and cook 5 minutes. Add bean sprouts, bamboo shoots, water chestnuts and chicken and bring to a boil. Add enough liquid from saucepan to cornstarch to make smooth paste. Add to saucepan and cook until mixture thickens. Add salt and pepper if needed. Garnish with reserved chicken and serve with rice. Serves 4 to 6.

Mrs. Edward T. Foote

Breast of Chicken Martinique

3 slices bacon, diced
1 cup wild rice
¼ cup finely chopped onions
¼ cup finely chopped chicken livers
2 cups chicken broth
½ cup fresh bread crumbs
½ cup freshly grated Parmesan cheese
1 egg
2 Tablespoons chopped parsley
Salt and freshly ground pepper to taste
6 chicken breasts, skinned, boned, halved and flattened
Melted butter
Salt and freshly ground pepper to taste
12 Holland rusks

Sauté bacon in a large skillet. Add wild rice, onions and chicken livers and sauté 5 minutes. Add chicken broth, cover and bake at 350°F for 45 minutes. Cool rice and add bread crumbs, cheese, egg, parsley, salt and pepper. Spread stuffing on chicken breasts, roll up and tie with string. Place in baking dish. Brush with butter and sprinkle with salt and pepper. Bake at 350°F for 1 hour. Place each breast on a rusk and cover with mushroom sauce. Serves 12.

Mushroom Sauce:

½ cup butter, divided
¼ cup rendered chicken fat
½ cup flour
2 cups chicken broth
1 cup thinly sliced mushrooms
2 Tablespoons sherry
Salt and freshly ground pepper to taste

Mushroom Sauce:

Heat ¼ cup butter and chicken fat in saucepan, stir in flour and when mixture foams add chicken broth. Bring sauce to a boil and simmer for 20 minutes. Sauté mushrooms in ¼ cup butter until they are soft; stir in sherry. Strain sauce into mushrooms and cook for 10 minutes longer. Season with salt and pepper to taste.

Ana Marie Anderson

Chicken Piccata

4 chicken breasts, skinned, boned and halved
½ cup flour
1½ teaspoons salt
¼ teaspoon freshly ground pepper
Paprika
¼ cup clarified butter
1 Tablespoon olive oil
2 to 4 Tablespoons dry Madeira or water
3 Tablespoons fresh lemon juice
1 lemon, thinly sliced
3 Tablespoons capers (optional)
¼ cup minced fresh parsley

Flatten chicken breasts between 2 sheets wax paper until ¼-inch thick. Combine flour, salt, pepper and paprika in bag. Add chicken and coat well. Shake off excess. Heat butter and oil in large skillet until bubbling. Sauté chicken breasts, a few at a time, 2 to 3 minutes on each side. Do not overcook. Drain and keep warm. Drain off all but 2 Tablespoons butter and oil. Stir Madeira or water into drippings, scraping bottom of skillet to remove any particles. Add lemon juice and heat briefly. Return chicken to skillet, add lemon slices and heat until mixture thickens. Add capers, if desired, and sprinkle with minced parsley. Serves 4 to 6.

Peggy McClellan

Chicken Verona

½ cup fine bread crumbs
⅓ cup freshly grated Romano cheese
¼ cup chopped fresh parsley
2 teaspoons salt
¼ teaspoon freshly ground pepper
⅛ teaspoon dry mustard
¼ cup butter
1 clove garlic, minced
4 chicken breasts, halved

Combine bread crumbs, cheese, parsley, salt, pepper and mustard in a pie plate. Melt butter in a baking dish and add garlic. Dip chicken in butter, roll in crumb mixture, and place skin side up in baking dish. Spread any extra crumb mixture over chicken. Bake at 375°F for 45 minutes. Serves 4 to 6.

Barbara S. Sullivan

Cherry Wine Chicken Breasts

3 chicken breasts, halved
⅓ cup flour
1½ teaspoons salt
1½ teaspoons garlic salt
1½ teaspoons paprika
¼ cup vegetable oil
1 (17 ounce) can pitted dark sweet cherries, drained
1 cup Sauterne wine
⅓ cup cherry liquid

Coat chicken with mixture of flour, salt, garlic salt and paprika. Heat oil in large skillet. Brown chicken in oil. Add cherries, wine and cherry liquid. Cover and simmer for 1 hour, or until chicken is tender. Serves 4.

Mildred K. Kaufman

Chicken Surprise

2 (10 ounce) packages chopped broccoli, cooked and well drained
½ pound fresh mushrooms, sliced
2 cups chicken chunks
2 (10¾ ounce) cans cream of chicken soup
1 cup mayonnaise
1 Tablespoon lemon juice
½ teaspoon curry powder
Velveeta or American cheese slices
½ cup Italian bread crumbs

Arrange broccoli in well-greased 9 x 13-inch baking dish. Place mushrooms on top. Cover with chicken. Combine soup, mayonnaise, lemon juice and curry powder. Pour over chicken. Cover with cheese slices. Sprinkle with bread crumbs. Bake at 350°F for 30 minutes. Serves 4 to 6.

Marleah Strominger

Chicken Artichoke Casserole

1 (3 pound) chicken, cut up
1½ teaspoons salt
½ teaspoon paprika
¼ teaspoon pepper
6 Tablespoons butter, divided
¼ pound fresh mushrooms, quartered
3 Tablespoons flour
⅔ cup chicken broth
3 Tablespoons sherry
1 (14 ounce) can artichoke hearts, drained

Sprinkle chicken with salt, paprika and pepper. Melt 4 Tablespoons butter in skillet and brown the chicken. Put browned chicken in 2-quart casserole. Add 2 Tablespoons butter to skillet; add mushrooms and sauté 5 minutes. Sprinkle flour over mushrooms, stir in chicken broth and sherry and cook for 5 minutes. Arrange artichoke hearts between chicken pieces. Pour mushroom sauce over chicken. Bake at 375°F for 40 minutes. Serves 4.

Tina M. Burke

Mother's Hot Chicken Salad

4 cups diced chicken
2 cups chopped celery
4 hard-boiled eggs, diced
1 Tablespoon minced onion
1 teaspoon salt
½ teaspoon MSG
1 (10¾ ounce) can cream of chicken soup
1 cup mayonnaise
2 Tablespoons lemon juice
1 cup grated sharp Cheddar cheese
⅔ cup toasted slivered almonds
1 cup herb stuffing mix

Combine chicken, celery, eggs, onion, salt and MSG in 2-quart casserole. Add soup, mayonnaise and lemon juice and mix well. Cover and refrigerate overnight. Remove 1 hour before serving. Sprinkle with cheese, almonds and stuffing mix. Bake at 400°F for 20 to 25 minutes. Serves 6 to 8.

Mrs. Paul Mansfield

If You Can't Get The Colonel's Fried Chicken

3 pounds chicken, cut up
2 (0.7 ounce) packages Good Seasons Italian Dressing mix
1½ cups flour, divided
¼ cup lemon juice
2 teaspoons salt
Butter, melted
1 teaspoon paprika
½ teaspoon powdered sage
¼ teaspoon freshly ground pepper
1 cup milk, club soda or beer
Vegetable oil

Halve chicken breasts and wipe chicken dry. Make a paste of salad dressing, 3 Tablespoons flour, lemon juice, salt and butter. Coat chicken by brushing or dipping in mixture. Cover and refrigerate for at least 2 hours. Combine remaining flour, paprika, sage and pepper. Dip chicken pieces individually into milk and then into flour mixture. Do not overcoat. Place pieces on wire rack to dry for 5 minutes. Heat 3 inches oil in 9-inch skillet to 425°F. Fry chicken in oil without turning for 5 to 6 minutes. Remove and arrange on shallow baking sheet so pieces do not touch. Bake at 350°F for 25 to 30 minutes. Serves 6.

Mary Jane Hutchinson

Barbecued Chicken Wings

48 chicken wings, tips removed
1 (12 ounce) jar chili sauce
½ cup cider vinegar
½ cup vegetable oil
½ cup brown sugar
½ cup grated onion
2 Tablespoons Worcestershire sauce
2 teaspoons chopped garlic
2 teaspoons salt
1 teaspoon freshly ground pepper

Place wings in large roasting pan. Combine chili sauce, vinegar, oil, sugar, onion, Worcestershire sauce, garlic, salt and pepper. Pour half the sauce mixture over wings. Bake at 375°F for 30 minutes. Turn wings and cover with remaining sauce. Bake at 375°F for 30 minutes more. Place under broiler for additional browning if desired. Serves 6 to 8.

Pearl Hanover

Good Gooey Chicken

1 (8 ounce) bottle Russian dressing
1 (10 ounce) jar apricot preserves
1 ($1\frac{3}{8}$ ounce) package onion soup mix
1 ($2\frac{1}{2}$ to 3 pound) chicken, cut up
Seasoned salt and freshly ground pepper to taste

Combine dressing, preserves and onion soup mix in bowl and pour into 9 x 13-inch baking dish. Sprinkle chicken with seasoned salt and pepper. Place chicken, skin side down, in baking dish. Bake at 375°F for 45 minutes, basting occasionally. Turn chicken over and baste. Bake for 35 minutes more, basting occasionally. Serves 4 to 6.

Julie Pogouler

Almond Sausage Stuffing

1 pound pork sausage
8 cups stale bread crumbs
¼ cup butter
2 cups chopped celery
2 cups shredded or sliced almonds
1 cup chopped onions
1 cup chopped fresh mushrooms
¼ cup chopped green pepper
¼ cup minced parsley
2 cloves garlic, crushed
2 teaspoons salt
1 teaspoon poultry seasoning
½ teaspoon freshly ground pepper
½ teaspoon fennel and/or anise seed
½ teaspoon basil
½ teaspoon oregano
¼ teaspoon nutmeg
Pinch cayenne
½ cup beef consommé
½ cup dry vermouth

Sauté sausage until brown in large skillet, stirring with fork to break up meat. Add bread crumbs. Stir well to mix sausage and crumbs and to let crumbs absorb sausage fat. Put in large bowl. Melt butter in skillet. Add celery, almonds, onions, mushrooms, green peppers, parsley, garlic, salt, poultry seasoning, pepper, fennel, basil, oregano, nutmeg and cayenne. Cook over low heat until onions are soft, stirring to blend. Add consommé and vermouth and heat. Combine with sausage mixture, tossing lightly. If stuffing is dry, add consommé and vermouth in equal parts. Cool. Stuffs a 10 pound turkey.

Janet Zanni

Beef

Flank Steak Teriyaki

1 (2 pound) flank steak
½ cup vegetable oil
¼ to ½ cup Kikkoman soy sauce
¼ cup dry sherry
2 Tablespoons grated fresh ginger root
1 Tablespoon grated fresh tangerine rind
3 cloves garlic, crushed

Place steak in shallow baking dish. Combine oil, soy sauce, sherry, ginger root, tangerine rind and garlic. Pour over steak. Marinate at room temperature for at least 5 hours, turning occasionally. Broil 1½ to 2 inches from heat for 6 to 7 minutes on each side. Brush with marinade when turning. Slice thin on the diagonal. Serves 6.

Lynn Hagee

Beef Wellington

1½ cups sifted flour
¾ cup butter
2 (3 ounce) packages cream cheese
1 (3½ to 4 pound) whole filet of beef
Salt and freshly ground pepper to taste
¼ pound fresh mushrooms, minced
2 tablespoons butter, melted
1 large onion, minced
2 tablespoons butter
1¼ pounds ground veal
2 slices white bread, soaked in water and squeezed dry
1 egg, beaten
2 Tablespoons heavy cream
2 Tablespoons minced fresh parsley
1½ teaspoons salt
¼ teaspoon freshly ground pepper
1 egg yolk
1 teaspoon cold water

Cut butter and cheese into flour with pastry blender. Shape dough into a ball, wrap in wax paper and refrigerate. Brown beef quickly on all sides. Roast at 350°F about 30 minutes or until rare. Remove meat and season with salt and pepper. Cool completely. Sauté mushrooms in melted butter until brown. Put in large bowl. Sauté onion, in 2 Tablespoons butter until golden. Add onion to mushrooms. Add veal, bread, egg, cream, parsley, salt and pepper. Mix well with hands. Roll pastry large enough to wrap around filet. Spread ¼ of filling down center of pastry. Remove any strings from filet and place meat on filling. Spread remaining filling on top and sides of beef and wrap loosely in pastry. Pinch edges of pastry together to seal. Place wrapped filet, seam side down, on cookie sheet. Combine egg yolk and water and brush over top. Cut several vents across top of pastry. Refrigerate until ready to bake. Bake at 375°F for 30 minutes, then raise temperature to 400°F and bake 10 minutes longer. Serves 10.

Sandra Mollica

Filet de Boeuf Français

2½ pounds filet of beef, well trimmed
4 Tablespoons butter, divided
2 Tablespoons oil, divided
½ pound fresh mushrooms, sliced
1 cup finely chopped onions
1 clove garlic, minced
1 cup brown stock or beef bouillon
2 Tablespoons tomato paste
1 teaspoon dry mustard
¼ teaspoon sugar
½ cup dry Madeira or dry sherry
1 Tablespoon cornstarch
1 cup heavy cream
Salt and freshly ground pepper to taste
3 Tablespoons chopped fresh dill
Chopped fresh parsley (garnish)

Cut filet into pieces about 2 inches long, 1½ inches wide and ½ inch thick. Dry thoroughly with paper towels. Heat 2 Tablespoons butter and 1 Tablespoon oil in large skillet until foam subsides. Brown beef quickly on both sides in 2 or 3 batches, adding more butter and oil if necessary. Remove meat. Discard fat. Heat 2 Tablepoons butter and 1 Tablespoon oil in same skillet. Add mushrooms and sauté for 3 minutes or until slightly wilted. Remove mushrooms with a slotted spoon. Add onions and garlic to skillet and sauté until onions are softened. Combine stock, tomato paste, mustard and sugar; add to skillet. Simmer rapidly over moderate heat for 5 minutes, stirring occasionally. Dissolve cornstarch in Madeira or sherry and add to mixture in skillet. Stir constantly and simmer until thickened. Simmer another 3 minutes. Add mushrooms and simmer for 1 minute. Add cream gradually while stirring. Blend well. Season beef lightly with salt and pepper; add to skillet with juices. Add dill. Baste beef with simmering sauce. Simmer just until heated through. Adjust seasonings. Serve over buttered noodles or rice. Sprinkle with chopped parsley. Serves 6 to 8.

Mary Beth Clifford

Chopped Steak Port du Salut

1 pound lean chopped beef
4 ounces Port du Salut cheese, sliced
Salt and freshly ground pepper to taste
Butter

Make beef into eight patties. Put slice of cheese in center of each of 4 patties. Cover with remaining patties. Seal edges and sprinkle with salt and pepper. Brown in hot butter in skillet for 3 to 5 minutes on each side. Serves 2 to 4.

Mrs. Leonard Harrison

Boeuf a la Flamande

1 (4 pound) beef brisket
4 cups sliced onions
¼ cup butter
2 Tablespoons flour
2 cups beer
3 Tablespoons minced parsley
1 Tablespoon vinegar
2 teaspoons salt
1 teaspoon sugar
½ teaspoon freshly ground pepper
½ teaspoon thyme
¼ teaspoon garlic powder
6 whole cloves
2 bay leaves

Remove fat from brisket. Brown onions in butter in roaster or large skillet. Remove onions and brown meat. Sprinkle flour on meat and continue browning. Transfer onions and meat to roasting pan, if not used for browning, being sure to include all onion and meat bits. Heat beer, parsley, vinegar, salt, sugar, pepper, thyme, garlic powder, cloves and bay leaves in saucepan. Pour over meat and onions. Cover and bake at 325°F for 3 hours, basting occasionally. Add water or beer if it starts to dry out. Slice diagonally in thin slices. Pour remaining juices into gravy boat and serve with meat. Serves 4 to 6.

Erma Richter

Beef Chianti

2 Tablespoons vegetable oil
2 pounds beef, cubed for stew
2 cloves garlic, chopped
2 Tablespoons flour
2 teaspoons salt
¼ teaspoon freshly ground pepper
2 (8 ounce) cans tomato sauce
2 cups Chianti wine
2 cups water
1 teaspoon Worcestershire sauce
1 teaspoon oregano
1 bay leaf
½ teaspoon basil
½ teaspoon thyme
⅛ teaspoon crushed red pepper
8 small white onions, peeled
4 carrots, sliced
4 medium potatoes, coarsely diced

Heat oil in large skillet. Add meat and garlic and brown. Sprinkle with flour, salt and pepper; mix well. Place in 3-quart casserole. Add tomato sauce, wine and water. Heat, scraping brown crust from bottom and sides. Add Worcestershire sauce, oregano, bay leaf, basil, thyme and red pepper. Pour over beef in casserole. Add onions, carrots and potatoes; mix well. Cover and bake at 300°F for 2 to 2½ hours. Serves 4.

Leona K. Whitley

Tournedos Flambé Dijonnaise

4 (4 ounce) filet mignons
Salt and freshly ground pepper to taste
¼ cup butter
¼ cup brandy
½ cup heavy cream
3 Tablespoons Dijon mustard
2 Tablespoons sour cream
1 Tablespoon Worcestershire sauce

Season steaks with salt and pepper. Heat butter in large skillet and sauté steaks, turn and cook to desired degree of doneness. Pour brandy into skillet and flambé. Add cream, mustard, sour cream and Worcestershire sauce. Cook and stir until heated through. Pour sauce over steaks to serve. Serves 4.

Madeline Monat

Beef on Skewers with Spices

1 (1½ pound) sirloin steak
2 Tablespoons Kikkoman soy sauce
1 Tablespoon fresh lemon juice
1 Tablespoon brown sugar
1 teaspoon ground caraway
1 teaspoon ground coriander
1 teaspoon ground garlic
Salt and freshly ground pepper to taste
15 bamboo skewers

Cut meat in ¾-inch cubes or short strips (cut across the grain). Combine soy sauce, lemon juice, sugar, caraway, coriander, garlic, salt and pepper; mix with meat. Marinate 3 hours. Place 5 or 6 pieces of meat on each skewer. Grill over charcoal fire, turning 2 or 3 times, for 10 minutes or until meat is done. Serve with Peanut Sauce or Peanut Butter Sauce. Serves 3.

Peanut Sauce:

1 cup water
1 onion, chopped
3 heaping Tablespoons chunky peanut butter
2½ Tablespoons fresh lemon juice
2 Tablespoons Kikkoman soy sauce
2 Tablespoons sugar

Peanut Sauce:

Combine water, onion, peanut butter, lemon juice, soy sauce and sugar in saucepan. Simmer over low heat until smooth. Should be of medium consistency. If too thick, add more water; if too thin, add more peanut butter.

Beef on Skewers

Peanut Butter Sauce (Hot):

1 cup water
3 Tablespoons peanut butter
2 Tablespoons fresh lemon juice
1 Tablespoon ground hot red pepper
Salt to taste
½ cup crisp fried onion flakes

Peanut Butter Sauce (Hot):
Mix water, peanut butter, lemon juice, red pepper and salt. Sprinkle onion flakes on top.

Mrs. Wallace Chappell

Boeuf Bourguignon

½ pound blanched salt pork, diced
3 pounds boneless lean chuck, cut in 2-inch cubes
Flour
1½ cups finely chopped onion
2 carrots, finely chopped
1 bouquet garni: 4 sprigs fresh parsley, 3 mashed cloves garlic, 1 teaspoon thyme, 1 bay leaf, 6 black peppercorns tied in cheesecloth
1½ teaspoons salt
1 Tablespoon tomato paste
2 cups burgundy wine, divided
1½ cups beef stock, divided
20 small white onions
5½ Tablespoons butter, divided
1½ Tablespoons vegetable oil
1 pound fresh mushrooms, quartered
2 Tablespoons finely chopped fresh parsley (garnish)

Fry pork in 6-quart casserole until crisp. Remove with slotted spoon and drain on paper towels. Dry beef cubes with paper towels and dredge with flour. Fry in hot pork fat, adding a little butter if necessary, until well browned on all sides. Do not crowd. Remove meat with slotted spoon. Add chopped onion and carrots to fat and brown, being careful not to burn. Return pork and meat to casserole. Tuck bouquet garni securely among beef cubes. Sprinkle with salt. Stir tomato paste into 1 cup wine. Add with rest of wine to casserole. Add 1 cup beef stock. Heat on top of stove until simmering. Bake at 300°F for 2 to 3 hours or until beef is fork tender. Prepare onions and mushrooms while beef is cooking. Peel and pierce the center of each onion with a thin skewer to prevent onion from popping. Heat 1½ Tablespoons butter and oil in skillet; add onions and sauté, turning to brown evenly. Pour in ½ cup stock and simmer on low heat for 30 minutes. Heat 4 Tablespoons butter in skillet, add mushrooms and sauté for 5 minutes. When beef is tender, remove bouquet garni and discard. Remove meat. Skim fat from surface of gravy. Thin or thicken sauce if necessary. Adjust seasonings. Return beef, mushrooms and onions to casserole. Simmer for 5 minutes. Serve over rice or noodles sprinkled with parsley. Serves 8.

Toni Henderson

Beef with Snow Pea Pods

1 pound flank steak
¼ cup Kikkoman soy sauce
1 Tablespoon dry sherry
2 teaspoons cornstarch
1 teaspoon sugar
¼ teaspoon MSG (optional)
¼ pound fresh snow pea pods or ½ (6 ounce) package frozen snow pea pods
¼ cup vegetable oil, divided
½ teaspoon salt
1 (⅛-inch) slice fresh ginger root or ¼ teaspoon ground ginger

Freeze steak until firm enough to slice easily. Cut, with grain of meat, into 2-inch strips. Cut across grain into ¼-inch slices. Combine soy sauce, sherry, cornstarch, sugar and MSG. Pour over meat and marinate for 30 minutes. Rinse pea pods and pat dry. Remove stems and strings. Heat 2 Tablespoons oil in a skillet for 2 minutes. Sprinkle in salt and add pea pods. Stir-fry for 1 minute. Remove pea pods to a plate. Add remaining oil, ginger and beef mixture. Cook, stirring briskly, until meat loses its pink color, about 2 to 4 minutes. Add pea pods and mix. Serve immediately over rice. Serves 4.

Karen S. Freihofer

Oven-Barbecued Short Ribs

4 pounds lean short ribs, trimmed of fat
3 Tablespoons vegetable oil
1½ cups minced onion
2 cloves garlic, minced
1½ cups tomato purée
⅓ cup lemon juice
3 Tablespoons Worcestershire sauce
2 Tablespoons Dijon mustard
2 Tablespoons dark brown sugar
2 Tablespoons red wine vinegar
1 Tablespoon ground cumin
1 teaspoon salt
¾ teaspoon cayenne
Minced fresh parsley

Pat short ribs dry with paper towels. Brown ribs in vegetable oil in large heavy skillet over high heat, turning to brown all sides. Place in single layer in baking dish. Reduce heat to moderate, add onion and garlic and cook for 3 minutes, scraping brown bits clinging to bottom and sides of skillet. Add tomato purée, lemon juice, Worcestershire sauce, mustard, sugar, vinegar, cumin, salt and cayenne and combine well. Cook, stirring, for 5 minutes. Pour mixture over short ribs. Cover and bake at 325°F for 3 hours, or until very tender, turning ribs every 30 minutes. Skim any excess fat. Sprinkle short ribs with parsley. Serves 6.

Suzy Wahl

Bar BQ Beef

1 (3 to 4 pound) chuck or arm roast
3 cups water
¼ cup Kikkoman soy sauce
1 (24 ounce) bottle ketchup
½ cup brown sugar
1 Tablespoon chili powder
1 Tablespoon Worcestershire sauce
1 Tablespoon molasses
1 Tablespoon onion juice
1 teaspoon dry mustard

Trim fat from meat. Place meat in stockpot with water and soy sauce. Simmer over low heat 4 to 5 hours, until meat falls apart. Remove meat, refrigerate and remove congealed fat. Combine ketchup, brown sugar, chili powder, Worcestershire sauce, molasses, onion juice and mustard; simmer for 3 minutes. Remove fat from meat; shred meat. Place meat in 3-quart casserole; add sauce and ½ cup broth from meat. Cover and bake at 350°F for 30 minutes; uncover and bake for 15 minutes. Serves 12 to 18.

Mrs. John P. Baird

Sweet Sour Beef and Cabbage with Potato Pancakes

1 (3 pound) beef brisket
2 pounds cabbage, shredded or chopped
1½ teaspoons salt
1 onion, finely diced
¾ cup vinegar
½ cup brown sugar
½ cup seedless white raisins
2 Tablespoons flour
Cold water

Sear brisket in Dutch oven over medium low heat. Sprinkle cabbage with salt and let stand a few minutes. Add cabbage and onion to pot, moving seared meat to one side. Lightly brown cabbage and onion. Add vinegar, sugar and raisins. Cover and cook over low heat for 1 hour. Uncover and turn meat. If additional liquid is needed add ¼ cup boiling water or chicken stock at a time. Cover and simmer 45 minutes. Combine flour and cold water to make paste, add to pot and cook 10 minutes.

Potato Pancakes:

3 large potatoes, grated
1 medium onion, grated
3 Tablespoons flour
1½ teaspoons baking powder
Salt to taste
1 Tablespoon chicken fat
2 eggs, slightly beaten
Vegetable oil

Potato Pancakes:

Drain water from potatoes. Combine potatoes, onion, flour, baking powder and salt; mix well by hand. Add chicken fat and mix well. Add eggs and mix well. Heat oil in skillet and fry pancakes. Serves 6 to 8.

Marsha Mason

Barbecued Brisket

1 (5 to 6 pound) beef brisket
¼ cup liquid smoke
Worcestershire sauce to taste
Celery salt
Onion salt
Garlic salt
Salt and freshly ground pepper to taste
¾ cup barbecue sauce

Place brisket in flat baking dish or roasting pan. Pour liquid smoke and Worcestershire sauce over both sides of meat. Generously sprinkle meat on both sides with celery salt, onion salt, garlic salt, salt and pepper. Cover with aluminum foil and bake at 275°F for 5 hours. Pour off half the juice and add barbecue sauce on the lean side of meat. Bake, uncovered, for 30 minutes. Recover and bake 30 minutes more. Cool meat in refrigerator 6 to 8 hours, or long enough to get cold and hard. Slice very thin. Before serving heat, covered, at 275°F to 300°F for 45 minutes. Serves 8 to 10.

Virginia Long

Vinaigrette Roast Beef

8 slices cooked roast beef
½ cup thinly sliced onion rings
9 Tablespoons olive oil
3 Tablespoons red wine vinegar
2 Tablespoons finely chopped capers
2 Tablespoons finely chopped parsley
1 teaspoon Dijon mustard
1 teaspoon salt
½ teaspoon freshly ground pepper
½ teaspoon finely chopped garlic
4 tomatoes, sliced
4 hard-boiled eggs, sliced
Chopped fresh parsley

Trim all fat and gristle from beef and spread slices in a glass bowl. Scatter onion rings over beef. Combine oil, vinegar, capers, parsley, mustard, salt , pepper and garlic; stir or shake until well blended. Pour vinaigrette over meat and onions. Marinate for several hours at room temperature, turning meat and onions occasionally. Remove meat and onions from marinade. Arrange meat on serving dish and scatter onions on top. Garnish with tomatoes, eggs and parsley. Serves 8.

Mrs. Peter Willingham

Sauerbraten

1 (4 pound) beef chuck, rump or round roast
Salt and freshly ground pepper to taste
1 onion, sliced
3 bay leaves
1 teaspoon peppercorns
3 cups water
3 cups vinegar
½ cup sugar, divided
¼ cup raisins
6 gingersnaps, crushed
1 cup sour cream

Rub meat well with salt and pepper. Place in deep earthenware dish with onion, bay leaves and peppercorns. Heat water, vinegar and ¼ cup sugar and pour over meat. Cover and refrigerate for 3 to 4 days. Remove meat from liquid, place in kettle, and roast in 450°F oven for 20 minutes or until well browned. Add 1 cup spiced liquid, cover and bake at 300°F for 3 hours or until tender, adding more liquid if necessary. Remove meat, slice and keep warm. Strain liquid and skim off fat. Melt ¼ cup sugar in skillet, add strained liquid gradually and stir in raisins and gingersnaps. Cook until thick and smooth; add sour cream and heat. Pour sauce over meat. Serves 10.

Mabel Niewoehner

Wine Flavored Baked Beef Hash

1½ pounds cooked roast beef or leftover brisket, cut in ½-inch cubes
2 large baking potatoes, coarsely diced
3 ribs celery, coarsely diced
1 large or 2 medium onions, coarsely diced
½ green pepper, coarsely diced
1 cup leftover gravy or 2 bouillon cubes in 1 cup water
¼ teaspoon freshly ground pepper
¼ teaspoon paprika
Salt to taste
1 clove garlic, pressed
2 Tablespoons flour
5 Tablespoons port wine
5 Tablespoons sherry
Paprika

Combine meat, potatoes, celery, onion and green pepper in bowl. Heat gravy and pour over meat and vegetables. Add pepper, paprika, salt and garlic. Mix well. Stir in flour as needed for thickening. Add port and sherry and pour mixture into greased baking dish or casserole. Sprinkle with additional paprika. Bake at 500°F for 20 minutes. Reduce heat to 350°F and continue baking for 20 to 25 minutes or until potatoes are soft. Serves 4.

Joan Goodson

Chunky Chili

4 Tablespoons vegetable oil, divided
1½ pounds stew beef, cubed
1½ cups chopped onion
1 cup green pepper slivers
2 teaspoons minced garlic
1 Tablespoon chili powder, or to taste
1½ teaspoons salt
½ teaspoon thyme, crumbled
½ teaspoon cumin
1½ cups water
1 cup pitted ripe olives
1 (8 ounce) can tomato sauce
½ (1 ounce) square unsweetened chocolate, chopped
1 (30 ounce) can small red beans
3 cups cooked rice or potatoes, cooked and quartered

Heat 3 Tablespoons oil in a Dutch oven. Brown meat well. Add remaining oil, onion, green pepper and garlic and cook until soft, not brown. Stir in chili powder, salt, thyme and cumin. Cook 1 minute more. Add water and heat to boiling. Reduce heat to low, cover and simmer for 45 minutes. Stir in olives, tomato sauce and chocolate. Simmer, uncovered, 25 to 30 minutes until thickened. Serve on top of a bean and rice bed or a bean and potato bed. Serves 4.

Mike Swan

Marzetti

2 pounds ground round
3 Tablespoons vegetable oil
1 pound fresh mushrooms, sliced and lightly sautéed in butter
⅔ cup chopped green pepper
1 large onion, chopped
1½ teaspoons salt
1 teaspoon oregano
½ teaspoon freshly ground pepper
2 (10 ounce) cans tomato soup
1 (6 ounce) can tomato paste
2 Tablespoons Worcestershire sauce
½ pound broad noodles
½ pound sharp Cheddar cheese, grated

Brown ground round in oil in heavy skillet. Drain well. Add mushrooms, green pepper, onion, salt, oregano and pepper; cook until tender. Add soup, tomato paste and Worcestershire sauce. Cook noodles until almost tender, drain and rinse. Spread half the noodles in large greased baking dish, cover with half the meat mixture and sprinkle with half the cheese. Repeat, using remaining ingredients. Bake at 375°F for 45 minutes or until heated through. Serves 8.

Joanne Kohn

Keshie Yena

15 ounces Edam cheese, sliced, divided

1 pound ground round

4 onions, finely chopped

4 carrrots, finely chopped

3 green peppers, finely chopped

1 (1 pound) box pitted prunes, halved

1 (15 ounce) box raisins

5 teaspoons Worcestershire sauce

4 teaspoons salt

1 teaspoon freshly ground black pepper

Line a greased 2-quart casserole with ⅔ of cheese. Brown the ground round in Dutch oven. Drain fat. Add onions, carrots, green peppers, prunes, raisins, Worcestershire sauce, salt and pepper. Cook over medium heat until thick and vegetables are well done. Cool. Pour cooled mixture into casserole and top with remaining cheese. Bake at 350°F for 20 minutes or until cheese has melted and mixture is hot. Serves 6 to 8.

Diane Newbury

Party Spaghetti Casserole

2 pounds lean ground beef

3 Tablespoons vegetable oil

½ pound fresh mushrooms, sliced

2 medium onions, chopped

1 (15 ounce) can tomato sauce

1 (6 ounce) can tomato paste

¼ cup chopped parsley

1 teaspoon dried oregano

1 teaspoon garlic powder

Salt and freshly ground pepper to taste

1 (8 ounce) package cream cheese, softened

2 cups cottage cheese

½ cup sour cream

½ cup chopped chives

1 pound green noodles or linguini, cooked and drained

½ cup bread crumbs

½ cup freshly grated Parmesan cheese

Butter

Brown ground beef and onions in oil. Drain excess fat. Sauté mushrooms until browned and add to meat mixture. Add tomato sauce and tomato paste. Add parsley, oregano, garlic powder, salt and pepper. Mix cream cheese, cottage cheese, sour cream and chives together until well blended. Layer half the noodles in bottom of a greased casserole. Cover with cheese mixture. Cover with remaining noodles. Top with meat sauce mixture. Mix bread crumbs and Parmesan cheese. Spread over top of casserole. Drizzle with melted butter. Bake at 350°F for 30 to 40 minutes. Serves 12.

Fran Browde

Oriental Meat Ball Dinner

1 pound ground round
1 pound mild pork sausage
1¾ cups beef broth, divided
1 (8 ounce) can water chestnuts, chopped
2 eggs, slightly beaten
⅔ cup quick-cooking rolled oats
⅓ cup chopped onion
1 Tablespoon sesame seeds
1½ teaspoons salt
1 teaspoon ground ginger
2 Tablespoons vegetable oil
2 small zucchini, sliced
1 medium green pepper, seeded and cut into strips
1 medium onion, sliced
4 stalks celery, diagonally sliced
4 cloves garlic, minced
1 (1 pound) can bean sprouts, drained
⅔ cup water
¼ cup Kikkoman soy sauce
3 Tablespoons cornstarch
4 cups hot cooked rice

Combine ground round, sausage, ⅔ cup beef broth, water chestnuts, eggs, oats, onion, sesame seeds, salt and ginger thoroughly. Shape into smooth balls, using 2 Tablespoons mixture for each ball. Place meatballs slightly apart on ungreased jelly roll pan. Bake at 450°F for 30 minutes or until meat is lightly brown and interior has lost all pinkness. Pour oil into wok or large skillet; place over medium heat. Add zucchini, green pepper, onion, celery and garlic. Cook, stirring, for 3 minutes; add bean sprouts and cook for 1 minute or until vegetables are tender crisp. Add hot meat balls, remaining broth and water; bring to a simmer. Blend soy sauce with cornstarch until smooth; add to meat mixture, stirring briskly to distribute. Cook, stirring, until sauce is thickened and clear. Serve over rice. Serves 8.

Mary Tureen

Party Pizza

Crust:

¾ cup warm water
1 (¼ ounce) package dry yeast
2 cups flour

Crust:

Mix warm water and yeast. Combine with flour. Knead about 24 times. Spread dough in 12 to 14-inch diameter and 1-inch deep pizza pan. Flute edges of dough high around side of pan. If thin crust is desired, do not use all of dough. Place in freezer while preparing filling.

Party Pizza

Filling:

Olive oil
1 (6 ounce) can tomato paste
1 pound ground beef
1 large onion
1 large green pepper
6 cups grated Mozzarella cheese
1 pint fresh mushrooms, sliced
1 link pepperoni, sliced
Sweet basil
Crushed red pepper

Filling:

Coat complete crust, including edges, with olive oil. Spread with tomato paste. Slice onion and green pepper. Reserve 4 slices of each and chop the rest. Cook ground beef with chopped onion and green pepper. Drain ground beef mixture and spread over tomato paste. Spread 2 cups cheese over meat mixture. Top with mushrooms; sprinkle with 1 cup cheese. Top with pepperoni; sprinkle with 2 cups cheese. Top with green pepper and onion slices. Sprinkle with sweet basil and crushed red pepper to taste. Spread last cup cheese over top. Bake at 375°F for 45 minutes or until done. Serves 4 to 6.

Marita Woodruff

Cincinnati Chili

4 cups water
2 pounds lean ground beef
2 medium onions, finely grated
2 (8 ounce) cans tomato sauce
5 whole allspice
¼ cup chili powder
4 cloves garlic
5 whole cloves
2 Tablespoons vinegar
2 teaspoons Worcestershire sauce
1½ teaspoons salt
½ (1 ounce) square unsweetened chocolate
1 teaspoon ground cumin seed
1 teaspoon cinnamon
1 large bay leaf
½ teaspoon red pepper
Spaghetti (optional)
Grated Cheddar cheese, onions or chili beans (optional)

Add ground beef to water in a 4-quart pot. Stir until beef separates to a fine texture. Boil slowly for 30 minutes. Add onions, tomato sauce, allspice, chili powder, garlic, cloves, vinegar, Worcestershire sauce, salt, chocolate, cumin seed, cinnamon, bay leaf and red pepper. Stir to blend, bringing to a boil. Reduce heat and simmer, uncovered, 30 minutes, or until sauce is thick. Can serve over spaghetti and top with grated Cheddar cheese, grated onions or chili beans. Serves 6 to 8.

Roberta Tureen

Cabbage Rolls

3 pounds ground beef
3 cups canned tomatoes, divided
1 onion, chopped
⅓ cup uncooked rice
2 Tablespoons salt, divided
1 teaspoon sugar
Freshly ground pepper, divided
1 large head cabbage
4 cups water
6 Tablespoons maple syrup
¼ cup fresh lemon juice
¼ cup raisins
½ teaspoon paprika

Combine ground beef, 1 cup tomatoes, onion, rice, 1 Tablespoon salt, sugar and pinch pepper. Shape into small meat balls. Put meat balls in large cabbage leaves and shape into rolls. Chop remaining cabbage and put in Dutch oven. Put cabbage rolls on top. Combine water, 2 cups tomatoes, maple syrup, lemon juice, raisins, 1 Tablespoon salt, paprika and pinch pepper; pour over cabbage rolls. Cover and simmer for 2 to 3 hours. Refrigerate overnight. Reheat over low heat, stirring occasionally, for 30 minutes. Serves 8.

Naomi Lebowitz

Beef and Rice Loaf

1 knackwurst, cut into ¼-inch slices
2 Tablespoons butter
1 cup diced onion
2 cloves garlic, minced
½ cup diced green pepper
1 pound ground chuck
2½ to 3 teaspoons chili powder
Salt and freshly ground pepper to taste
1½ cups peeled, seeded and chopped tomatoes
2 cups cooked brown rice
1 cup cooked peas, divided

Sauté knackwurst in butter in large skillet until lightly browned, turning once. Remove with slotted spoon. Add onion and garlic to skillet and sauté until onion is soft. Stir in green pepper and sauté for 3 minutes. Add ground chuck and sauté over medium high heat until brown. Stir in chili powder, salt and pepper and cook for 2 minutes. Add tomatoes. Reduce heat to low, cover and simmer for 25 minutes, stirring occasionally. Stir in rice and ½ cup peas. Arrange a layer of alternating rows of knackwurst slices and ½ cup peas in a buttered 8 x 4-inch loaf pan. Spoon in beef and rice mixture and press down slightly. Cover pan with buttered foil. Set in a baking dish and add boiling water to reach halfway up sides. Bake at 350°F for 15 minutes. Remove pan from water, remove foil and let loaf stand for 5 minutes. Invert onto serving dish. Serves 4 to 6.

Mrs. Lester Crancer Jr.

Mozzarella Meat Roll

1½ pounds lean ground beef
½ cup tomato juice
2 eggs, beaten
½ cup soft bread crumbs
3 Tablespoons dried parsley flakes
1½ teaspoons salt
½ teaspoon freshly ground pepper
½ teaspoon garlic powder
¼ teaspoon oregano
6 to 8 thin slices ham, trimmed of fat
2 cups grated Mozzarella cheese

Combine beef, tomato juice, eggs, bread crumbs, parsley flakes, salt, pepper, garlic powder and oregano. On wax paper, form meat mixture into 10 x 16-inch rectangle. Arrange ham slices on top of meat mixture, overlapping slightly and leaving a small border around edges. Sprinkle cheese on top of ham. Using wax paper, roll meat into loaf and place in a 9 x 13-inch baking pan. Remove paper and seal ends of roll securely. Bake at 350°F for 1 hour. Serves 6.

Mrs. William Reis

Cranberry Meat Balls

2 pounds ground beef
½ cup ice water
1 onion, grated
1 green pepper, chopped
1 egg
¼ cup dry bread crumbs
1½ teaspoons salt
Pinch garlic salt
Pinch paprika
Pinch freshly ground pepper
Butter
1 (1 pound) can whole cranberry sauce
2 (8 ounce) cans tomato sauce
1 green pepper, chopped
1 clove garlic, chopped

Combine ground beef, water, onion, green pepper, egg, bread crumbs, salt, garlic salt, paprika and pepper. Roll into 12 balls. Melt butter in skillet and brown meat balls. Remove with slotted spoon and put in Dutch oven. Combine cranberries, tomato sauce, green pepper and garlic. Pour over meatballs. Cover and simmer for 1½ hours. Refrigerate overnight. Reheat over low heat, stirring occasionally. Serves 6.

Naomi Lebowitz

Hamburger Stroganoff

½ cup minced onion
¼ cup butter
1 pound ground round
1 pound fresh mushrooms, sliced
1 cup sour cream
1 (10¾ ounce) can cream of chicken soup
2 Tablespoons flour
2 teaspoons salt
1 clove garlic, minced
½ teaspoon parsley or chives
¼ teaspoon freshly ground pepper
¼ teaspoon paprika

Brown onions in butter. Add ground beef and brown. Add mushrooms, sour cream, soup, flour, salt, garlic, parsley, pepper and paprika. Simmer for 45 minutes. Serve over noodles. Serves 4.

Margie Falk

Zucchini Moussaka

2 Tablespoons vegetable oil
3 zucchini, cut in ¼-inch slices
1 onion, sliced
1 pound lean ground beef
1 (8 ounce) can tomato sauce
1 clove garlic, minced
½ teaspoon salt
¼ teaspoon cinnamon
1 cup small curd cottage cheese
1 egg, slightly beaten
¼ cup freshly grated Parmesan cheese or Feta cheese
Cinnamon
Nutmeg

Put oil in skillet, add zucchini and onion and lightly brown. Remove from skillet and place in a shallow 1½ to 2-quart baking dish. Brown ground beef in same skillet. Drain fat. Stir in tomato sauce, garlic, salt and cinnamon. Spoon mixture over zucchini and onion in baking dish. Blend egg and cottage cheese. Spoon over meat. Sprinkle Parmesan or Feta over cottage cheese mixture. Sprinkle cinnamon and nutmeg over top. Bake at 350°F for 30 minutes. Serves 6.

Janet Speroulias

Pork

Sweet and Sour Pork

2 eggs, well beaten
½ cup flour
1 teaspoon salt
½ teaspoon white pepper
½ teaspoon garlic powder
2 pounds lean pork, cut into 1-inch cubes
Vegetable oil
1½ cups chicken broth
1 cup brown sugar
⅔ cup vinegar
1 cup pineapple chunks
2 large green peppers, seeded and cut into large pieces
1 large onion, cut into eighths
1 Tablespoon ketchup
1 Tablespoon Kikkoman soy sauce
½ cup pineapple juice
2 Tablespoons cornstarch
2 tomatoes, cut into sixths

Combine eggs, flour, salt, pepper and garlic powder in large bowl. Dip pork in batter and fry, a few pieces at a time, in hot oil at least 1 inch deep. Combine chicken broth, brown sugar and vinegar in saucepan. Stir in pineapple, green pepper, onion, ketchup and soy sauce; bring to a boil. Combine pineapple juice and cornstarch; add to sauce. Cook and stir until thickened. Add pork and tomatoes; stir carefully to combine. Cook for 2 minutes. Serve over hot cooked rice. Serves 8.

Patti Lewis

Loin of Pork Vermouth

4 to 5 pound loin of pork
1 cup dry vermouth, divided
1 Tablespoon hickory salt
2 teaspoons dried sage
½ teaspoon nutmeg
½ teaspoon freshly ground pepper

Wipe pork loin with paper towel. Brush with some of vermouth. Combine hickory salt, sage, nutmeg and pepper; rub over pork. Roast at 325°F for 1¾ to 2 hours. Combine any excess seasonings with vermouth and baste every twenty minutes during roasting. Use additional vermouth if necessary. Serves 4 to 6.

Lynn Caldwell

Hungarian Pork Stew

3 pounds boneless pork
Flour
2 Tablespoons vegetable oil
1 onion, diced
1 clove garlic, diced
4 cups chicken broth
4 stalks celery, chopped
2 carrots, peeled and chopped
1 green pepper, chopped
3 Tablespoons sweet Hungarian paprika
1 teaspoon dry mustard
Salt and freshly ground pepper to taste
Water
1 pound fresh mushrooms, quartered
3 potatoes, peeled and cubed
3 tomatoes, peeled and cubed
1 cup sour cream (garnish)

Trim fat from pork, cut into cubes and dredge with flour. Heat oil in large skillet; add pork, onion and garlic and brown on all sides. Put pork mixture in large kettle. Add chicken broth, celery, carrots, green pepper, paprika, mustard, salt, pepper and enough water to cover. Cover and cook over medium heat for 1½ hours. Add mushrooms, potatoes and tomatoes and cook 1 hour. Top each serving with 1 Tablespoon sour cream. Serves 8.

Patti Lewis

Scrapple

1 pound pork steak
3 cups water
1 cup cornmeal
1½ teaspoons salt
¼ teaspoon marjoram
¼ teaspoon thyme
⅛ teaspoon crushed sage
Freshly ground pepper to taste

Simmer pork in water until it is very tender and the meat falls from the bone. Cool meat in broth. Drain, reserving broth. Stir cornmeal into 1 cup cold broth. Bring 1 cup broth to a boil and add to cornmeal mixture. Stir in salt, marjoram, thyme, sage and pepper. Cook, stirring constantly, until mixture boils. Cover and cook over low heat, stirring occasionally. Shred meat and combine with cornmeal mix. Pack into 9 x 5-inch loaf pan. Refrigerate at least 8 hours. Cut into slices and pan fry until brown on both sides. Serve with eggs for breakfast. Serves 6 to 8.

Eleanor Waldau

Pork with Sour Cherry Sauce

1 clove garlic
2 Tablespoons salt
1 teaspoon cracked pepper
½ teaspoon thyme
5 pound boned rolled loin of pork

Crush garlic with salt, pepper and thyme. Rub surface of pork loin with mixture and let stand 2 hours. Roast at 450°F for 30 minutes. Reduce heat to 325°F and roast for 2 hours or until meat thermometer registers 185°F. Serve cold or hot with sour cherry sauce. Serves 8 to 10.

Sour Cherry Sauce:
1 (1 pound) can pitted sour cherries
½ cup port wine
¼ cup red currant jelly
¾ cup lemon juice
¼ cup orange juice
1 Tablespoon Dijon mustard
1 teaspoon grated orange rind

Sour Cherry Sauce:
Simmer cherries and wine for 10 minutes; cool completely. In small saucepan set over hot water, soften, but do not melt, currant jelly. Put jelly in bowl; combine with lemon juice, orange juice, mustard and orange rind. Stir in cherry mixture. Serve at room temperature if meat is hot; chill to serve with cold meat. Makes 2 cups.

Fleur Hampton

Ham Rolls

2 Tablespoons butter
1 small onion, chopped
1½ Tablespoons flour
1 teaspoon Dijon mustard
1 teaspoon horseradish
1 teaspoon Worcestershire sauce
1 egg yolk
½ cup pineapple juice
½ cup milk
4 slices Swiss cheese
4 slices baked ham
8 spears broccoli, steamed 7 minutes, or uncooked fresh asparagus

Melt butter in saucepan and sauté onion until clear. Blend in flour, mustard, horseradish and Worcestershire sauce. Mix egg yolk with pineapple juice; slowly stir in milk. Cook over medium heat until sauce is thick. Lay Swiss cheese on ham slice and roll around broccoli or asparagus. Place in greased 8 x 10-inch baking dish. Pour sauce over ham rolls and bake at 350°F for 20 to 25 minutes. Serves 4.

Michael Drennan

Hickory Smoked BBQ Pork Loin

1 (4 to 5 pound) boneless pork loin, rolled and tied
½ cup Lawry seasoned salt
¼ cup oregano flakes
1 cup water
Hickory chips
Parsley (garnish)

Sprinkle meat evenly with seasoned salt and oregano. Place in roasting pan and pour water into pan. Roast at 350°F for 2 hours or until meat thermometer reaches 150°F. Remove meat from pan; place on barbeque grill over medium hot coals which have been generously sprinkled with hickory chips. Leave thermometer in roast. Lower lid on grill, leaving one vent open, and smoke roast until thermometer reaches 170°F. Check roast from time to time and rotate for even smoke flavor. Remove any strings. Slice and serve heated sauce on the side. Serves 8 to 10.

Sweet Richard BBQ Sauce:
1¾ cups ketchup
1½ cups brown sugar
1 Tablespoon fresh lemon juice
1 Tablespoon Worcestershire sauce
1 teaspoon garlic salt

Sweet Richard BBQ Sauce:
Combine ketchup, brown sugar, lemon juice, Worcestershire sauce and garlic salt in saucepan. Cook until heated through. Serve hot. Makes 3 cups.

Charlotte's Rib BBQ Restaurant

Raisin Sauce

½ cup brown sugar
1 Tablespoon cornstarch
¼ teaspoon salt
¾ cup ham broth or cold water
½ cup seedless raisins
¼ cup fresh orange juice
3 Tablespoons fresh lemon juice
1 Tablespoon butter

Combine sugar, cornstarch and salt in saucepan; add broth or water and heat to boiling, stirring constantly. Add raisins, orange juice, lemon juice and butter. Simmer 5 minutes. Keep warm in double boiler. Do not refrigerate, freeze or reheat. Serve over slices of baked ham. Serves 6.

Susan Greta

Mushroom-Sausage Strudel

2 pounds sweet Italian sausage
2 pounds fresh mushrooms, minced
¼ cup minced shallots
6 Tablespoons butter
2 Tablespoons vegetable oil
Salt and freshly ground pepper to taste
2 (8 ounce) packages cream cheese, softened
12 sheets filo dough
1 cup butter, melted
Bread crumbs

Remove sausage meat from casing and bake at 325°F until no longer pink; crumble into small pieces. Squeeze mushrooms dry in towel. Sauté mushrooms and shallots in butter and oil over moderately high heat, stirring frequently. Cook until pieces separate and liquid has evaporated. Add salt and pepper. Combine with sausage and blend in cream cheese. Spread a sheet of filo dough on a damp towel. Brush with butter and sprinkle on bread crumbs. Repeat with second and third sheets, and butter, but do not crumb fourth sheet. Pat ⅓ the sausage-mushroom mixture on narrower edge of dough, leaving a 2-inch border at sides. Fold in sides, then using edge of towel, roll. Put strudel on buttered cookie sheet and brush with melted butter. Repeat for second and third strudels. Bake at 400°F about 20 minutes or until brown. Cut with shears. Serves 8.

Roberta Franklin

Scandinavian Pork Chops

1 cup cut up mixed dried fruit
¼ cup raisins
1 cup white wine
½ teaspoon curry powder
¼ cup butter
¼ cup hot water
2 cups herb stuffing mix
¼ cup diced celery
2 Tablespoons diced onion
Salt and freshly ground pepper to taste
4 rib pork chops (1½ inches thick), cut with pocket

Plump mixed fruit and raisins in wine and curry powder. Drain and reserve wine. Melt butter in hot water. Combine fruit, stuffing mix, celery, onion, salt and pepper; add butter and stir. Add more water if necessary. Blend well. Stuff each pork chop. Put remaining stuffing in bottom of casserole; place meat on top; pour wine over meat. Cover and bake at 350°F for 30 minutes. Uncover and cook 20 to 30 minutes more, or until meat is done. Serves 4.

Delie Holmes

Party Pork Casserole

1 pound fresh mushrooms
2 cups chicken bouillon
1 cup chopped onion
6 Tablespoons butter, divided
2 cups cubed cooked lean pork
2 cups cooked tiny shrimp
8 ounces green noodles, cooked and drained
1 (16 ounce) can tomatoes
1 cup sliced ripe olives
1 cup finely chopped fresh parsley
⅓ cup flour
1½ cups milk
2 (3 ounce) packages cream cheese
1 teaspoon basil
1 teaspoon salt
½ teaspoon freshly ground pepper
½ teaspoon thyme
2 cups grated Cheddar cheese

Remove stems from mushrooms; simmer stems in bouillon for 10 minutes. Remove and discard stems. Slice mushroom crowns. Sauté sliced mushrooms and onion in 2 Tablespoons butter. Combine mushrooms, onion, pork, shrimp, noodles, tomatoes, olives and parsley in large bowl. Melt 4 Tablespoons butter in saucepan. Add flour and stir until well blended. Add chicken bouillon and milk; cook over medium heat, stirring frequently, until thick and smooth. Cut cream cheese in small pieces and melt in sauce. Add basil, salt, pepper and thyme. Combine with meat mixture. Spoon into 2 (2-quart) buttered casseroles. Sprinkle with cheese. Bake at 350°F for 30 minutes or until cheese browns slightly. Serves 8 to 10.

Carol Drennan

Pork a la Lane

8 to 10 pork frenchettes or 4 large pork cube steaks
1 teaspoon salt
Freshly ground pepper to taste
½ to 1 teaspoon finely minced fresh ginger root
¼ cup butter, melted
2 Tablespoons brown sugar
1½ Tablespoons flour
1 Tablespoon Dijon mustard
1 Tablespoon tarragon white wine vinegar
1 cup fresh orange juice
⅛ cup Cointreau or bourbon

To make a frenchette, pound a 1-inch thick slice of pork tenderloin very thin. Sprinkle pork with salt and pepper. Sauté pork and ginger in butter in large skillet until brown. Remove frenchettes. Add brown sugar, flour, mustard and vinegar to skillet. Stir in orange juice and Cointreau or bourbon gradually. Cook until thickened. Pour sauce over frenchettes. Serves 4.

Pat Lane

Székely Gulyás (Transylvanian Goulash)

2 pounds boneless pork
6 medium onions, chopped
1½ (10½ ounce) cans beef broth
¼ cup snipped fresh dill or 1 teaspoon ground dill seed
1 Tablespoon salt
1 clove garlic, minced
1 teaspoon caraway seeds
4 teaspoons Hungarian paprika
1 (27 ounce) can sauerkraut, rinsed and drained
2 cups sour cream
Sour cream (garnish)
Snipped fresh dill or ground dill seed (garnish)

Combine pork, onions, broth, dill, salt, garlic and caraway seeds in Dutch oven. Bring to boil, cover and simmer for 1 hour. Dissolve paprika in 1 cup hot broth from goulash and add to goulash. Stir in sauerkraut. Cover and simmer for 1 hour more or until meat is tender. Stir in sour cream. Cover and refrigerate at least 24 hours. Reheat, uncovered, over very low heat, stirring occasionally, for 45 minutes. Serve with sour cream and dill. Serves 6.

Skippy Dennis

Stir Fry Pork

1½ to 2 cups julienne strips of pork, 1-inch long
½ cup sliced green onions, white part only
3 Tablespoons vegetable oil
2 cups sliced small zucchini
¾ cup chicken broth, divided
2 Tablespoons Kikkoman soy sauce
1 teaspoon ground cardamom
¾ cup fresh bean sprouts
½ cup sliced water chestnuts
½ cup dry sherry
2 Tablespoons cornstarch
⅓ cup cashews

Brown pork and onions in oil. Add zucchini, ½ cup chicken broth, soy sauce and cardamom. Cover and steam for 5 minutes. Add sprouts, water chestnuts and sherry. Dissolve cornstarch in ¼ cup chicken broth and add only enough to thicken sauce. If there is not enough sauce, add more chicken broth and thicken with cornstarch mixture. Add cashews. Serve over rice or Chinese noodles. Serves 4.

Carol Drennan

Creole Pie in Scone Shell

Scone Shell:

1½ cups flour

1 teaspoon baking powder

1 teaspoon salt

⅓ cup shortening

1 egg

⅓ cup milk

Creole Filling:

½ pound pork sausage

¼ cup chopped green pepper

¼ cup chopped onion

¼ cup flour

1 teaspoon salt

⅛ teaspoon freshly ground pepper

⅛ to ½ teaspoon filé powder (optional)

3 dashes Tabasco (optional)

1 cup cooked or canned tomatoes, chopped

2 cups cooked vegetables (garbanzos, lentils, green beans, corn or peas)

Scone Shell:

Sift flour, baking powder and salt together in bowl. Cut in shortening. Stir in egg and milk. Gather into ball, and roll out on lightly floured board, 1½ inches larger than a deep 9-inch pie pan. Place loosely in pie pan and press gently in place so there are no air pockets. Build up edge and flute; prick bottom and sides with a fork. Bake at 425°F for 15 minutes. Keep warm until ready to fill with creole mixture.

Creole Filling:

Brown sausage lightly in large skillet. Add green pepper and onion. Cook over low heat, stirring constantly, until vegetables are soft, not brown. Stir in flour, salt, pepper, filé powder and Tabasco. Add tomatoes and stir until blended. Cook until thickened, about 5 minutes. Add vegetables. Cook just long enough to heat vegetables. Pour into hot scone shell. Cut into wedges. Serves 2 to 4.

Adelaide Earnest

Grilled Butterflied Leg of Lamb

1 (5 to 6 pound) boned leg of lamb, butterflied
½ cup vegetable oil
¼ cup dry vermouth
¼ cup grated onion
1 teaspoon salt
1 teaspoon tarragon
1 clove garlic, minced
½ teaspoon thyme
½ teaspoon freshly ground pepper

Place lamb in large baking dish. Combine oil, vermouth, onion, salt, tarragon, garlic, thyme and pepper. Pour over lamb and marinate 1 to 3 hours at room temperature or overnight in refrigerator. Drain and save marinade. Place meat in wire broiler basket. Roast over medium coals for 1½ hours, turning every 15 minutes, for medium rare. Baste often with reserved marinade. Cut against grain into thin slices. Serves 8 to 10.

Joan Thomas

Peasant Lamb

3 pounds lean lamb shoulder
2 or 3 onions, chopped
1 cup water
1 cup tomato sauce
1 teaspoon tarragon, basil or oregano
Salt and freshly ground pepper to taste

Choice of:
1½ to 3 pounds fresh spinach
1 to 2 pounds fresh green beans
1 to 2 pounds new potatoes
1 to 2 pounds fresh zucchini
1 to 2 pounds fresh peas

Cut lamb into cubes and brown with onions in oil in Dutch oven. Add water, tomato sauce, herb, salt and pepper. Lower heat to simmer. Cover and cook for 1 to 1½ hours. Add one or two vegetables and allow time to cook before meat is done. Serves 6 to 8.

Mrs. Robert Pettus

Gingered Leg of Lamb

1 (5 to 6 pound) boned leg of lamb, butterflied
⅓ cup white wine
⅓ cup olive oil
⅓ cup fresh lemon juice
¼ cup slivered ginger root
1 small onion, diced
2 Tablespoons honey
1 clove garlic
1½ teaspoons salt
1 teaspoon coriander
½ teaspoon cumin
Pinch cayenne

Place lamb in shallow pan. Place wine, oil, lemon juice, ginger root, onion, honey, garlic, salt, coriander, cumin and cayenne in blender and purée. Pour over lamb and refrigerate for 12 hours. Turn lamb occasionally. Place lamb on broiler pan and broil 4 inches from heat for 20 minutes, basting once. Turn and broil 20 minutes, basting frequently. Turn off heat and let lamb remain in oven for 15 minutes. Remove skin. Carve in thin slices and serve with meat juices. Serves 6 to 8.

Phyl Maxwell

Surprise Lamb Chops

2 slices ham, finely diced
1 small chicken breast, finely diced
2 large mushrooms, finely chopped
2 cloves shallots, finely chopped
2 Tablespoons butter
Pinch thyme
Salt and freshly ground pepper to taste
1 cup dry white wine, divided
2 leaves fresh tarragon, chopped
Freshly ground black pepper to taste
¼ pound puff pastry dough
12 lean lamb chops, trimmed
Melted butter

Sauté ham, chicken, mushrooms and shallots in butter. Season with thyme, salt and pepper and remove from heat when half cooked. Simmer tarragon leaves and freshly ground pepper in ½ cup wine until wine is reduced by half. Stir into meat mixture, add remaining wine and finish cooking meat. Roll out dough until paper thin and cut into 4-inch square pieces. Season lamb chops with salt and pepper and grill until rare. Let chops cool slightly. Cover top of each chop with meat mixture and wrap with a square of dough. Brush with melted butter and bake at 350°F for 10 minutes. Serves 6.

Marilyn Merker

Lamb Korma

¼ cup butter
½ cup minced onion
¼ teaspoon ground ginger
1 clove garlic, crushed
6 whole cloves
6 whole cardamom seeds
1 (2-inch) stick cinnamon
2 teaspoons salt
2 teaspoons ground coriander
2 teaspoons ground cumin
1 teaspoon ground turmeric
½ teaspoon ground chili pepper
1 cup yogurt
2 Tablespoons tomato paste
2 Tablespoons chopped almonds
2 pounds boneless lamb, cubed
¼ cup sherry
2 Tablespoons flour
Cooked rice

Condiments:
Chutney
Raisins soaked in cognac or sherry
Shredded coconut
Chopped salted peanuts
Chopped salted almonds
Thinly-sliced green onions
Sieved hard-boiled eggs
Crumbled crisp bacon

Melt butter in Dutch oven. Add onion, ginger and garlic and cook, stirring occasionally, until onions are golden. Tie cloves, cardamom and cinnamon in cheesecloth bag. Add to mixture with salt, coriander, cumin, turmeric and chili pepper. Stir and cook for 5 minutes. Add yogurt, tomato paste and almonds; blend together and heat to boiling. Add the lamb and stir to coat all the cubes. Cover and simmer for 45 minutes. Remove cover and simmer for 15 minutes. Remove cheesecloth bag. Dissolve flour in sherry. Remove pan from heat. Pour flour mixture into pan, stirring carefully until gravy thickens. Return pan to heat and simmer, uncovered, for 10 minutes. Serve on rice with condiments as desired. Serves 6.

Lillian Sherman

Moroccan Tajine of Lamb

3 Tablespoons butter
2 teaspoons olive oil
1 large onion, thinly sliced
1½ teaspoons ground ginger
1¼ teaspoons salt
½ teaspoon freshly ground pepper
⅛ teaspoon saffron
2 cinnamon sticks
2 pounds lean leg of lamb, cubed
1 clove garlic, mashed
1 cup moist dried apricots
1½ Tablespoons honey
1½ Tablespoons fresh lemon juice
½ cup chopped pistachios
Lemon wedges

Heat butter and oil over medium heat in Dutch oven. Add onion, ginger, salt, pepper, saffron and cinnamon sticks. Sauté for 4 minutes. Add lamb and garlic and stir to coat with onion mixture. Cover and simmer for 1½ hours, stirring occasionally. Add apricots, cover and cook for 20 minutes. Remove meat with slotted spoon, put on serving plate and arrange apricots on top. Add honey to Dutch oven and cook over high heat to make thin sauce. Add lemon juice and pour over lamb. Top with pistachios and lemon wedges. Serves 6 to 8.

Mrs. Richard M. Jones

Lamb Crown Roast

1 (5 pound) crown roast of lamb
Seasoned salt and freshly ground pepper to taste
1 (6 ounce) package curried rice mix
1 pound ground lamb
½ cup chicken broth
½ cup chopped green pepper
⅓ cup seedless raisins
2 Tablespoons fresh lemon juice
½ teaspoon seasoned salt
½ teaspoon salt
Freshly ground pepper to taste

Sprinkle roast with seasoned salt and pepper and roast at 325°F for 1½ hours. Prepare rice according to directions, using only 2¼ cups water. Brown ground lamb in skillet, drain well. Combine rice, lamb, chicken broth, green pepper, raisins, lemon juice, seasoned salt, salt and pepper in large bowl. Fill center of crown of lamb with stuffing and cover with foil. Put remaining stuffing in uncovered casserole. Bake at 325°F for 1 hour or until meat thermometer registers 175°F. Serves 6 to 8.

Mrs. Clarence T. Wilson

Lamb Tarragon

6 lamb chops
Seasoned salt and freshly ground pepper to taste
½ cup dry vermouth
3 Tablespoons butter
½ teaspoon tarragon

Sprinkle lamb chops with salt and pepper. Broil to desired doneness. Pour drippings from broiler pan into skillet. Add vermouth, butter and tarragon. Bring to a boil and boil for 1 minute. Pour sauce over chops. Serves 3 to 4.

Diane Linsin

Lamb Shanks

2 large lamb shanks
Garlic slivers
Kitchen Bouquet
2 Tablespoons chili sauce
2 Tablespoons red wine
2 Tablespoons water
1 teaspoon dry instant onion
Salt and freshly ground pepper to taste

Rinse and dry lamb shanks. Make tiny slits in fleshy parts of shanks and insert garlic slivers. Rub with Kitchen Bouquet. Place on rack in baking dish. Combine chili sauce, wine, water, onion, salt and pepper and pour over shanks. Cover and bake at 325°F for 1 hour. Serves 2.

Mrs. William Marré

Marinade for Lamb

1 cup olive oil
½ cup tarragon white wine vinegar
1 Tablespoon Worcestershire sauce
1 Tablespoon Dijon mustard
1 teaspoon salt
1 bay leaf, crushed
1 clove garlic, crushed
Pinch rosemary

Combine oil, vinegar, Worcestershire sauce, mustard, salt, bay leaf, garlic and rosemary. Stir until well blended. Pour over lamb and marinate for 1 to 3 hours before cooking. Makes 1½ cups.

Beverly Clarkson

Grenadin de Veau

1½ pounds veal filet
Paprika to taste
Salt and freshly ground pepper to taste
8 paper-thin slices Canadian bacon
8 paper-thin slices Jarlsberg cheese
Flour
2 whole eggs, beaten
2 Tablespoons vegetable oil
2 cups fine bread crumbs
½ cup butter
Fresh lemon juice
Lemon slices (garnish)
Parsley (garnish)

Cut veal into 8 pieces and pound to very thin slices, about 4 x 6 inches. Sprinkle with paprika, salt and pepper. Put 1 slice of bacon and 1 slice of cheese in center of each piece of veal; fold in half. Dip veal lightly in flour, then in eggs, then in oil, and then in bread crumbs. Pound or pinch edges gently to seal. Melt butter in large skillet over low heat and sauté veal 10 minutes on each side. Sprinkle with lemon juice while cooking. Place veal on platter, cover with sauce, and garnish with lemon slices and parsley. Serves 4.

Sauce:
4 slices Canadian bacon
Paprika to taste
Salt and freshly ground pepper to taste
½ cup cognac
2 cups beef consommé
¼ cup butter, melted
1 cup heavy cream
2 egg yolks
¼ cup capers
2½ Tablespoons fresh lemon juice

Sauce:
Slice bacon into very narrow strips and sauté with paprika, salt and pepper. Add cognac and ignite, shaking pan until flame dies. Add consommé and butter and cook for 10 minutes. Reduce heat, add cream, egg yolks, capers and lemon juice. Cook, stirring constantly, until sauce is creamy and smooth.

Marilyn Merker

Veal Cleopatra

1 pound thin veal scallops
7 Tablespoons butter, divided
4 Tablespoons olive oil, divided
⅓ cup freshly grated Parmesan cheese
⅓ cup freshly grated Romano cheese
⅓ cup crumbled Fontina cheese
3 Tablespoons milk
½ teaspoon oregano
Salt and freshly ground pepper to taste
1 egg
1 Tablespoon water
1 cup very fine bread crumbs

Sauté veal scallops in 2 Tablespoons butter and 2 Tablespoons oil for 1½ minutes on each side. Set aside and keep warm. Combine Parmesan, Romano and Fontina cheeses, 3 Tablespoons butter, milk, oregano, salt and pepper in saucepan. Cook, stirring constantly, over low heat to make a smooth sauce. Dip veal scallops in hot cheese sauce and place on wax paper until scallops have cooled and cheese has formed a firm coating. Beat egg and water together thoroughly. Dip scallops in egg mixture, then in bread crumbs. Heat 2 Tablespoons butter and 2 Tablespoons oil in clean skillet. Sauté scallops until lightly browned on both sides. Serves 4.

Mrs. Jack Taylor

Veal Piemontese

24 (2 ounce) very thin veal scallops
Flour
2 cups sliced artichoke bottoms
½ cup butter
¾ cup white wine
3 cups heavy cream
¾ cup veal stock (if not available, substitute beef bouillon)
Salt and freshly ground pepper to taste

Lightly flour veal scallops. Sauté scallops and artichokes in butter. Pour off butter, add wine and reduce to half. Add cream and veal stock. Season. Remove scallops from pan and arrange on platter; reduce cream and stock to half and pour over scallops. Serve with rissotta or pasta with butter. Serves 4.

Tony's

Veal Chasseur

1½ pounds veal cutlet, sliced ¼-inch thick
¼ cup butter
½ cup dry white wine, divided
1 pound fresh mushrooms, trimmed and sliced
1 onion, chopped
2 cups brown sauce
¼ cup chopped fresh parsley
1 teaspoon salt
Freshly ground pepper to taste
Paper thin lemon slices (garnish)
Parsley (garnish)

Trim fat from veal and cut into 1¼-inch pieces. Sauté in butter for 8 to 10 minutes. Add splash of wine to loosen pieces stuck to pan. Remove with slotted spoon and keep warm. Add mushrooms and onions and sauté for 5 minutes. Add remaining wine and simmer until reduced by half. Stir in brown sauce, parsley, salt and pepper. Add meat and simmer 3 minutes. Garnish with lemon slices and parsley. Serves 4.

Brown Sauce:

½ cup butter
1 onion, chopped
1 large carrot, chopped
¼ cup diced celery
1 clove garlic, chopped
3 cups beef bouillon, divided
3 Tablespoons cornstarch
2 Tablespoons dry Madeira
½ teaspoon thyme
½ teaspoon salt
6 peppercorns
1 large bay leaf

Brown Sauce:

Melt butter in skillet. Add onion, carrot, celery and garlic and sauté for 10 minutes. Dissolve cornstarch in ½ cup cold bouillon and add to mixture. Add remaining bouillon, Madeira, thyme, salt, peppercorns and bay leaf. Cover and simmer 30 minutes, stirring occasionally. Strain. Makes 2 cups.

Carol Salomon

Veal Cream with Mushrooms

1½ pounds boneless veal
¼ cup butter
3 Tablespoons finely chopped shallots
½ pound fresh mushrooms, thinly sliced
1 teaspoon paprika
½ cup dry white wine
½ cup chicken broth
½ cup heavy cream
½ teaspoon rosemary
Salt and freshly ground pepper to taste
½ Tablespoon fresh lemon juice
Parsley (garnish)

Pound veal thin and cut into ½-inch strips. Melt butter in large skillet. Add shallots and sauté until soft. Add veal and sauté over high heat 8 minutes, stirring frequently. Add mushrooms and paprika. Add wine, broth, cream, rosemary, salt and pepper. Lower heat and cook 8 minutes or until veal is tender. Add lemon juice. Garnish with parsley. Serves 4.

Frank Walsh

Veal with Cream and Brandy

2½ pounds veal from leg
2 Tablespoons butter
1 Tablespoon oil
½ pound fresh mushrooms, thinly sliced
2 Tablespoons cognac
⅓ cup heavy cream
2 pounds fresh asparagus
2½ Tablespoons fresh lemon juice
Salt and freshly ground pepper to taste

Cut veal into 12 slices and pound until very thin. Heat butter and oil until foamy and brown veal. Add mushrooms. Heat brandy and ignite. Pour flames over veal. Add cream and simmer for 5 minutes. Peel and cook asparagus until tender. Purée in food processor or blender and season with lemon juice, salt and pepper. Put veal on serving platter and spread a spoonful of puréed asparagus between each veal slice. Serves 6.

Beverly Clarkson

Scallopini of Veal Roma

2½ pounds veal steak sliced ¼-inch thick
½ cup flour
2 teaspoons paprika
2 teaspoons salt
1 teaspoon freshly ground pepper
5 Tablespoons butter
1 clove garlic
½ cup water
1 teaspoon fresh lemon juice
1 teaspoon basil
¼ teaspoon rosemary
2 cups sour cream
2 cups sliced water chestnuts
8 dried apricot halves, chopped
½ cup dry Marsala
Chopped dried apricots
2 Tablespoons cornstarch (optional)
¼ cup cold water (optional)

Remove fat from veal and pound thin. Cut into strips 2 inches long and 1 inch wide. Mix flour, paprika, salt and pepper together and use to coat veal. Melt butter in very large skillet; add garlic. When sizzling hot, add veal. Brown, stirring frequently, being careful not to burn. Add water, lemon juice, basil and rosemary; scrape bottom of skillet with spatula. Add sour cream and lower heat to simmer. When meat is tender, add water chestnuts, chopped apricot halves and wine. Cook mixture to just under a boil. Check seasonings and thicken with cornstarch and water if necessary. Pour into 2-quart casserole and sprinkle with a few chopped apricots. Cover and bake at 350°F for 20 to 30 minutes. Serves 8.

Marian O'Brien

Madeira Sauce for Veal

3 Tablespoons butter, divided
3 shallots, chopped
2 Tablespoons flour
1½ cups beef broth
½ cup Madeira
Salt and freshly ground pepper to taste

Melt 2 Tablespoons butter in skillet. Add shallots and sauté until soft. Add flour and cook for 1 minute. Add broth gradually, stirring constantly with wire whisk. Lower heat to lowest setting and simmer 10 minutes. Add Madeira and simmer 5 minutes. Add salt and pepper. Swirl in 1 Tablespoon butter to make sauce shiny. Serve with veal chops and roasts. Makes 2 cups.

Mrs. Charles Wilson

Breads

Banana Nut Bread a la South

1½ cups sugar
½ cup butter
2 eggs
1½ cups sifted flour
½ teaspoon salt
½ cup buttermilk
1 teaspoon baking soda
1 cup mashed bananas
½ cup chopped pecans

Cream sugar and butter in large bowl. Beat in eggs. Stir in flour and salt and mix well. Combine buttermilk and baking soda and add to batter. Stir in bananas and pecans. Pour into greased and floured 9 x 5-inch loaf pan. Bake at 350°F for 1 hour or until toothpick inserted in center comes out clean. Makes 1 loaf.

Shirley Williams

Biscuits

2 cups flour
4 teaspoons baking powder
1 teaspoon salt
1 teaspoon sugar
½ cup butter
1 egg in measuring cup with milk to equal ⅔ cup

Combine flour, baking powder, salt and sugar. Cut in butter until well blended and the mixture resembles corn meal. Add egg and milk and stir until there are no dry particles. Turn out onto floured board and work gently for a moment until dough looks smooth. Do not over handle. Roll out ½ inch thick. Cut . Bake at 450°F for 8 to 10 minutes until barely brown. Makes 10 to 12.

Maria Schweizer

Amaretto Nut Bread

8 eggs, separated
3 cups sugar, divided
2 cups butter, softened
3 cups sifted flour
½ cup Amaretto
4 teaspoons vanilla
1 cup chopped almonds

Beat egg whites until soft peaks form. Add 1 cup sugar gradually and beat until it holds stiff peaks. Set aside. Cream butter with remaining sugar. Add egg yolks, one at a time, beating well after each addition. Add flour in thirds, alternating with Amaretto. Mix well. Stir in vanilla and nuts. Fold in egg whites gently. Pour batter into 3 well-greased 8 x 4-inch loaf pans. Bake at 350°F for 1 hour or until done. Makes 3 loaves.

Marilyn Wilson

Apple Bread

1 cup sugar
¾ cup vegetable oil
2 eggs
1½ cups flour
1 teaspoon cinnamon
1 teaspoon baking soda
¼ teaspoon salt
¼ cup nuts
1½ cups chopped apples
Sugar and cinnamon

Mix together sugar, oil and eggs. Add flour, cinnamon, baking soda and salt. Add nuts and apples. Pour into greased 9 x 5-inch loaf pan. Sprinkle top with sugar and cinnamon. Bake at 350°F for 55 minutes. Makes 1 loaf.

Pam Cole

Bacon Flavored Corn Sticks

6 Tablespoons warm bacon drippings, divided
½ cup boiling water
1 cup yellow cornmeal
2 eggs, well beaten
1 cup milk
1 cup sifted flour
2½ teaspoons baking powder
2 teaspoons sugar
½ teaspoon salt

Brush insides of 2 cast iron corn stick pans with 2 Tablespoons bacon drippings. Put in preheated 375°F oven while preparing batter. Pour boiling water over cornmeal in large bowl. Add remaining 4 Tablespoons bacon drippings, stirring until thick. Add eggs, then milk mixing well. Sift flour, baking powder, sugar and salt together and mix well with cornmeal mixture. Remove pans from oven and spoon in batter level with top. Bake at 375°F for 30 minutes or until tops are nicely browned. Makes 14.

Jeannette A. Kelley

Old Fashioned Coconut Toast

8 slices bread
Butter
¾ cup coconut
⅓ cup sugar
1 egg, beaten

Toast bread in toaster on medium-light setting. Butter toast and cut in half. Place bread on ungreased cookie sheet. Mix together coconut, sugar and egg and spread on bread. Bake at 350°F for 15 minutes. Makes 16.

Betty Umbach

Poppy Seed Loaf Delight

3 cups flour
2¼ cups sugar
1½ cups milk
1⅛ cups vegetable oil
3 eggs
1½ Tablespoons poppy seeds
1½ teaspoons salt
1½ teaspoons baking powder
1½ teaspoons vanilla
1½ teaspoons almond extract
1½ teaspoons butter flavoring

Combine flour, sugar, milk, oil, eggs, poppy seeds, salt, baking powder, vanilla, almond extract and butter flavoring. Mix 1 to 2 minutes with electric mixer. Pour into 2 greased 9 x 5-inch loaf pans. Bake at 350°F for 1 hour. Let cool about 5 minutes; then glaze. Makes 2 loaves.

Glaze:

¾ cup sugar
¼ cup orange juice
½ teaspoon butter flavoring
½ teaspoon almond extract
½ teaspoon vanilla

Glaze:

Mix together sugar, orange juice, butter flavoring, almond extract and vanilla. Pour over warm bread before removing from pans.

Megan Brooks

Pumpkin Nut Bread

1 cup butter, softened
3 cups sugar
3 eggs
1 (1 pound) can pumpkin
1 teaspoon vanilla
3 cups sifted flour
1 Tablespoon baking soda
1½ teaspoons salt
1 teaspoon baking powder
1 teaspoon cinnamon
1 teaspoon ground cloves
½ teaspoon nutmeg
1 cup chopped pecans
1 cup raisins

Cream butter and add sugar. Beat in eggs. Add pumpkin and vanilla and mix. Sift together flour, baking soda, salt, baking powder, cinnamon, cloves, and nutmeg. Add to butter mixture. Add nuts and raisins. Pour into 2 greased and lightly floured 9 x 5-inch loaf pans. Bake at 350°F for 60 to 75 minutes. Refrigerate overnight before slicing or bread will crumble. Makes 2 loaves.

Karen Krumm Murphy

Applesauce Puffs

2 cups buttermilk baking mix
1 cup chunky applesauce
¼ cup sugar
¼ cup milk
1 egg, beaten
2 Tablespoons vegetable oil
1 teaspoon cinnamon

Combine baking mix, applesauce, sugar, milk, egg, oil and cinnamon. Beat vigorously for 30 seconds. Fill greased muffin tins ⅔ full. Bake at 400°F for 12 minutes. Cool slightly. Remove. Makes 12.

Topping:
4 Tablespoons butter, melted
½ cup sugar
½ teaspoon cinnamon

Topping:
Combine sugar and cinnamon. Dip tops of puffs in melted butter and then into sugar mixture.

Donna Karney

Quick Molasses Rye Bread

2½ cups rye flour, divided
1 teaspoon baking powder
1 teaspoon baking soda
1 teaspoon salt
1½ cups sour milk
½ cup molasses
½ cup wheat germ
¼ cup butter, melted
2 Tablespoons grated orange rind

Sift ½ cup flour, baking powder, baking soda and salt into large bowl. Stir in 2 cups flour, milk, molasses, wheat germ, butter and orange rind. Spoon into greased 9 x 5-inch loaf pan. Let stand 20 minutes. Bake at 375°F for 50 minutes. Makes 1 loaf.

Laurie Orgel

Anchovy Bread

1 loaf crusty bread
½ cup butter, softened
6 anchovies, mashed
1 (2 ounce) tube anchovy paste
Freshly ground black pepper to taste

Slice bread almost through to bottom. Combine butter, anchovies, anchovy paste and pepper. Spread slices with mixture. Tie together with string and place on cookie sheet. Heat at 400°F for 10 minutes or until crusty and brown. Makes 1 loaf.

Irene Conrad

Best Bran Muffins

4 cups Bran Buds, divided
1½ cups sugar
1 cup boiling water
10 Tablespoons butter
2 cups buttermilk
¾ cup dark molasses
2 eggs
2½ cups flour
2½ teaspoons baking soda
1½ teaspoons salt
1 or 2 cups raisins (optional)

Mix 1 cup Bran Buds, sugar, water and butter in large bowl. Let stand until cool. Stir in buttermilk, molasses and eggs. Sift flour, baking soda and salt together and add to bran mixture. Turn gently a few times. Lightly fold in 3 cups Bran Buds and raisins. Spoon into paper cups in muffin tins, filling ⅔ full. Bake at 400°F for 20 minutes. Batter can be stored in refrigerator for 1 week. Do not stir again. Makes 36.

Mrs. Craig Andrews

Strawberry Bread

3 cups flour
1½ teaspoons cinnamon
1 teaspoon baking soda
1 teaspoon salt
2 cups sugar
2 (10 ounce) packages frozen sliced strawberries in syrup, thawed and undrained
4 eggs, beaten
1¼ cups vegetable oil
1 cup chopped pecans

Sift flour, cinnamon, baking soda and salt together; combine with sugar in large bowl. Make well in center; put strawberries, eggs, oil and pecans in well and stir until moistened. Pour batter into 2 greased and floured 9 x 5-inch loaf pans. Bake at 350°F for 60 to 75 minutes or until toothpick inserted in center comes out clean. Makes 2 loaves.

Gloria Levin

Port du Salut Bread

8 ounces Port du Salut cheese, softened
1 cup unsalted butter, softened
2 cloves garlic, minced
1 loaf French bread

Combine cheese and butter. Add garlic and mix well. Cut bread into 12 slices. Spread cheese mixture thickly on bread slices. Broil until cheese is browned, but not burned. Can be frozen. Makes 12 pieces.

Lynn Allen

Mississippi Spice Muffins

2 cups sugar
1 cup butter, softened
2 eggs
2 cups unsweetened applesauce
1 Tablespoon cinnamon
2 teaspoons allspice
1 teaspoon cloves
4 cups flour
2 teaspoons baking soda
1 teaspoon salt
1 cup chopped nuts
Confectioners' sugar (optional)

Cream sugar and butter together. Add eggs; beat well. Mix in applesauce, cinnamon, allspice and cloves. Sift flour, baking soda and salt together; add to creamed mixture. Stir in nuts. Fill lightly greased miniature muffin tins ⅔ full. Bake at 350°F for 8 to 10 minutes. If desired, fill lightly greased regular muffin tins ⅔ full and bake at 350°F for 15 to 17 minutes. Sprinkle with confectioners' sugar, if desired. Batter keeps for 6 weeks in refrigerator. Makes 84 miniature muffins or 40 regular muffins.

Margaret Moss

Zucchini Parmesan Bread

3 cups sifted flour
¾ pound unpeeled zucchini, shredded
¼ cup sugar
¼ cup freshly grated Parmesan cheese
5 teaspoons baking powder
1½ teaspoons salt
½ teaspoon baking soda
1 cup buttermilk
2 eggs, beaten
6 Tablespoons butter, melted
3 Tablespoons grated onion

Combine flour, zucchini, sugar, cheese, baking powder, salt and baking soda in large bowl. Combine buttermilk, eggs, butter and onion; add to flour mixture and mix well. Batter should be somewhat dry. Pour into greased 9 x 5-inch loaf pan. Bake at 350°F for 1 hour or until toothpick inserted in center comes out clean and bread pulls away from pan. Makes 1 loaf.

Amanda Tate

Zucchini Bread

2 cups whole wheat flour
1 cup flour
1 teaspoon salt
1 teaspoon cinnamon
1 teaspoon baking soda
¼ teaspoon baking powder
2 cups sugar
1 cup vegetable oil
2 eggs, beaten
2 teaspoons vanilla
2 cups grated unpeeled raw zucchini
½ cup chopped nuts (optional)
½ cup raisins (optional)

Sift flours, salt, cinnamon, baking soda and baking powder into large bowl. Combine sugar, oil, eggs and vanilla and stir into flour mixture until well blended. Stir in zucchini, nuts and raisins. Pour into 2 greased 8 x 4-inch loaf pans. Bake at 350°F for 60 minutes. Makes 2 loaves.

Marcia Bernstein

Mexican Cornbread

1 cup flour
1 cup cornmeal
½ teaspoon baking soda
½ teaspoon salt
1 cup buttermilk
1 (8 ounce) can creamed corn
2 eggs
⅓ cup vegetable oil
1 small onion, chopped
1½ Jalapeño peppers, chopped
2 cloves garlic, chopped
½ pound grated Cheddar cheese

Mix together flour, cornmeal, baking soda and salt. Add buttermilk, corn, eggs, oil, onion, peppers and garlic. Mix thoroughly. Pour half the batter into greased 9-inch square pan. Sprinkle on cheese. Pour remaining batter on top. Bake at 350°F for 35 to 40 minutes, or until firm. Allow to cool. Cut in squares. Serve warm. Serves 6 to 8.

Karen McDonaugh

Blender Fruit Bread

3 cups flour
1½ teaspoons baking powder
1 teaspoon baking soda
1 teaspoon salt
1⅓ cups sugar
½ cup shortening
½ cup orange juice
2 eggs
1½ apples, cored and sliced
¼ unpeeled orange
1 cup raisins
½ cup nuts

Sift flour, baking powder, baking soda and salt together. Place sugar, shortening, orange juice and eggs in blender; blend well. Add apples and orange and blend until chopped fine. Add raisins and nuts; blend. Stir fruit mixture into dry ingredients. Pour into greased and floured 9 x 5-inch loaf pan. Bake at 350°F for 1 hour and 15 minutes. Makes 1 loaf.

Valerie B. Safron

Cracked Wheat Bread

½ cup warm water
2 (¼ ounce) packages dry yeast
1 Tablespoon brown sugar or molasses
1 cup buttermilk
1 cup water
¼ cup honey
3 Tablespoons butter
1 Tablespoon salt
4 cups whole wheat flour
1 cup cracked wheat
¼ teaspoon baking soda
2 cups flour

Combine warm water, yeast and brown sugar in large bowl; let stand for 10 minutes. Combine buttermilk, water, honey, butter and salt in saucepan and heat over low heat until lukewarm (110° to 120°F); pour into yeast. Add whole wheat flour, cracked wheat and baking soda and mix thoroughly. Cover and let rise until doubled, about 1 hour. Stir dough until deflated and work in 1 cup flour. Turn out onto well floured surface and knead for 5 minutes, using only as much remaining flour as needed to prevent sticking. Place dough in greased bowl; turn to grease top. Cover and let rise until doubled, about 30 minutes. Punch down dough, turn onto floured surface and cut in half. Shape each piece into loaf and place in 2 9 x 5-inch loaf pans. Cover and let rise until doubled, about 45 minutes. Place pans in cold oven, set heat at 375°F and bake for 50 to 60 minutes or until done. Cool on wire rack. Makes 2 loaves.

Bernard Watson Gerdelman

Cereal Bread

1 cup Malt-o-Meal, Cream of Wheat, Ralston or other quick cooking (but not instant) cereal
2 cups boiling water
½ cup vegetable oil
½ cup honey
2 teaspoons salt
1 cup lukewarm water
3 (¼ ounce) packages dry yeast
3½ cups whole wheat flour
½ cup wheat germ
1 to 2 cups unbleached flour

Put dry cereal in large bowl and pour boiling water over it. Add oil, honey and salt. Cool to lukewarm. Add yeast to lukewarm water and stir with fork until dissolved. Add to cereal mixture. Add whole wheat flour and wheat germ. If dough does not pull away from sides of bowl, add enough unbleached flour until it does. Turn out on floured board and use as much of remaining unbleached flour as necessary while kneading dough for 8 to 10 minutes, until it is smooth and elastic. It should be a little sticky. Put dough in a greased bowl, turn and cover. Let rise until doubled. Turn out on floured board and divide into 3 pieces; let rest 10 minutes. Shape into loaves and put into 3 greased 9 x 5-inch loaf pans or one pound coffee cans. Cover and let rise until dough reaches rims of pans. Bake at 350°F about 40 minutes or until hollow sounding when thumped. Turn out of pans and cool on racks. Makes 3 loaves.

Etta Taylor

Honey-Wheat Bread

3 cups whole wheat flour
2 (¼ ounce) packages dry yeast
1 Tablespoon salt
1 cup milk
1 cup water
½ cup honey
2 Tablespoons solid vegetable shortening
1 egg
3 to 3½ cups flour

Combine whole wheat flour, yeast and salt in large bowl. Heat milk, water, honey and shortening until very warm (120° to 130°F); add to flour mixture with egg and blend on low speed until ingredients are moistened. Beat 3 minutes on medium speed. Gradually add enough flour to form a stiff dough. Knead on lightly floured surface until smooth and elastic, about 5 minutes. Place in lightly greased bowl; cover and let rise until light and doubled, 1 to 1½ hours. Shape into 2 loaves and place into greased loaf pans. Cover, let rise until doubled, 30 to 60 minutes. Bake at 350°F for 35 to 45 minutes. Makes 2 loaves.

Carol Ziemann

Sourdough Starter

2 cups warm water
1 (¼ ounce) package dry yeast
2½ cups flour
1 Tablespoon sugar

Combine water and yeast in a 2-quart crock or glass container; stir to dissolve. Beat in flour and sugar until smooth. Cover with double layer of cheese cloth and place in warm, protected spot. Leave until sponge rises and falls back, about 8 to 10 hours. Stir down; cover and let stand until thick and sponge has a fresh, sour aroma (about 2 days). Stir down, place in jar and refrigerate.

To replenish: each time starter is used, add equal amounts of warm water and flour with 1 teaspoon sugar. Stir with whisk until smooth; cover with cheesecloth and allow to bubble overnight. Store in refrigerator.

Sourdough Rye Bread

2 cups unbleached flour
¼ cup gluten flour
¾ cup sourdough starter
Water
2 Tablespoons molasses
1 Tablespoon caraway seeds
1 teaspoon cardamom
1 teaspoon salt
½ teaspoon baking soda
1 cup whole wheat flour
1 cup rye flour
Unbleached flour
Melted butter

Put 2 cups unbleached flour and gluten flour in large bowl. Add sourdough starter and enough water to make a semi-thick paste. Put plastic wrap over bowl; cover with dish towel. Let sit in warm place overnight. In the morning add molasses, caraway seeds, cardamom, salt and baking soda and stir with wooden spoon. Add whole wheat and rye flour, and mix well, adding enough unbleached flour to make a manageable dough. Place on floured board and knead for 15 minutes. Place in greased bowl. Cover with cloth and let rise until doubled, about 1½ hours. Knead dough lightly and divide into 2 equal parts. Roll each part with rolling pin until about ¾ inch thick. Roll as for jelly roll and tuck both ends under to form ball. Place on greased cookie sheet. Make three ½ inch slashes across top of loaf with razor blade. Place in slightly warm oven and let rise until doubled. Bake at 400°F 45 to 60 minutes. Brush tops of baked loaves with melted butter. Cool on racks. Makes 2 loaves.

Joyce Anicker

Apple Cinnamon Coffee Cake

Cake:

2 cups sourdough starter
2 cups flour
1 cup sugar
2 teaspoons cinnamon
1½ teaspoons baking soda
½ teaspoon salt
⅔ cup vegetable oil
2 eggs
2 cups chopped apples

Cake:

Combine sourdough starter, flour, sugar, cinnamon, baking soda and salt in large bowl. Add oil and eggs and mix well. Stir in apples. Pour into greased 9 x 13-inch pan. Sprinkle with topping. Bake at 350°F for 50 minutes. Makes 1 cake.

Topping:

1 cup brown sugar
¼ cup butter, melted
2 Tablespoons flour
1 teaspoon cinnamon
½ cup chopped nuts

Topping:

Combine sugar, butter, flour and cinnamon in small bowl. Stir in nuts.

Midge Aufderheide

Grandma's Christmas Bread

1 (¼ ounce) package dry yeast
2 Tablespoons warm water
1⅓ cups milk, scalded
½ cup sugar
⅓ cup butter
1 teaspoon salt
4⅓ cups flour, divided
2 eggs, beaten
2 cups raisins
1 cup fruitcake mix
1 teaspoon ground cardamom
Milk
¼ cup sugar
2 teaspoons cinnamon

Dissolve yeast in water. Combine milk, sugar, butter and salt in large bowl and cool. Add 1⅓ cups flour and beat thoroughly. Stir in yeast and eggs. Add raisins, fruitcake mix and cardamom and mix thoroughly. Add 3 cups flour gradually and mix until dough leaves sides of bowl. Turn out onto lightly floured pastry cloth and knead lightly. Cover and let rise until doubled. Punch dough down. Put into 2 greased 8 x 4-inch loaf pans. Brush top with milk; combine sugar and cinnamon and sprinkle on top. Cover and let rise until doubled. Bake at 350°F for 1 hour. Makes 2 loaves.

Linda Falk

Garlic French Bread

1 Recipe French bread dough
½ cup butter, softened
¼ cup grated Parmesan cheese
2 Tablespoons minced parsley
2 to 3 cloves garlic, minced
¼ teaspoon Italian herbs
¼ teaspoon salt
1 egg white
1 Tablespoon water

Prepare French bread dough according to directions and let rise 2 times. Divide dough into 2 equal parts; cover and let rest 10 to 15 minutes. Combine butter, cheese, parsley, garlic, herbs and salt; blend well. Roll each portion of dough into a 15 x 10-inch rectangle and spread with half the butter mixture, leaving a 1-inch edge around all sides. Cut dough in half lengthwise. Roll up each half as for jelly roll, beginning with cut edge. Pinch edges and sides of roll to seal. Place seam side down in lightly greased French bread pans. Gash tops. Beat egg white with water and brush tops. Let rise, lightly covered, until doubled, about 1 hour. Brush again with egg white mixture. Bake at 450°F for 30 minutes or until deep golden brown. Makes 4 loaves.

Carol Ziemann

Cheesy Casserole Bread

2¼ to 2¾ cups flour, divided
¼ cup cornmeal
1 Tablespoon sugar
1½ teaspoons salt
1 (¼ ounce) package dry yeast
1 cup milk
2 Tablespoons butter
1 Tablespoon instant minced onion or ¼ cup minced fresh onion
1 egg
¼ teaspoon Tabasco
½ cup grated Cheddar cheese

Combine 1 cup flour, cornmeal, sugar, salt and yeast in large bowl. Heat milk, butter and onion to 120° to 130°F. Add to flour mixture with egg and Tabasco and beat on high speed for 2 minutes. Add cheese and enough remaining flour to make a soft dough. Turn into a 1½ to 2-quart greased and cornmeal-sprinkled casserole. Cover and let rise until doubled, about 45 minutes. Spread with topping mixture and bake at 375°F for 35 to 45 minutes or until golden brown. Makes 1 loaf.

Cheesy Casserole Bread

Topping:

½ cup grated Cheddar cheese

1 Tablespoon cornmeal

½ teaspoon dry mustard

½ teaspoon poppy or sesame seeds

1 egg

1 Tablespoon milk

Topping:

Combine cheese, cornmeal, mustard and seeds in bowl. Stir in egg and milk and mix well.

Tricia Reay

French Bread

2½ cups warm (105° to 115°F) water

2 (¼ ounce) packages dry yeast

6 to 7 cups flour

1 Tablespoon salt

1 egg white

1 Tablespoon water

Combine warm water and yeast in large mixer bowl. Add 3 cups flour and salt. Beat with electric mixer on low speed until all ingredients are moistened, then on high speed for 3 minutes. Gradually add enough flour to form a soft dough. Knead until smooth and elastic, about 10 minutes. Place in lightly greased bowl; cover and let rise in warm place until doubled, 1 to 1½ hours. Punch dough down; cover and let rise until doubled again, 45 to 60 minutes. Divide dough into 4 pieces; cover and let rest 10 to 15 minutes. Shape each piece into a loaf and place in lightly greased French bread pans. Gash tops. Beat egg white with 1 tablespoon water and brush tops. Let rise, lightly covered, for 1 hour or until doubled. Brush loaves again with egg white mixture. Bake at 450°F for 25 to 30 minutes. If desired, spray cold water on loaves occasionally during baking to enhance crustiness. After baking, remove loaves from pans. If bottom crust is not brown and crusty, return bread to oven upside down in pans and bake until brown. Cool. Serve bread within 4 hours of baking. If not possible, wrap bread in foil and freeze. To serve, reheat frozen bread at 350°F for 15 minutes. If reheated in foil, unwrap last 5 minutes of warming. Makes 4 loaves.

Carol Ziemann

Elephant Ears

1 (¼ ounce) package dry yeast
¼ cup lukewarm water
2 cups sifted flour
1½ Tablespoons sugar
½ teaspoon salt
½ cup butter
½ cup scalded milk, cooled
1 egg yolk
2 Tablespoons butter, softened
2½ cups sugar, divided
3½ teaspoons cinnamon, divided
Chopped walnuts or pecans
Melted butter

Soften yeast in water. Mix flour, 1½ Tablespoons sugar and salt; cut in ½ cup butter. Combine milk, egg yolk and yeast mixture; add to flour mixture and mix well. Cover and chill until firm enough to handle, at least 2 hours. Turn out on a lightly floured board, punch down, cover and allow to rest 10 minutes. Roll into a 10 x 18-inch rectangle. Spread with softened butter. Mix ½ cup sugar and 2 teaspoons cinnamon and sprinkle evenly over dough. Starting with long side, roll as for jelly roll, sealing the edge. Cut into 1-inch slices. Mix remaining sugar and cinnamon on a large square of wax paper. Place slices, one at a time, on sugar mixture and roll into 5-inch rounds. Place on ungreased cookie sheets. Sprinkle nuts on top and press in gently. Brush with melted butter and sprinkle each with 1 teaspoon sugar-cinnamon mixture. Bake at 400°F about 12 minutes. Cool on wire racks. Makes 18.

Virginia Horton

Rum Buns

Buns:
2 Tablespoons lukewarm water
1 (¼ ounce) package dry yeast
Pinch sugar
½ cup shortening
⅓ cup sugar
1 teaspoon salt
½ cup boiling water
1 egg
½ cup cold water
3 cups flour

Buns:
Combine water, yeast and sugar in small bowl. Let stand for 10 minutes. Cream shortening, sugar and salt together. Add boiling water to creamed mixture; beat for 1 minute. Beat egg with cold water. Add to yeast mixture. Pour into creamed mixture in a stream, beating for 5 minutes. Beat in flour, ½ cup at a time, until dough is smooth. Cover and chill for 4 or more hours. Roll half the dough into a 16 x 10-inch rectangle. Spread with half the filling and sprinkle with half each of raisins and nuts. Starting with long side, roll as for jelly roll, sealing the edge. Cut into 1-inch slices. Arrange in a buttered 9-inch square baking dish. Repeat with remaining dough and filling. Cover and let rise for 1 hour. Bake at 350°F for 30 minutes. Let cool 1 minute and remove from pan. Let cool completely and spread with glaze. Makes 32.

Rum Buns

Filling:

1¼ cups butter
1¼ cups brown sugar
2½ teaspoons cinnamon
¼ teaspoon salt
1 cup chopped nuts
1 cup raisins

Filling:

Cream butter, sugar, cinnamon and salt together until thoroughly combined.

Glaze:

1½ cups confectioners' sugar
3 Tablespoons rum
2 Tablespoons butter, softened
Milk as needed

Glaze:

Combine sugar, rum and butter in small bowl. Add milk gradually to make mixture of glaze consistency.

Christine M. Randall

Herb Bubble Loaf

3 to 3½ cups flour
2 Tablespoons sugar
1½ teaspoons salt
1 (¼ ounce) package dry yeast
1¼ cups milk
2 Tablespoons vegetable oil
1 egg
½ cup butter, melted
2 Tablespoons Parmesan cheese
1 Tablespoon sesame seed
1 teaspoon garlic salt
½ teaspoon paprika
½ teaspoon parsley flakes
½ teaspoon rosemary leaves
½ teaspoon thyme leaves

Combine 1 cup flour, sugar, salt and yeast in large bowl. Heat milk and oil until very warm (120° to 150°F). Add egg and warm liquid to flour mixture. Beat ½ minute at low speed and 3 minutes at medium speed. Clean bowl and beaters frequently. Stir in remaining flour with wooden spoon to make soft dough. Turn out onto lightly floured board. Knead until smooth and elastic, about 3 minutes. Place dough in warm, greased bowl; turn to grease top. Cover and let rise until doubled. Punch down dough. Pinch off walnut-sized balls of dough and dip into melted butter. Place in greased 2½-quart round deep casserole, forming one layer. Combine Parmesan cheese, sesame seed, garlic salt, paprika, parsley, rosemary and thyme. Sprinkle half over layer of bubbles. Make another layer of bubbles, pour remaining butter over top and sprinkle with remaining seasonings. Cover and let rise until light; bubbles will almost reach top of casserole. Bake at 400°F for 23 to 30 minutes. Loaf sounds hollow when tapped when done. Makes 1 loaf.

Bro. Roland Pepperling, F.S.C.

Shaker Style Whole Wheat Bread

2 cups milk
2 (¼ ounce) packages dry yeast
3 Tablespoons molasses
2 teaspoons salt
½ cup runny mashed potatoes
5 to 6 cups whole wheat flour, divided
3 Tablespoons vegetable oil

Warm milk to 115°F in a large saucepan. Add yeast while stirring. Add molasses and salt and stir. Add cooked potatoes. Set aside about 10 to 15 minutes until mixture bubbles. Put about 2 cups flour in large mixing bowl, sprinkle with oil and stir. Add half the yeast mixture and mix with wooden spoon. Add 3 to 4 cups flour, then rest of yeast mixture and stir well. Place on floured board and start kneading. If dough is sticky, sprinkle with flour. Knead 10 minutes. Put dough in greased bowl. Turn and cover with hot wet dish towel and put in warm place to rise. Check after an hour; if it is well risen and top is smooth, take out and cut in half. If top is rough and uneven, it needs more kneading. Put unkneaded dough in warm place to rise. Shape ready dough into 2 loaves and put in greased 8 x 4-inch loaf pans. Let rise in pans 30 minutes or until dough is ½ inch above edge of pan. Bake at 360°F about 30 minutes until brown and hollow sounding. Remove from pans at once; cool on racks. Makes 2 loaves.

Terry Nicholson

Peachy Muffins

2 cups sifted flour
1 Tablespoon baking powder
¼ teaspoon baking soda
⅛ teaspoon allspice
⅓ cup dark brown sugar
⅓ cup butter, melted
1 egg, beaten
1 cup milk or sour cream
⅔ cup chopped fresh peaches

Sift flour, baking powder, baking soda and allspice together. Add sugar and sift again. Stir butter and egg into milk or sour cream. Add to flour mixture, stirring just enough to moisten. Add peaches and stir only until mixed. Batter should be lumpy. Fill greased muffin tins ⅔ full. Bake at 400°F for 25 minutes or until golden brown. Makes 10 to 12 muffins.

Barbara Leonard

Pita Pocket Bread

2 cups warm water
1 (¼ ounce) package dry yeast
1 teaspoon sugar
5½ cups flour
2 teaspoons salt
2 Tablespoons vegetable oil
2 Tablespoons cornmeal for cookie sheets
½ teaspoon vegetable oil for bowl

Combine water, yeast and sugar in small bowl; stir well. Cover and let rest for 8 to 10 minutes. Combine 3 cups flour and salt in large bowl. Stir carefully while adding yeast mixture and oil. Beat hard with wooden spoon until smooth. Add 1½ cups flour; stir well. Add remaining flour and stir until most of flour is worked in. Knead on very lightly floured (1 teaspoon flour) surface for 8 to 10 minutes. Wash bowl with warm water. Put ½ teaspoon oil in bowl. Place dough in bowl; turn to oil all surfaces. Cover with wax paper and towel. Let rise in warm place for 45 minutes. Push risen dough down. Knead in bowl for 1 minute. Cover and return to warm place for 30 minutes. Sprinkle 1 Tablespoon cornmeal on each of 2 ungreased cookie sheets. A 15 x 18-inch sheet holds 6 pitas. On lightly floured surface shape dough into a long salami shape. Cut into 12 equal portions. Form each piece into a round little cushion; bring four corners together, pinch to seal, turn pinched side down. Pat down into a pancake. Set aside until 6 are formed. Gently roll from center out to 5½ to 6-inch circles, about ¼-inch thick. Place circles on prepared sheets. Cover and let rest 10 to 20 minutes. Preheat oven to 475°F for 15 minutes. Bake on bottom rack of oven for 9 minutes. Tops will not brown much. Shape, roll out and bake remaining 6 circles. Wrap warm pitas carefully in large piece of foil, 6 to a package, then place in plastic bag. Freeze or refrigerate. Warm in foil before using. Some may not puff into pocket. These can be split and toasted. Makes 12.

Sharon Winstein

Pumpernickel Bread

¾ cup cold water
6 Tablespoons cornmeal
¾ cup boiling water
¾ cup dark molasses
1 Tablespoon butter
1 Tablespoon salt
2 teaspoons sugar
1½ teaspoons caraway seed
½ (1 ounce) square unsweetened chocolate
1 (¼ ounce) package dry yeast
¼ cup warm water (105° to 110°F)
1 cup cooled mashed potatoes
3 cups rye flour
1 cup whole wheat flour
Butter
Cornmeal
1 egg white, slightly beaten
Cold water

Combine cold water and cornmeal in very heavy saucepan. Add boiling water and cook mixture, stirring with wooden spoon, until thickened. Add molasses, butter, salt, caraway seed and chocolate. Blend mixture well and let stand until lukewarm. Add yeast to warm water and stir with fork until dissolved. Add to mixture in saucepan. Blend in potatoes. Stir in rye flour and whole wheat flour to make a stiff dough. Turn dough out onto a floured board and knead for 20 minutes, or until it is no longer sticky, dusting board with more flour if necessary. Butter a large bowl. Put dough in bowl and turn until coated with butter on all sides. Cover dough and let rise in warm, draft-free place for 1 hour, or until doubled in bulk. Punch down dough and form into a large round loaf. Transfer dough to a cookie sheet that has been well sprinkled with cornmeal. Cover dough and let rise in warm place for 50 to 75 minutes, or until doubled in bulk. Combine egg white with small amount of cold water. Brush bread with egg mixture. Bake at 375°F for 35 to 50 minutes, or until crust is brown and bread sounds hollow when tapped. Put bread on rack to cool. Makes 1 loaf.

The Elsah Landing Restaurant

Desserts

Gateau Citron Meringue

Cake:

4 egg yolks
⅔ cup sugar
1 teaspoon lemon extract
1 cup cake flour, sifted
⅛ teaspoon salt
4 egg whites, stiffly beaten
2 Tablespoons butter, melted and cooled

Cake:

Beat egg yolks with sugar until pale yellow in color. Stir in lemon extract. Sift in flour and salt. Fold in beaten egg whites and melted butter. Pour into 8-inch buttered and floured cake pan. Bake at 350°F for 30 minutes or until toothpick in center comes out clean. Remove from pan and cool.

Cream:

1 cup plus 2 Tablespoons sugar
⅝ cup butter, divided
1 egg
1 egg yolk
3 Tablespoons lemon juice, strained
2 teaspoons grated lemon rind

Cream:

Combine sugar, ¼ cup butter, egg, egg yolk, lemon juice and lemon rind in top of double boiler. Heat over barely simmering water and whisk until consistency of lightly whipped cream. Cool completely. Beat in remaining butter and chill until firm but still spreadable. Cut cake in 2 layers. Spread ⅓ of cream on bottom layer; cover with other layer. Ice cake with remainder of cream. Chill.

Meringue:

1 cup sugar
¼ teaspoon cream of tartar
⅓ cup water
2 egg whites, well beaten

Meringue:

Dissolve sugar and cream of tartar in water in saucepan. Cook syrup until candy thermometer reaches 240°F. Pour syrup in thin stream into egg whites, beating until mixture is cool and thick enough to spread. Cover cake completely with meringue and place under broiler until it is lightly browned. Serves 8 to 10.

Nancy Turner

Chocolate-Raspberry Cheese Cake Exquisite

Crust:

2½ cups chocolate wafer crumbs

¾ cup butter, melted

½ cup sugar

Crust:

Combine crumbs, butter and sugar in a bowl. Press mixture ½ inch deep into a lightly greased 9-inch springform pan.

Filling:

3 (8 ounce) packages cream cheese, softened

1 cup sugar

2 eggs

1 (8 ounce) package semisweet chocolate

2 Tablespoons heavy cream

1 cup sour cream

¼ cup strong coffee

¼ cup Framboise

1 teaspoon vanilla

Chocolate shavings or whipped cream (garnish)

Filling:

Cream cheese and sugar. Add eggs, one at a time, beating well after each addition. Melt chocolate with cream in top of double boiler. Add chocolate mixture, sour cream, coffee, Framboise and vanilla to cheese mixture. Mix until smooth. Pour over crust. Bake at 350°F for 45 to 60 minutes. Top will be a little creamy in center. Cool completely. Chill at least 3 to 4 hours in refrigerator. Remove side of springform pan. Garnish with chocolate shavings or whipped cream. Serves 8 to 12.

Rachel Kent

Kahlúa Chocolate Mousse

6 ounces semisweet chocolate

2 Tablespoons Kahlúa

1 Tablespoon fresh orange juice

2 eggs

2 egg yolks

¼ cup sugar

1 teaspoon vanilla

1 cup heavy cream

Melt chocolate in Kahlúa and orange juice over very low heat. Cool. Put eggs, egg yolks, sugar and vanilla in blender on medium high speed for 2 minutes. Add cream and blend for 1 minute more. Add chocolate mixture and blend until smooth. Pour into serving bowl or individual serving dishes. Refrigerate until set. Serves 6.

Louise Morton

Amaretto Whisper Cheese Cake

Crust:

1½ cups chocolate wafer crumbs

1 cup finely chopped lightly toasted almonds

¾ cup butter, softened

⅓ cup sugar

Crust:

Combine crumbs, almonds, butter and sugar in a bowl. Press into bottom and sides of a 9-inch springform pan.

Filling:

3 (8 ounce) packages cream cheese, softened

1 cup sugar

4 eggs

⅓ cup heavy cream

¼ cup plus 1 teaspoon Amaretto

Filling:

Cream cheese and sugar together in a large mixer bowl. Add eggs, one at a time, beating well after each addition. Add cream and Amaretto. Beat until light. Pour into crust. Bake at 375°F for 40 minutes. Let stand for 5 minutes on wire rack. Filling will not be set.

Topping:

2 cups sour cream

2 Tablespoons sugar

1 teaspoon Amaretto

Lightly toasted slivered almonds (garnish)

Topping:

Combine sour cream, sugar and Amaretto. Spread evenly on cake. Bake 5 to 10 minutes; top will still be jiggly in center. Cool completely on rack. Cover lightly and chill overnight. Remove from springform pan. Place almond slivers around outside edge of top of cake. Serves 8 to 12.

Suzy Wahl

Frozen Peanut Butter Delight

Crust:

½ cup brown sugar
½ cup smooth peanut butter
¼ cup butter, softened
1 cup flour

Crust:

Cream sugar, peanut butter and butter in large bowl. Add flour and mix until crumbly. Sprinkle in 9x13-inch pan. Bake at 350°F for 10 minutes, stirring occasionally. Reserve ⅓ for topping, and press remaining mixture evenly in bottom of pan.

Filling:

1 (8 ounce) package cream cheese, softened
½ cup sugar
¼ cup peanut butter
1 teaspoon vanilla
2 eggs
1 (4 ounce) container frozen non-dairy whipped topping, thawed
1 cup semisweet chocolate morsels

Filling:

Combine cream cheese, sugar, peanut butter and vanilla in large bowl and beat until smooth. Add eggs, one at a time, and beat well. Fold in topping. Pour over crust. Melt chocolate morsels over low heat and drizzle over filling. Marble chocolate through filling with knife. Sprinkle with reserved crumbs and freeze. Remove from freezer 15 to 20 minutes before serving. Serves 12.

Sylvia Fait

Blackberry Sauce for Fresh Peaches

1 pound frozen blackberries
3 Tablespoons sugar
1 Tablespoon Kirsch
4 ripe fresh freestone peaches
Heavy cream, whipped (garnish)
Sugar or honey (garnish)

Defrost blackberries, strain excess juice. Press berries through a sieve with back of spoon until only seeds remain. Scrape pulp from back of sieve and discard seeds. Mix berry pulp with sugar and Kirsch. Blanch peaches for 1 minute in boiling water. Peel skin, remove pits. Place each peach in a bowl. Cover with ¼ of berry sauce and garnish with whipped cream lightly sweetened with sugar or honey. Serves 4.

Duff's Restaurant

Linzertorte

1½ cups flour
½ cup dark brown sugar
¼ cup sugar
1 teaspoon cinnamon
½ teaspoon baking powder
¼ teaspoon salt
⅛ teaspoon cloves
½ cup butter
½ cup ground almonds
2 teaspoons grated lemon rind
1 egg, slightly beaten
1 cup thick raspberry jam or preserves
1 egg yolk
1 teaspoon water

Stir flour, sugars, cinnamon, baking powder, salt and cloves together in a large bowl. Cut in butter with pastry blender until fine and crumbly. Add almonds and lemon rind and blend well. Stir in egg with fork until thoroughly moistened. Gather particles into a dough. Set aside ½ cup of dough. Place remainder in ungreased 9-inch square pan, pressing to even layer. Set aside. Flatten the reserved dough and place between 2 sheets of wax paper. Roll out to a 9-inch square. Put on cookie sheet in freezer for 10 minutes. Spread jam evenly over dough in pan to within ¼ inch of edges. Remove dough from freezer. Cut into 18 ½-inch strips. Make a lattice of strips over jam. Combine egg yolk with water. Brush top crust with egg yolk mixture. Bake at 375°F for 30 minutes or until top is rich golden brown. Cool completely in pan on wire rack. Cut into 1½-inch squares. Store in covered container. Makes 36.

Mary Aleese Schreiber

Summer Fruit Dessert

1 cup cold water
2 Tablespoons unflavored gelatin
1½ cups milk
¼ teaspoon salt
⅛ teaspoon nutmeg
2 (3 ounce) packages cream cheese, softened
2 cups grated Swiss cheese
1 cup heavy cream, whipped
3 cups mixed summer fruits

Sprinkle gelatin over water in saucepan. Stir over low heat until gelatin dissolves, about 4 or 5 minutes. Remove from heat and stir in milk, salt and nutmeg. Gradually beat ½ cup of gelatin mixture into cream cheese. Stir in remaining gelatin mixture and Swiss cheese. Fold in whipped cream. Turn into 6-cup ring mold. Chill until firm. Unmold. Fill center of mold with fruit. Serves 8.

Dona Cooley

Coffee Nut Tortoni

½ cup finely chopped almonds
1 cup corn flake crumbs
2 cups heavy cream
½ cup confectioners' sugar
3 Tablespoons instant coffee
2 teaspoons vanilla
2 drops almond extract
3 egg whites
6 Tablespoons sugar

Toast almonds on cookie sheet in 350°F oven until edges turn golden brown. Add corn flake crumbs to almonds and divide in half. Cool. Whip cream until almost stiff and add confectioners' sugar. Beat until stiff. Add coffee, vanilla and almond extract. In another bowl, beat egg whites until foamy, gradually add sugar and beat until stiff. Fold half the crumb mixture into egg white mixture and gently fold into whipped cream. Spoon into 12 large cupcake papers which have been set into a cupcake tin. Sprinkle remaining crumb mixture over tops. Freeze until firm. Serves 12.

Jean L. Davis

Forgotten Cake

Meringue:
5 egg whites
¼ teaspoon cream of tartar
1¼ cups sugar

Filling:
5 egg yolks
½ cup sugar
3 Tablespoons lemon juice
2 teaspoons lemon rind
1 cup heavy cream
Sugar
Vanilla
2 (10 ounce) packages frozen raspberries, thawed, undrained

Meringue:
Beat egg whites and cream of tartar until foamy. Add sugar, 1 tablespoon at a time, beating until stiff and shiny. Spread in buttered 9 x 13-inch glass baking dish. Put in 450°F oven. Turn oven off. Leave 8 hours or overnight.

Filling:
Combine egg yolks, sugar, lemon juice and lemon rind in top of double boiler. Heat over simmering water until thickened. Cool. Whip cream until thick. Add sugar and vanilla to taste. Spread half of whipped cream over meringue. Cover with lemon filling. Top with other half of whipped cream. Chill 4 hours. Cut in squares and spoon raspberries over top. Serves 12.

Mrs. J. Bruce McBrayer

Elegant Lemon Charlotte Russe

⅔ cup fresh lemon juice
1 Tablespoon unflavored gelatin
1½ cups sugar, divided
5 Tablespoons butter, softened
4 eggs, separated
1 teaspoon vanilla
1½ pints, heavy cream divided
1 Tablespoon grated fresh lemon rind
1½ (3 ounce) packages lady fingers
Sugar
Candied violets and/or fresh mint leaves (garnish)

Dissolve gelatin in lemon juice in top of double boiler over hot, not boiling, water. Add 1 cup sugar and stir until liquified. Add butter and stir until melted and blended. Beat egg yolks slightly and stir 3 Tablespoons of hot mixture into them, blending well. Add egg yolks to lemon mixture, stirring constantly. Continue to cook for about 5 minutes, stirring constantly. Remove from heat and add vanilla. Strain mixture into large mixing bowl and chill until the consistency of raw egg whites. While mixture is chilling, beat egg whites slowly, adding ½ cup sugar and beat until medium to firm peaks form. Beat 1 pint cream with the lemon rind until stiff. Gently fold the whipped cream and egg whites into gelatin mixture, folding only until well blended. Pour into a 9-inch springform pan which has been sprayed with non-stick coating and lined on bottom and sides with ladyfingers. Refrigerate until firm. Just before serving, whip ½ pint cream with sugar to taste. Top unmolded charlotte russe with whipped cream and garnish with candied violets and/or mint leaves. Serves 12.

Pat Campos

Huguenot Torte

2 eggs
1½ cups sugar
¼ cup flour
2 teaspoons baking powder
1 teaspoon vanilla
¼ teaspoon salt
1 cup peeled, chopped tart apples
1 cup chopped pecans
Sherry-flavored whipped cream (optional)
Vanilla ice cream (optional)

Beat eggs until frothy in medium bowl. Fold in, by hand, flour, baking powder, vanilla and salt. Stir in apples and pecans. Pour into greased and floured 9 x 13-inch baking dish. Bake at 325°F for 45 minutes. Batter will swell, form a crust on top, then collapse. Serve warm with sherry-flavored whipped cream or vanilla ice cream. Serves 8.

Mrs. J. Glennon Schreiber

Italian Chocolate Nut Meringue

4 egg whites
⅛ teaspoon cream of tartar
⅛ teaspoon salt
¼ cup sugar
2 cups heavy cream
1 Tablespoon vanilla
2 teaspoons sugar
1 (6 ounce) package semisweet chocolate morsels
½ cup toasted slivered blanched almonds

Beat egg whites until foamy. Add cream of tartar and salt. Continue beating until soft peaks form, then add ¼ cup sugar gradually and stop beating. Beat cream until thick; add vanilla and 2 teaspoons sugar. Egg whites and cream should be the same consistency. Fold cream into egg whites. Put meringue in freezer and freeze until ice crystals form in meringue. Melt chocolate. Remove meringue from freezer and add hot melted chcolate and almonds. Working quickly, fold together. Spoon into bowl or silver-foil cupcake papers and return to freezer until ready to serve. Makes 12 in bowl, 16 in cupcake papers.

Hope Edison
Audrey Rothbarth

Swirl-Top Cheesecake

Crust:

2 cups graham cracker crumbs

½ cup sugar

¼ teaspoon cinnamon

⅛ teaspoon nutmeg

½ cup butter

Crust:

Combine graham cracker crumbs, sugar, cinnamon and nutmeg. Cut in butter until completely blended. Press mixture evenly on bottom and sides of a heavily buttered 9-inch springform pan. Chill while preparing filling.

Filling:

1 (1 ounce) square unsweetened chocolate

2 (8 ounce) packages cream cheese, softened

1 cup sugar

6 eggs, separated

1 Tablespoon grated fresh orange rind

1 Tablespoon fresh orange juice

1 teaspoon vanilla

1 cup heavy cream

Filling:

Melt chocolate over hot water. Blend cream cheese and sugar until creamy and fluffy. Add egg yolks, one at a time, beating well after each addition. Stir in orange rind, orange juice and vanilla. Beat egg whites until stiff but not dry. Whip cream; fold with egg whites into cheese mixture until well blended. Spoon ⅓ of filling into crust; drizzle a little of the melted chocolate over the surface and swirl lightly into the filling with tip of a knife. Repeat twice ending with chocolate. Bake at 300°F for 1 hour. Turn heat off and leave cake in oven with door closed for another hour. Remove and cool at room temperature. Loosen crust around sides with knife and remove from pan. Serves 12 to 16.

Sandra Mollica

Fluffy Cheese Cake

Crust:

¾ cup graham cracker crumbs

2 Tablespoons sugar

2 Tablespoons butter, melted

Filling:

4 eggs, separated

¼ teaspoon salt

2 (8 ounce) packages cream cheese, softened

1 cup light cream

¾ cup sugar

2 Tablespoons flour

1 teaspoon vanilla

1 teaspoon fresh lemon juice

1 teaspoon grated fresh lemon rind (optional)

Crust:

Butter sides of 9-inch springform pan. Mix graham cracker crumbs, sugar and butter thoroughly. Press crumb mixture into bottom of pan.

Filling:

Beat egg whites with salt until stiff. Set aside. Using electric mixer, gradually beat cream into cream cheese until smooth. Blend in sugar, flour, vanilla, lemon juice and lemon rind. Beat egg yolks lightly and blend into cheese mixture. Gently fold in egg whites. Pour into crust. Bake at 325°F for 1 hour. When done, turn oven off. Open door, but leave cake in oven 30 minutes. Serves 8 to 10.

Mary Alice Steinman

Three Layer Party Torte

Layers:

12 egg whites at room temperature

2 teaspoons vanilla

1½ teaspoons white vinegar

3 cups sifted granulated sugar

Filling:

1 (20 ounce) can crushed pineapple, drained

1 cup maraschino cherries

1 cup chopped pecans

3 cups heavy cream, whipped

1 teaspoon vanilla or almond extract

Layers:

Combine eggs, vanilla and vinegar and beat until soft peaks form. Add sugar, 1 Tablespoon at a time, and beat until very stiff. Spread into 3 greased and floured 9-inch cake pans. Bake at 300°F for 1 hour and 15 minutes. Cool.

Filling:

Combine pineapple, cherries and pecans. Fold in whipped cream and vanilla. Spread on layers and stack layers. Cover and refrigerate overnight. Serves 12.

Lois Rea

Charlotte Almond Mousse

Meringue Layers:

3 egg whites at room temperature

⅜ teaspoon cream of tartar

¾ cup sugar, divided

Meringue Layers:

Cut 3 (8-inch) circles of wax or brown paper; place on cookie sheet. Beat egg whites and cream of tartar to soft peaks. Add ½ cup sugar gradually until eggs are shiny and hold stiff peaks. Fold in ¼ cup sugar. Divide and spread on circles. Bake at 250°F for 1 hour. Turn heat off and leave meringues in oven 3 hours to cool and dry completely. Peel off paper.

Filling:

½ cup sugar

3 Tablespoons butter, softened

¾ teaspoon almond extract

2 egg yolks

1 cup finely ground lightly toasted blanched almonds

1 cup heavy cream, divided

2 Tablespoons lightly toasted sliced almonds (garnish)

Whole or halved strawberries (garnish)

Filling:

Cream sugar and butter until light and fluffy. Add almond extract and blend well. Add egg yolks, one at a time, beating well. Stir in ground almonds. Add ½ cup cream, beating until smooth and thick. Spread half of mixture on one layer of meringue. Add second layer and spread with remaining mixture. Put third layer of meringue on top and cover tightly with plastic wrap. Chill 18 hours. At least 4 hours before serving, whip ½ cup cream until it holds a peak. Spread on top. Cover and chill. Garnish with almonds and strawberries before serving. Serves 8 to 10.

Tina M. Burke

Wine Gelatin Dessert

¼ cup cold water

1 Tablespoon unflavored gelatin

½ cup sugar

¼ teaspoon salt

1 cup red wine

¾ cup fresh orange juice

1 Tablespoon fresh lemon juice

Whipped cream (garnish)

Sprinkle gelatin in water in small bowl. Add sugar and salt. Heat wine and pour into gelatin. Stir until solids are dissolved. Add orange juice and lemon juice. Pour into 4 stemmed glasses. Chill until firm. Top with a dollop of whipped cream. Serves 4.

Etta Taylor

Bavarian Apple Torte

Pastry:

⅓ cup sugar
⅓ cup butter
¼ teaspoon vanilla
⅛ teaspoon salt
1 cup sifted flour

Pastry:

Cream sugar, butter, vanilla and salt together. Blend in flour. Pat into bottom of 9-inch springform pan.

Filling:

4 cups peeled and sliced apples
1 (8 ounce) package cream cheese, softened
¼ cup sugar
1 egg
2 teaspoons grated lemon rind and/or 1 teaspoon lemon juice
¼ teaspoon vanilla or almond extract
⅛ teaspoon salt

Filling:

Place apples in shallow pan, cover with foil and bake at 400°F for 15 minutes while preparing filling. Beat cheese with sugar. Add egg, lemon rind, vanilla and salt and beat until smooth. Turn into pastry-lined pan. Top with apple slices.

Topping:

¼ to ⅓ cup sugar
½ teaspoon cinnamon
¼ to ⅓ cup sliced or slivered almonds

Topping:

Combine sugar and cinnamon and sprinkle over apples. Sprinkle almonds on top. Bake at 350°F for 40 minutes to 1 hour, or until crust is nicely browned. Serves 8 to 10.

Jane Ross

Dacquoise au Chocolat Blanc

8 egg whites
1 cup sugar
8 ounces ground blanched almonds

Butter and flour 2 baking sheets and trace a 9-inch circle on each. Beat egg whites until very stiff, adding a spoonful of sugar halfway through. Combine remaining sugar and almonds; carefully fold into egg whites. Fill pastry bag fitted with #9 tip and press spirals onto baking sheets. Bake at 250°F for 1 to 1¼ hours or until crisp. Remove and cool a few minutes. Remove from sheets carefully. If necessary, store in covered container in cool, dry place, or freeze.

White Chocolate Ganache:

¾ pound white chocolate, grated
1½ cups heavy cream
Confectioners' sugar
Chopped toasted almonds (garnish)

White Chocolate Ganache:
Combine white chocolate and cream in saucepan; bring just to a boil, whisking constantly. Allow to cool until cold and slightly thickened. Whip with wire whisk until thick and soft peaks form. Reserve small amount for decoration. Spread cream between meringue layers with spatula or use pastry bag fitted with star tip. Sprinkle top of cake with confectioners' sugar and decorate with remaining ganache. Sprinkle with almonds. Serves 10 to 12.

Frank Waldman

Kentucky Delight

½ pound miniature marshmallows
½ cup bourbon
24 almond macaroons, crumbled
1 pint heavy cream, whipped

Soak marshmallows in bourbon for 1 hour. Add macaroons and whipped cream. Chill slightly. Serve over angel food cake or ice cream. Makes 4 cups.

Carolyn Clarke

Chocolate Ice Box Cake

- *2 (3 ounce) packages lady fingers, split*
- *3 (4 ounce) bars German sweet chocolate*
- *3 Tablespoons sugar*
- *½ cup water*
- *6 eggs, at room temperature, separated*
- *1 teaspoon vanilla*
- *½ pint heavy cream*
- *Confectioners' sugar (optional)*
- *Shaved chocolate (garnish)*

Line ungreased 9-inch springform pan on sides and bottom with lady fingers. Melt chocolate in top of double boiler. Add sugar; slowly stir in water and cook until smooth. Beat egg yolks; add, one at a time, stirring until well blended. Cook 3 minutes. Add vanilla. Cool mixture. Beat egg whites until stiff. Fold into chocolate mixture. Pour into springform pan. Whip cream with confectioners' sugar, if desired, and cover top of cake. Garnish with shaved chocolate. Refrigerate. Serves 8.

Nancy Monson

Maple Walnut Sponge

- *½ cup cold water*
- *2 Tablespoons unflavored gelatin*
- *2 cups pure maple syrup*
- *2 egg whites, at room temperature*
- *Pinch cream of tartar*
- *3 cups heavy cream*
- *1⅓ cups finely chopped walnuts*
- *Walnuts (garnish)*

Soften gelatin in cold water for 10 minutes. Combine maple syrup and gelatin in saucepan. Heat over moderate low heat, stirring constantly, until gelatin is dissolved and mixture is hot, but not boiling. Combine egg whites and cream of tartar; beat with electric mixer to stiff peaks. Add hot maple syrup in a slow stream, beating constantly. Beat meringue until it is cool and holds stiff glossy peaks. Beat cream until it holds stiff peaks; fold into meringue with chopped walnuts. Lightly grease a 3-quart mold with vegetable oil. Spoon mixture into mold; rap mold sharply to remove any air bubbles. Cover and chill at least 4 hours or until set. Run a thin knife around inside rim of mold. Dip mold in hot water for a few seconds. Invert chilled serving plate over mold. Invert, giving mold a sharp rap. Garnish with walnuts. Serves 6 to 8.

Wolfgang Bierer C.E.C.
St. Louis Club

White Chocolate Mousse De Bergerac

Mousse:

2 cups double heavy cream
1 cup confectioners' sugar
1½ Tablespoons water
½ cup egg whites
1 pound white chocolate, coarsely chopped
4 to 6 Tablespoons dark Jamaican rum

Mousse:

Whip cream until moderately stiff. Mix sugar and water in saucepan and heat to melt sugar. Beat egg whites until firm, about 3 or 4 minutes. When sugar mixture reaches 250°F, add to beaten egg whites, beating continuously. Beat about 3 minutes more. Add white chocolate while beating. Mixture will reduce to a liquid. Beat for 1 minute more. Stir in rum. Fold in whipped cream. Refrigerate for at least 2 hours. Garnish with chocolate-dipped strawberries and serve with sauce. Serves 8.

Sauce:

1 quart fresh strawberries
¼ cup Kirsch

Sauce:

Mix strawberries and Kirsch in blender and spin until smooth. Pour into dish and serve with mousse.

Garnish:

Strawberries
Grand Marnier
Bittersweet coating chocolate

Garnish:

Marinate strawberries in Grand Marnier. Drain berries. Melt chocolate over low heat or in top of double boiler over hot water. Hold berries by stems and dip partially into melted chocolate. Place on rack to cool.

De Bergerac's

Cold Raspberry Soufflé

2 (10 ounce) packages frozen red raspberries, thawed
2 Tablespoons unflavored gelatin
½ cup cold water
8 eggs, separated
1½ cups sugar, divided
¼ teaspoon salt
2 cups heavy cream

Prepare 2-quart soufflé dish by adding 6-inch collar secured by string or tape. Purée raspberries, using blender or forcing through sieve. Sprinkle gelatin over cold water to soften. Beat egg yolks in top of double boiler and gradually beat in 1 cup sugar and salt. Cook over simmering water until thickened, beating constantly. Remove from heat. Stir in gelatin until dissolved. Let mixture stand until cool, but not set. Stir in raspberry purée. Beat egg whites until they hold soft peaks, then gradually beat in ½ cup sugar to make a meringue. Whip cream until it holds stiff peaks. Gently fold meringue and whipped cream into raspberry mixture. Pour into prepared soufflé dish. Chill 2 to 3 hours. Remove collar carefully. Sprinkle top with crushed praline powder. Serves 8.

Praline Powder:

½ cup blanched almonds
1 cup sugar
3 Tablespoons water
¼ teaspoon cream of tartar

Praline Powder:

Place almonds in pan in 300°F oven and heat until golden, about 15 to 20 minutes. Shake pan frequently to prevent burning. Combine sugar, water and cream of tartar in heavy saucepan. Boil, without stirring, until syrup takes on color. Add almonds and boil syrup until it is golden brown. Pour mixture into buttered pan; cool and chill until it hardens. Pulverize mixture in blender, a small amount at a time. Store in refrigerator.

Nancy Turner

Greek Walnut Torte

Torte:

9 eggs, separated
1 cup sugar
3 cups ground walnuts
½ cup dry bread crumbs
1 Tablespoon grated orange rind
2 teaspoons grated lemon rind
2 teaspoons baking powder
1 teaspoon cinnamon
½ teaspoon cloves
½ teaspoon salt
½ cup water
1 teaspoon vanilla

Torte:

Combine egg yolks and sugar in medium bowl; beat with mixer at high speed until very thick and light colored. Stir walnuts, bread crumbs, orange rind, lemon rind, baking powder, cinnamon, cloves and salt in very large bowl. Add water and vanilla to egg yolk mixture and stir well. Stir into walnut mixture. Beat egg whites until stiff but not dry. Fold gently into walnut batter until thoroughly combined. Pour batter into 3 8-inch cake pans which have been lined with wax paper and lightly buttered. Bake at 350°F for 30 minutes. Invert layers, in pans, on racks to cool. Loosen around edges and turn out of pans; remove wax paper. Several hours before serving, make brandy butter cream. Fill and frost 3 layers; lightly press broken walnuts into butter cream on top of torte. Serves 8 to 12.

Brandy Butter Cream:

½ cup butter, softened
1 (1 pound) box confectioners' sugar
⅛ teaspoon salt
1 egg
2 Tablespoons brandy
1 teaspoon vanilla
⅔ cup broken walnuts

Brandy Butter Cream:

Beat butter until creamy in small bowl. Beat in sugar and salt until smooth. Beat in egg, brandy and vanilla until creamy.

Judith Bettendorf

Chocolate Amaretto Mousse Cake

1 (6 ounce) package semisweet chocolate morsels
18 whole blanched almonds
½ cup Amaretto
2 Tablespoons unflavored gelatin
¼ cup water
4 eggs, separated
2 cups milk
⅓ cup sugar
2 cups heavy cream, whipped
2 (3 ounce) packages lady fingers, split

Melt chocolate morsels. Dip bottom half of almonds into chocolate and place on wax paper; chill until firm. Gradually stir Amaretto into remaining chocolate. Set aside. Combine gelatin and water in a saucepan. Stir in egg yolks, milk and sugar. Stir over low heat until mixture thickens slightly and coats a metal spoon. Stir in chocolate mixture. Chill until mixture mounds. Beat egg whites until stiff. Fold into mixture. Remove 1 cup whipped cream and set aside. Fold remaining cream into chocolate mixture. Chill until mixture mounds. Line the bottom and sides of a 9-inch springform pan with split lady fingers. Pour in chocolate mixture. Chill until firm. Remove sides of pan and pipe rosettes of reserved cream around outer edge of cake. Press a chocolate almond into each rosette. Chill until ready to serve. Serves 10 to 12.

Nancy Clifton

Chocolate Mousse

3 (1 ounce) squares semisweet chocolate
1 (1 ounce) square unsweetened chocolate
¼ cup honey
1 Tablespoon brandy
1 teaspoon instant coffee
2 cups heavy cream
1 teaspoon vanilla

Melt semisweet and unsweetened chocolate in top of a double boiler. Add honey. Dissolve instant coffee in brandy and add to chocolate. Cool mixture. Whip cream to stiff peaks and add vanilla. Fold chocolate mixture into whipped cream. Refrigerate overnight. Serves 6 to 8.

Affairs to Remember Catering

Cherry Cheese Cake

Crust:

1¼ cups zwieback crumbs
¼ cup sugar
¼ cup butter
1 teaspoon cinnamon

Crust:

Combine zwieback crumbs, sugar, butter and cinnamon. Spread on bottom and a little up sides of greased 9-inch springform pan.

Filling:

3 (8 ounce) packages cream cheese, softened
1 cup sugar
5 eggs
1 teaspoon vanilla

Filling:

Beat cheese and sugar together; add eggs, one at a time; continue beating until light and fluffy. Add vanilla. Pour mixture into crust in pan. Bake at 350°F for 35 minutes or until toothpick inserted in center comes out clean.

Topping:

2 cups sour cream
¼ cup sugar
1 teaspoon vanilla

Topping:

Combine sour cream, sugar and vanilla. Spread on top of baked cake. Bake at 350°F for 5 minutes.

Cherry Topping:

2 (1 pound) cans waterpacked cherries, undrained
¾ cup sugar
2 Tablespoons cornstarch
¼ teaspoon salt

Cherry Topping:

Drain cherries; save ¾ cup juice. Combine sugar, cornstarch and salt with juice in saucepan. Boil about 7 minutes or until thick and clear. Add cherries. Allow to cool. Spread on top of cooled cake. Refrigerate at least 8 hours. Serves 10 to 12.

Selma H. Soule

Chocolate Roll with Rum Filling

Roll:

1 cup cake flour
¼ cup cocoa
1 teaspoon baking powder
⅛ teaspoon salt
3 eggs
1 cup sugar
⅓ cup water
1 teaspoon vanilla
Confectioners' sugar

Roll:

Sift flour, cocoa, baking powder and salt together. Beat eggs in small mixer bowl until very thick and lemon colored, about 5 minutes. Transfer to large mixer bowl and gradually beat in sugar. Blend in water and vanilla on low speed. Add flour mixture, gradually, beating just until smooth. Pour into a foil-lined and greased jelly roll pan. Bake at 375°F for 12 to 15 minutes. Invert onto towel sprinkled with confectioners' sugar. Remove foil; roll cake and towel from narrow end. Cool on wire rack. Unroll, remove towel and fill with pastry cream. Roll cake from narrow end and spread with glaze. Refrigerate. Serves 8 to 10.

Filling:

1 egg
1 egg yolk
3 Tablespoons sugar
3 Tablespoons flour
⅛ teaspoon salt
2 teaspoons unflavored gelatin
1 cup milk, scalded
2 egg whites
3 Tablespoons rum
1 cup heavy cream, whipped stiff

Filling:

Beat egg, egg yolk, sugar, flour and salt with whisk until light and fluffy. Stir in gelatin and mix in milk. Put in heavy saucepan over low heat and beat with whisk until thick and smooth. Put pan in bowl of ice and stir until mixture cools. Beat egg whites to soft peaks and add to mixture with rum. Continue to stir over bowl of ice until mixture is on point of setting. Add whipped cream slowly.

Glaze:

2 (1 ounce) squares unsweetened chocolate
3 Tablespoons butter
1 cup sifted confectioners' sugar
1 teaspoon vanilla
2 Tablespoons hot water

Glaze:

Melt chocolate and butter over low heat. Remove from heat and stir in sugar and vanilla. Add water, 1 teaspoon at a time, until of proper consistency.

Judy Geoghean

Lemon Ice Cream Dessert

Crust:

1 cup butter, softened
½ cup brown sugar
2 cups flour
1 cup finely chopped pecans
1 quart vanilla ice cream, softened

Crust:

Cream butter and sugar. Stir in flour and pecans and mix well. Pat into bottom of 9 x 13-inch pan and bake at 350°F for 20 minutes. Cool. Spread ice cream over crust and freeze.

Custard:

2 cups sugar
¾ cup butter
⅔ cup fresh lemon juice
Pinch salt
4 eggs
4 egg yolks

Custard:

Combine sugar, butter, lemon juice and salt in saucepan. Beat eggs and egg yolks slightly; stir into lemon mixture. Cook, stirring frequently, over low heat until mixture thickens and boils. Chill. Spread over ice cream and freeze.

Meringue:

4 egg whites
½ cup sugar
2 Tablespoons grated fresh lemon rind

Meringue:

Beat egg whites very stiff. Gradually add sugar. Beat until thick and shiny; add lemon rind. Spread over frozen dessert and seal against crust. Bake at 500°F for 3 minutes until golden brown. Serves 12.

Tina M. Burke

Kahlúa Flan Delight

Cake:

1 (18½ ounce) package chocolate fudge cake mix

1 (3¾ ounce) package instant chocolate pudding

4 eggs

1½ cups Kahlúa, divided

½ cup water

Cake:

Combine cake mix, pudding mix, eggs, ¾ cup Kahlúa and water in large mixer bowl. Beat with mixer for 4 minutes. Pour into 2 greased flan pans, filling half full. Bake at 350°F for 25 to 30 minutes. Cool 15 minutes and remove from pans. Drizzle each cake with equal amounts of remaining Kahlúa.

Filling:

1 (3¼ ounce) package regular chocolate pudding

1½ cups milk

½ cup Kahlúa

Filling:

Combine pudding and milk and cook according to package directions. Remove from heat and add Kahlúa. Pour into cake shells. Cover with foil. Refrigerate for 2 days or freeze.

Topping:

1½ cups heavy cream

3 Tablespoons confectioners' sugar

2 Tablespoons Kahlúa

1 Tablespoon instant coffee

2 teaspoons cocoa

Toasted sliced almonds (garnish)

Chocolate curls (garnish)

Topping:

On day of serving, combine cream, sugar, Kahlúa, coffee and cocoa and beat until stiff. Cover filling. Garnish with almonds and chocolate curls. Makes 2 flans.

Gwen Springett

Christmas Plum Pudding

10 eggs
25 ounces Guiness Stout
1¼ pounds dried bread cubes
15 ounces ground beef suet
2½ cups flour
3½ teaspoons allspice
2½ teaspoons baking powder
2½ teaspoons ground nutmeg
1¼ teaspoons cinnamon
1¼ teaspoons salt
15 ounces dark brown sugar
5 Tablespoons English marmalade
5 pounds dried fruits; raisins, currants, sultanas, apricots, prunes and figs in proportion according to taste (cut larger fruits into pieces)
Brandy
½ cup brandy or rum

Mix eggs, stout and bread cubes and beat until smooth. Stir in suet. Combine flour, allspice, baking powder, nutmeg, cinnamon and salt; add to mixture with sugar and marmalade. Mix well. Add dried fruits and mix well; mixture will be very stiff and sticky. Pack mixture into greased molds or coffee cans. Cover with wax paper and aluminum foil; secure with string. Steam in large pot for 6 hours. Cool and pour brandy, to taste, on each pudding. Re-cover and store in refrigerator or freezer. Puddings improve with age and can be made up to a year in advance. Before serving, steam again for 2 or 3 hours. Warm ½ cup brandy or rum, pour over pudding and ignite. Serve with foamy hard sauce. Makes 10 pounds pudding.

Foamy Hard Sauce:

½ cup butter, softened
1 cup confectioners' sugar
1 egg or 2 egg yolks, well beaten
Dash salt
Vanilla, sherry or brandy to taste
½ cup heavy cream

Foamy Hard Sauce:

Cream butter until light. Beat sugar, eggs and salt in gradually. Place over hot water and beat until smooth and light, about 7 minutes. Add vanilla, sherry or brandy. Beat cream until stiff. Fold into mixture. Serves 6 to 8.

Mrs. David Frank

Baklava

1 pound frozen filo dough
2¼ cups sugar, divided
1½ cups honey
1½ cups water
1½ lemons
1 cinnamon stick
1 teaspoon vanilla
1 pound walnuts, finely chopped
1 Tablespoon cinnamon
1 pound unsalted butter
Whole cloves (optional)

Put frozen dough into refrigerator overnight. Mix 1½ cups sugar, honey, water, juice and skin of the lemons, cinnamon stick and vanilla in saucepan. Boil 10 minutes. Strain, cool and chill at least 4 hours or overnight. Take filo dough out of refrigerator 2 or 3 hours before ready to use. Mix walnuts, ¾ cup sugar and cinnamon. Set aside. Melt butter slowly. Keep butter warm while working on pastry. Open filo and spread flat. Work fast so filo will not dry out. Place 18 x 12 x 1-inch pan on filo. (9 x 13-inch pan may be used, but there will be fewer pieces of Baklava.) Cut all the sheets to fit the pan. Cover filo with towel. Butter pan using pastry brush to spread melted butter. Lay 1 sheet of filo in pan. Brush thoroughly with butter. Repeat until there are 8 buttered sheets. Lay on another sheet. Spread on ¼ the nut mixture. Top with another sheet and brush with butter. Repeat 3 times, until the nut mixture has been used. Lay on another sheet of filo and brush with butter. Repeat until all the filo has been used. Be sure top layer is very well buttered. Refrigerate ½ hour. Using a sharp knife, cut pastry into diamonds. Make first cut parallel to long side of pan, 1¼ to 1½ inches from edge. Continue long cuts, dividing width evenly. Then cut at an angle. Be sure to cut all the way through. A clove may be placed in center of each diamond if desired. Bake at 325°F for 45 to 55 minutes until golden chestnut in color and pastry is flaky. Spoon chilled syrup over Baklava. Cool in pan. Best served after it has set several hours. Baklava will keep at room temperature for 2 to 3 days, refrigerated for 2 to 3 weeks; or it may be frozen. Makes 60 to 70 diamonds.

Garie Perry

Pies

Tartelettes aux Fraises

Pastry:

16 baked tart shells, cooled
¼ cup fine bread crumbs
¼ cup sugar
½ teaspoon ground cardamom

Pastry:
Combine bread crumbs, sugar and cardamom. Spread 1 teaspoon of mixture on bottom of each tart shell. This will keep shells crisp after filling.

Filling:

1 egg
1 egg yolk
3 Tablespoons sugar
3 Tablespoons flour
⅛ teaspoon salt
2 teaspoons unflavored gelatin
1 cup milk, scalded
2 egg whites
3 Tablespoons rum
1 cup heavy cream, whipped
2 quarts strawberries, washed and hulled

Filling:
Combine egg, egg yolk, sugar, flour and salt in bowl and beat with wire whisk until light and fluffy. Stir in gelatin. Add milk. Put in saucepan over low heat and beat with wire whisk until thick and smooth. Put pan in bowl of ice and stir until filling cools a little. Beat egg whites to soft peaks and add to filling with rum. Continue to stir over ice until filling is on point of setting. Slowly add whipped cream. Fill tart shells level and refrigerate until set. Cover tops with strawberries, point up, as close together as possible. Brush strawberries with cooled glaze. Makes 16 tarts.

Glaze:

½ cup red currant jelly
1 Tablespoon sherry

Glaze:
Combine jelly and sherry in saucepan. Melt over low heat. Strain and cool.

Mrs. J. Glennon Schreiber

Lemon Chess Pie

2 cups sugar
1 cup butter (do not substitute)
5 eggs, beaten
¼ cup fresh lemon juice
2 Tablespoons flour
1 Tablespoon cornmeal
1 teaspoon vanilla
2 unbaked 8-inch pie shells

Cream sugar and butter. Add eggs, lemon juice, flour, cornmeal and vanilla. Mix well. Pour into pie shells. Bake at 300°F for 1 hour. Makes 2 pies.

Peggy McClellan

Louise Hagan's Cheese Pie

Crust:

2 cups graham cracker crumbs
½ cup sugar
½ cup butter, melted

Crust:

Combine graham cracker crumbs, sugar and butter. Press in 9 or 10-inch pie pan at least 1½ inches deep. Chill 1 hour.

Filling:

2 (8 ounce) packages cream cheese, softened
2 eggs
⅔ cup sugar
1 teaspoon vanilla

Filling:

Beat cream cheese until smooth. Add eggs, sugar and vanilla. Pour into crust. Do not overfill. Bake at 375°F for 20 minutes. Let stand for 20 to 25 minutes.

Topping:

1 cup sour cream
2 Tablespoons sugar
1 teaspoon vanilla
Frozen berries, thawed (optional)

Topping:

Combine sour cream with sugar and vanilla. Carefully spread over baked filling. Bake at 425°F for 10 minutes. Cool and refrigerate. Can be served with berries poured over top, if desired. Makes 1 pie.

Mrs. Howard Carter III

Italian Plum Torte

Dough:

2 cups flour
2 Tablespoons sugar
1 cup butter
⅛ teaspoon salt

Dough:

Combine flour, sugar, butter and salt. Mix thoroughly with pastry blender. Refrigerate 2 hours. Pat into 10-inch round glass pie pan, making sure crust goes up sides of pan.

Filling:

¼ cup bread crumbs
1½ pounds Italian plums, halved and pitted
½ to ¾ cup sugar
2 egg yolks, beaten
3 Tablespoons heavy cream

Filling:

Sprinkle bread crumbs over bottom of crust. Place plum halves in bottom of pie, in decorative arrangement. Mix sugar, egg yolks and cream together. Pour in center of each plum, then over all. Bake at 400°F for 30 minutes. Cannot be frozen. Makes 1 torte.

Sarajoan Rezak

Cotton Patch Pie

3 (1 ounce) squares unsweetened chocolate
⅓ cup butter
4 eggs
2 cups sugar
1 teaspoon vanilla
¼ teaspoon salt
1 cup chopped pecans
1 unbaked 9-inch pie shell
1 cup pecan halves

Melt chocolate and butter in double boiler over low heat. Cool. Beat eggs lightly and add sugar, vanilla and salt. Stir in chopped pecans and chocolate mixture. Pour into pie shell. Top with pecan halves. Bake at 350°F for 35 to 45 minutes. Pie is done when crust is slightly brown and center is slightly firm when pan is gently moved. It is better to undercook than overcook. Makes 1 pie.

Deborah Randall

Pecan Pie

1 cup white corn syrup
1 cup dark brown sugar
⅓ cup butter, melted
1 teaspoon vanilla
⅓ teaspoon salt
3 eggs, slightly beaten
1 unbaked 9-inch pie shell
1¼ cups pecan halves

Combine syrup, sugar, butter, vanilla and salt; mix well. Add eggs and blend well. Pour into pie shell and sprinkle pecans over top. Bake at 350°F for 45 minutes. Makes 1 pie.

Carolyn Clarke

Clafoutis aux Cerises

1 (16½ ounce) can pitted bing cherries, drained
1 unbaked 9-inch pie shell
½ cup unsalted butter
4 ounces sugar
3 egg yolks
1 egg
4 ounces flour
1 cup milk
1 Tablespoon rum
1 teaspoon vanilla
Confectioners' sugar (garnish)

Spread cherries over bottom of pie shell. Cream butter and sugar in bowl. Add egg yolks and egg; beat for 2 minutes. Stir in flour. Add milk, rum and vanilla; beat until smooth. Pour batter over cherries. Bake at 375°F for 40 minutes. Sprinkle with confectioners' sugar. Serve very hot. Makes 1 pie.

Andre Gotti
C. Exe. Chef
Old Warson Country Club

Rum Black Bottom Pie

4 eggs, separated
1 cup sugar, divided
1 Tablespoon cornstarch
2 cups milk, scalded
¼ cup cold water
1 Tablespoon unflavored gelatin
1 cup semisweet chocolate morsels
3 Tablespoons rum or ¾ teaspoon rum flavoring
2 cups heavy cream
¼ cup confectioners' sugar
2 baked 9-inch pie shells or graham cracker crusts
Shaved chocolate (garnish)

Beat egg yolks. Add ½ cup sugar and cornstarch and stir to blend. Combine yolk mixture and milk in top of double boiler. Cook over low heat until mixture coats a metal spoon. Soak gelatin in water. Pour 1 cup hot mixture over chocolate morsels and blend until smooth. Pour half of chocolate mixture into each crust to cover bottom. Add soaked gelatin and rum to remaining custard; Stir until gelatin is dissolved. Chill until slightly thickened. Beat egg whites until very stiff, adding ½ cup sugar gradually. Add chilled custard and blend until smooth. Pour over chocolate layer. Chill for several hours. Whip cream and confectioners' sugar. Spread over top. Garnish with shaved chocolate. Makes 2 pies.

Norma Lea Shelp

Bourbon Chiffon Pie

Crust:

1½ cups graham cracker crumbs
6 Tablespoons sugar
6 Tablespoons butter, melted
½ teaspoon nutmeg

Crust:

Combine graham cracker crumbs, sugar, butter and nutmeg. Press into a 9-inch pie pan. Bake at 350°F for 10 minutes. Cool.

Filling:

1 Tablespoon unflavored gelatin
¼ cup cold black coffee
⅔ cup sugar, divided
¼ teaspoon salt
3 eggs, separated
6 Tablespoons bourbon
¼ cup Kahlúa
1 cup heavy cream, whipped
Bourbon flavored whipped cream (garnish)
Shaved chocolate (garnish)

Filling:

Dissolve gelatin in coffee in saucepan. Add ⅓ cup sugar and salt; bring to a simmer. Beat egg yolks lightly. Add a small amount of hot mixture to egg yolks; stir into mixture in saucepan. Stir in bourbon and Kahlúa. Chill until it begins to thicken. Beat egg whites until stiff, adding ⅓ cup sugar gradually. Fold meringue and whipped cream into bourbon mixture. Pour into pie shell and chill overnight. Spread bourbon flavored whipped cream on top of pie and sprinkle with shaved chocolate before serving. Makes 1 pie.

Jefferson Avenue Boarding House

Old Tavern Walnut-Raisin Pie

3 eggs
¾ cup sugar
⅓ cup butter, melted
½ teaspoon cinnamon
½ teaspoon ginger
½ teaspoon salt
⅔ cup raisins
⅓ cup English walnuts
1 unbaked 9-inch pie shell
Whipped cream (garnish)
Cinnamon or nutmeg (garnish)

Combine eggs, sugar, butter, cinnamon, ginger and salt in a bowl. Beat for 2 minutes. Stir in raisins and walnuts. Pour into pie shell. Bake at 375°F for 40 to 45 minutes or until set. Combine whipped cream and cinnamon or nutmeg to taste. Put a dollop of cream on each piece of pie. Makes 1 pie.

Deanna Swift

Buttermilk Custard Pie

1 unbaked 9-inch pie shell
3 eggs
1 cup sugar
½ cup butter, melted
2 Tablespoons flour
1 teaspoon vanilla
2 cups buttermilk
⅛ teaspoon nutmeg
Fresh berries

Bake pie shell at 425°F for 4 to 5 minutes. Blend eggs, sugar, butter, flour and vanilla. Stir in buttermilk. Pour into pie shell. Sprinkle with nutmeg. Bake at 350°F for 35 to 40 minutes. Cool and chill. Serve with berries. Makes 1 pie.

Sarajoan Rezak

Raspberry Cobbler

3 cups fresh or unsweetened frozen raspberries
¾ cup sugar
½ cup chopped pecans
½ cup butter
1 cup sugar
1 cup flour
2 eggs, beaten

Spread raspberries in 8-inch pie plate. Cover with sugar and sprinkle with pecans. Melt butter and mix in sugar, flour and eggs. Pour mixture over raspberries. Bake at 325°F for 1 hour. Makes 1 pie.

Pam Cole

Grasshopper Pie

Crust:

1½ to 2 cups chocolate wafer crumbs

¼ cup sugar

⅓ cup butter, melted

Crust:

Combine crumbs, sugar and butter. Press into bottom and sides of 9-inch greased pie plate. Set aside.

Filling:

1 Tablespoon unflavored gelatin

½ cup sugar, divided

⅛ teaspoon salt

½ cup cold water

3 eggs, separated

¼ cup green creme de menthe

¼ cup white creme de cacao

1 cup heavy cream, whipped

Filling:

Combine gelatin, ¼ cup sugar and salt in top of double boiler. Add water and egg yolks, one at a time, stirring until gelatin dissolves and mixture thickens slightly, about 5 minutes. Remove from water. Stir in creme de menthe and creme de cacao. Chill, stirring occasionally, until mixture is the consistency of unbeaten egg whites. Beat egg whites until stiff, but not dry. Gradually add remaining ¼ cup sugar to whites, beating until very stiff. Fold in gelatin mixture, then fold in whipped cream. Turn into chocolate crumb crust. Chill several hours or overnight. Makes 1 pie.

Mrs. Hubert C. Moog

Derby Pie

1 cup sugar

¼ cup butter

2 eggs

¾ cup light corn syrup

1 teaspoon vanilla

¼ teaspoon salt

½ to 1 cup chopped pecans

½ cup semisweet chocolate morsels

2 Tablespoons bourbon

1 unbaked 8-inch pie shell

Cream sugar and butter. Add eggs, corn syrup, vanilla and salt. Stir in pecans, chocolate morsels and bourbon. Pour into pie shell. Bake at 375°F for 40 to 45 minutes. Makes 1 pie.

Lucia Ward

Old Fashioned Chocolate Pie

Filling:

2 (1 ounce) squares unsweetened chocolate

1 cup sugar

3 Tablespoons flour

1½ cups scalding water

3 egg yolks, well beaten

½ teaspoon vanilla

Baked pie shell

Filling:

Melt chocolate in top of double boiler. Add sugar, flour and water, stirring well. Add egg yolks, stirring quickly into chocolate mixture. Cook over boiling water for 10 minutes, or until it thickens, stirring constantly. Stir in vanilla. Pour into pie shell.

Meringue:

3 egg whites

¼ teaspoon cream of tartar

6 Tablespoons sugar

1 teaspoon vanilla

Meringue:

Add cream of tartar to egg whites and beat until they hold a peak. Gradually beat in sugar. Add vanilla and beat just long enough to blend. Pile gently on filled pie, making sure it touches crust all the way around. Bake at 350°F until golden brown, about 15 minutes. Makes 1 pie.

Mrs. Howard Nussbaum

Mystery Pecan Pie

1 (8 ounce) package cream cheese, softened

1 egg

⅓ cup sugar

1 teaspoon vanilla

1 unbaked 9-inch pie shell

1¼ cups chopped pecans

Combine cream cheese, egg, sugar and vanilla; beat until fluffy. Spread in bottom of pie shell. Sprinkle pecans over cheese mixture.

Topping:

3 eggs

1 cup white corn syrup

¼ cup sugar

1 teaspoon vanilla

¼ teaspoon salt

Topping:

Beat eggs until fluffy. Do not overbeat. Add syrup, sugar, vanilla and salt. Mix well. Pour over pecans. Bake at 350°F for 40 minutes. Makes 1 pie.

The Elsah Landing Restaurant

Lemon Chiffon Pie

Shell:

1 cup sugar
¼ teaspoon cream of tartar
4 egg whites

Shell:

Sift sugar with cream of tartar. Beat egg whites stiff. Slowly add sugar and cream of tartar to stiff egg whites. Spread in 8-inch pie pan thicker on edges than on bottom. Bake at 275°F for 1 hour, until light brown. Cool.

Filling:

4 egg yolks
½ cup sugar
3 Tablespoons lemon juice
1 Tablespoon grated lemon rind
⅛ teaspoon salt
1 to 2 cups heavy cream, whipped, divided

Filling:

Beat egg yolks slightly. Stir in sugar, lemon juice, lemon rind and salt. Cook until thick. Cool. Fold 1 cup whipped cream into custard mixture. Slowly pour into shell. Refrigerate 12 to 24 hours. May top with additional whipped cream, if desired. Makes 1 pie.

Mrs. Arthur Niemoeller

Pie Crust

2 cups flour
⅔ cup lard
1 teaspoon salt
1 Tablespoon cider vinegar
Cold water

Cut lard into flour until mixture is size of peas. Add salt. Put vinegar in measuring cup and add water to equal ¼ cup. Pour over flour mixture and mix well until dough forms ball. Divide in half. Roll thin. Fit into pie pans. Prick with fork. Bake at 350°F for 15 minutes or until brown. Makes 2 (9-inch) pie shells.

Dorothea Lowe

Never Fail Pie Crust

4 cups flour
1 Tablespoon sugar
1 Tablespoon salt
2 cups lard
½ cup cold water
1 Tablespoon cider vinegar
1 egg

Mix flour, sugar and salt. Cut in lard. Measure water, add vinegar and whisk in egg. Mix together. Shape into 4 balls. Chill or freeze. Roll thin. Fit into pie pans. Prick with fork. Bake at 350°F for 15 minutes. Makes 4 (9-inch) pie shells.

Dorothea Lowe

Cakes

Pecan Raisin Cake

2 cups chopped pecans or walnuts
2 cups raisins
3½ ounces candied red or green cherries
½ cup bourbon
3½ cups sifted flour
1½ teaspoons baking powder
1 teaspoon nutmeg
½ teaspoon salt
2 cups sugar
1½ cups butter
1 teaspoon vanilla
7 eggs
½ cup bourbon for cheesecloth wrap

Combine pecans, raisins and quartered candied cherries with ½ cup bourbon; mix well. Let stand at room temperature several hours until liquid is absorbed. Sift flour, baking powder, nutmeg and salt together. Combine butter, sugar and vanilla; beat with electric mixer. Add eggs, one at a time, beating well after each addition. Beat 4 minutes. At low speed gradually beat in flour mixture until smooth. Add fruit and mix well with spoon. Pour batter into greased and floured 10-inch bundt pan. Bake at 350°F for 70 to 75 minutes or until toothpick inserted in center comes out clean. Cool 20 minutes before inverting on a wire rack. Soak a large piece of cheesecloth in ½ cup bourbon. Stretch cheesecloth on a large piece of foil. Place cake in center, wrap cake in soaked cheesecloth and wrap foil over tightly. Refrigerate several days to mellow. Warm to room temperature before serving. Makes 1 cake.

Grace Wilkins

White Chocolate Cake

¼ pound white chocolate
½ cup boiling water
2 cups sugar
1 cup butter
4 eggs, separated
1 teaspoon vanilla
2½ cups cake flour
1 teaspoon baking powder
1 cup buttermilk
1 cup pecans
1 cup flaked coconut

Melt chocolate in boiling water. Cream butter and sugar. Beat in egg yolks, one at a time. Add melted chocolate and vanilla. Sift together flour and baking powder. Add to creamed mixture alternately with buttermilk. Fold in stiffly beaten egg whites. Gently stir in pecans and coconut. Pour batter into 3 greased and floured 9-inch cake pans. Bake at 350°F for 30 to 35 minutes. Ice with cooked fluffy white icing. Makes 1 cake.

Maxine Range

Cranberry Torte

Cake:

2¼ cups sifted flour
1 cup sugar
1 teaspoon baking powder
1 teaspoon baking soda
¼ teaspoon salt
1 cup chopped dates
1 cup chopped pecans
1 cup fresh cranberries, washed
¼ cup grated orange rind
1 cup buttermilk
¾ cup vegetable oil
2 eggs, beaten

Glaze:

1 cup orange juice
1 cup sugar

Cake:

Sift flour, sugar, baking powder, baking soda and salt together in large bowl. Stir in dates, pecans, cranberries and orange rind. Combine buttermilk, oil and eggs; add to dry ingredients and stir until well blended. Pour batter into a 10-inch greased Bundt pan; bake at 350°F for 1 hour or until toothpick inserted in center comes out clean. Cool on rack for 20 minutes, then turn out on foil. Glaze, wrap and refrigerate. Do not freeze. Makes 1 cake.

Glaze:

Bring orange juice and sugar to a boil, stirring constantly. Cool before spooning over cake.

Mrs. R. C. ter Kuile

Backers' Surprise Coffee Cake

1 (18½ ounce) package yellow cake mix
1 (3¾ ounce) package instant vanilla pudding
4 eggs
1 cup sour cream
½ cup vegetable oil
¼ cup water
¾ cup sugar
¾ cup finely chopped walnuts
1½ Tablespoons cinnamon
1½ Tablespoons cocoa

Combine cake mix, pudding, eggs, sour cream, oil and water in large mixer bowl. Beat on medium speed for 5 minutes. Batter will be stiff. Put ¼ of batter in greased and floured bundt pan. Combine sugar, walnuts, cinnamon and cocoa. Sprinkle ⅓ of mixture over batter. Alternate batter and filling, ending with batter. Bake at 350°F for 60 to 70 minutes or until cake springs back when lightly touched. Cool in pan for 10 minutes before inverting on large cake plate. Makes 1 cake.

Peggy Miller

Soused Apple Cake

4 cups coarsely chopped peeled apples
¾ to 1 cup bourbon
2 cups sugar
½ cup vegetable oil
2 eggs
2 cups flour
2 teaspoons baking soda
2 teaspoons cinnamon
1 teaspoon salt
1 teaspoon nutmeg
¼ teaspoon cloves
1 cup coarsely chopped nuts
1 cup coarsely chopped raisins
1 cup heavy cream, whipped (garnish)

Put apples in bowl, pour over as much bourbon as they will absorb. Beat sugar, oil and eggs together with electric beater. Sift flour, soda, cinnamon, salt, nutmeg and cloves together. Stir into sugar mixture. Add nuts and raisins and stir until well mixed. Pour into greased 9 x 13-inch pan. Bake at 350°F for 45 minutes to 1 hour or until toothpick inserted in center comes out clean. Serve warm or cold with whipped cream. Makes 1 cake.

Josefa Wolff

White Pound Cake

Cake:

3 cups sugar
1 cup unsalted butter, softened (do not substitute)
6 eggs
3 cups sifted flour
1 cup heavy cream
½ teaspoon almond extract
½ teaspoon vanilla

Cake:

Cream butter and sugar. Add eggs, one at a time, beating 1 minute after each addition. Add flour and heavy cream alternately, using low speed on mixer. Blend well. Add almond extract and vanilla. Pour into greased and floured solid bottom 10-inch tube pan. Put cake in cold oven and set oven at 300°F. Bake 1½ hours. Cool 10 minutes before removing from pan. Ice when cold. Makes 1 cake.

Icing:

½ cup unsalted butter, softened
1 (1 pound) box confectioners' sugar
½ teaspoon salt
⅓ cup cold milk

Icing:

Cream butter, add sugar and salt, mix well. Add milk; stir until smooth.

Nancy Monson

Bakery Fruitcake Gifts

6 cups diced glazed fruits
5 cups dark and light raisins
3 cups chopped pecans
1 cup red candied cherries
½ cup unsweetened grapefruit juice
½ cup brandy
¼ cup dark molasses
2½ cups sugar
1 cup butter, softened
1 cup shortening
3 cups flour
1½ Tablespoons cinnamon
1½ Tablespoons allspice
1 Tablespoon ground cloves
½ Tablespoon baking powder
½ teaspoon salt
15 eggs
Milk
Whole glazed fruit slices, cherries, pecan halves (garnish)
Good brandy
Cheesecloth

Combine diced glazed fruits, raisins, chopped pecans, cherries, grapefruit juice, brandy and molasses in large container. Cover and let stand at room temperature overnight. The next day, cream sugar, butter and shortening together and set aside. Sift flour, cinnamon, allspice, cloves, baking powder and salt together; place in very large bowl. Beat eggs in separate bowl until creamy. Make well in center of dry ingredients and add eggs. Beat together well. Using your hands may be necessary. Add creamed mixture and beat. Fold in fruit and nut mixture with your hands. Place in 9 x 5-inch loaf pans that have been well greased and lined with wax paper using 1 pound of batter for each pan. Press batter down well in pans. Dip fingers in milk and press batter down again. This will give fruitcakes a light glaze. Bake no more than 4 loaves at a time at 275°F for 1½ to 1¾ hours or until toothpick inserted in center comes out clean. Cool completely on racks before removing from pans. Decorate tops with glazed fruits and pecan halves. Drizzle brandy over tops. Wrap in cheesecloth and store in air tight containers. Pour more brandy on cheesecloth every week for at least a month. Makes about 14 fruitcakes.

Suzy Wahl

Truly Differents

1 cup butter
4 (1 ounce) squares semisweet chocolate
Pinch salt
1¾ cups sugar
1 cup flour
4 eggs
1 teaspoon vanilla
¼ teaspoon butter flavoring

Melt butter, chocolate and salt over low heat. Mix sugar, flour, eggs, vanilla and butter flavoring together well with spoon. Stir in chocolate mixture; mix well again. Fill paperlined muffin cups ¾ full. Bake at 325°F for 30 minutes. Makes 18 cupcakes.

Agnes T. Koenig

Eggnog Pound Cake

2 Tablespoons butter, softened
½ cup sliced almonds
1 (18½ ounce) package yellow cake mix
2 eggs
1½ cups commercial eggnog
¼ cup butter, melted
2 Tablespoons rum
⅛ teaspoon nutmeg

Butter a 10-inch tube or bundt pan. Press almonds against buttered sides and bottom. Blend together cake mix, eggs, eggnog, melted butter, rum and nutmeg. Beat batter at medium speed until smooth. Pour batter into prepared pan. Bake at 350°F for 45 to 55 minutes or until toothpick inserted in center comes out clean. Cool cake in pan 10 minutes; invert cake onto a rack, and cool thoroughly. Makes 1 cake.

Mrs. Richard McGillis

Oat Cake

1½ cups boiling water
1 cup quick cooking rolled oats
½ cup butter
1 cup sugar
1 cup brown sugar
3 eggs
2¼ cups flour
1 teaspoon salt
1 teaspoon baking soda
1 teaspoon baking powder
1 teaspoon cinnamon
1 teaspoon nutmeg
1 teaspoon cloves
½ teaspoon ginger
2 Tablespoons dark rum or brandy
1 teaspoon vanilla
1 cup applesauce
1 cup raisins
1 cup chopped walnuts

Add boiling water to oats, and set aside. In a large bowl, cream the butter; add sugars, and beat until fluffy. Beat in eggs, one at a time. Stir together flour, salt, baking soda, baking powder, cinnamon, nutmeg, cloves and ginger. Add to butter mixture together with vanilla and rum or brandy. Beat in oats and applesauce. Stir in raisins and walnuts. Spoon batter into a well-greased 10-inch tube pan. Bake at 350°F for 60 to 80 minutes or until toothpick inserted in center comes out clean. Set pan on rack, and let cake cool completely before turning out of pan. Makes 1 cake.

Mrs. David Frank

Date Nut Cake with Penuche Icing

Cake:

1¼ cups finely cut dates
1 cup very hot water
1 cup sugar
¼ cup butter
1 egg
1 teaspoon vanilla
1¾ cups sifted cake flour
1 teaspoon baking soda
¼ teaspoon salt
½ cup chopped pecans

Cake:

Pour hot water over dates; let cool. Combine sugar, butter, egg and vanilla, and beat 3 to 4 minutes at high speed. Sift together flour, baking soda and salt. With mixer on low speed, add flour mixture alternately with date mixture. Blend just until smooth. Fold in nuts by hand. Pour batter into greased and floured 9-inch square pan. Bake at 350°F for 35 to 45 minutes. Cool before icing. Makes 1 cake.

Penuche Icing:

¼ cup butter
½ cup brown sugar
2 Tablespoons milk
1 cup sifted confectioners' sugar
1 teaspoon vanilla

Icing:

Melt butter in saucepan. Add brown sugar and milk, and boil over low heat for 2 minutes, stirring constantly. Cool to lukewarm. Gradually add confectioners' sugar and vanilla; beat until thick.

Irene Malick

Black Bottom Cups

Cake:

1½ cups sifted flour
1 cup sugar
¼ cup cocoa
1 teaspoon baking soda
½ teaspoon salt
1 cup water
⅓ cup vegetable oil
1 Tablespoon vinegar
1 teaspoon vanilla

Cake:

Sift together flour, sugar, cocoa, baking soda and salt. Add water, oil, vinegar and vanilla. Beat until well mixed. Fill paper-lined muffin pans ⅓ full with cake mixture. Add heaping teaspoonful cream cheese mixture. Sprinkle with sugar and almonds, if desired. Bake at 350°F for 30 minutes. Makes 18 cupcakes.

Black Bottom Cups

Filling:

1 (8 ounce) package cream cheese

1 egg

⅓ cup sugar

⅛ teaspoon salt

1 cup semisweet chocolate morsels

Topping: (optional)

Sugar

Chopped blanched almonds

Filling:

Combine cream cheese, egg, sugar and salt. Beat until smooth. Sir in chocolate morsels.

Linda S. Heater

Kentucky Prune Cake

Cake:

1½ cups sugar

1 cup vegetable oil

3 eggs, beaten

1 teaspoon vanilla

2 cups flour

1 teaspoon cinnamon

1 teaspoon nutmeg

1 teaspoon allspice

½ teaspoon salt

1 cup buttermilk

1 teaspoon baking soda

1 cup cooked prunes, chopped

1 cup chopped pecans

Cake:

Beat sugar, oil, eggs and vanilla until mixture becomes light. Mix together flour, cinnamon, nutmeg, allspice and salt. Stir baking soda into buttermilk, and add to creamed mixture alternately with the flour mixture. Fold in prunes and pecans. Pour batter into 2 greased and floured 9-inch cake pans. Bake at 325°F for 35 to 40 minutes. Put layers on rack at once, and pour hot glaze over them. When glaze is all absorbed, arrange one on top of the other. Makes 1 cake.

Glaze:

1 cup sugar

½ cup butter

½ cup buttermilk

1 Tablespoon light corn syrup

½ teaspoon baking soda

½ teaspoon vanilla

Glaze:

Boil sugar, butter, buttermilk, corn syrup, baking soda, and vanilla for one minute. Pour over hot cake layers.

Mrs. J. Glennon Schreiber

Hummingbird Cake

Cake:

3 cups flour
2 cups sugar
1 teaspoon salt
1 teaspoon baking soda
1 teaspoon cinnamon
3 eggs, beaten
1½ cups vegetable oil
2 cups chopped bananas
1 (8-ounce) can crushed pineapple, undrained
1 cup chopped pecans
1½ teaspoons vanilla

Cake:

Combine flour, sugar, salt, baking soda and cinnamon. Add eggs and oil, stirring until moistened. Do not beat. Stir in bananas, pineapple, pecans and vanilla. Pour batter into 3 well-greased and floured 9-inch cake pans. Bake at 350°F 25 to 30 minutes. Cool in pans for 10 minutes. Remove and cool completely. Makes 1 cake.

Frosting:

2 (8 ounce) packages cream cheese, softened
1 cup butter, softened
2 (1 pound) boxes confectioners' sugar
2 teaspoons vanilla

Frosting:

Cream butter and cream cheese until smooth. Add confectioners' sugar, beating until light and fluffy. Stir in vanilla. Spread frosting between layers and on top and sides of cake.

Mrs. J. Glennon Schreiber

Mocha Cream Cake

Cake:

1½ cups sifted flour
1½ teaspoons baking powder
¾ teaspoon salt
4 eggs, separated
½ cup water
1½ teaspoons grated fresh lemon rind
¾ teaspoon vanilla
1½ cups sugar
3 Tablespoons fresh lemon juice

Cake:

Sift together flour, baking powder and salt. Combine egg yolks, water, lemon rind and vanilla and beat well. Gradually add sugar and lemon juice. Blend in dry ingredients carefully. Beat egg whites until stiff but not dry and fold into batter. Pour batter into 2 greased and wax paper-lined 9-inch cake pans. Bake at 350°F for 25 minutes. When cool, split the layers, ice and refrigerate for at least 4 hours before serving. Makes 1 cake.

Mocha Cream Cake

Mocha Cream Frosting:

2 (1 ounce) squares unsweetened chocolate

½ cup water

½ cup sugar

2 teaspoons instant coffee

½ teaspoon vanilla

2 cups heavy cream

Frosting:

Melt chocolate in water over low heat, stirring constantly. Add sugar, coffee and vanilla and boil for 3 minutes. When cool, stir in cream, whipped stiff.

Mrs. Walt Yesberg

Lemon Cake

¾ cup butter, softened

⅔ cup sugar

2 eggs, separated

1⅓ cups flour

¾ teaspoon baking soda

¾ teaspoon baking powder

¼ teaspoon salt

¾ cup sour cream

Pinch cream of tartar

Sifted confectioners' sugar

Cream butter and sugar i large bowl. Beat in egg yolks. Sift flour, baking soda, baking powder and salt together. Add to butter mixture alternately with sour cream and beat until well combined. Beat egg whites with cream of tartar to stiff peaks and fold gently but thoroughly into batter. Pour batter into a buttered 9 x 5-inch loaf pan. Bake at 350°F for 45 to 50 minutes or until toothpick inserted in center comes out clean. Cool in pan for 10 minutes, turn onto rack and sool completely. Slice cake horizontally into 3 layers. Spread bottom layer with half the filling, leaving a ½-inch border and top with second layer and repeat. Press layers together and dust top of cake with confectioners' sugar. Makes 1 cake.

Filling:

¾ cup sugar

2 eggs, beaten

2 egg yolks, beaten

⅔ cup fresh lemon juice

2 Tablespoons grated fresh lemon rind

½ cup butter

Filling:

Combine sugar, eggs, egg yolks, lemon juice and rind in a heavy saucepan and cook, whisking, over medium low heat until mixture is smooth. Add butter, but into bits, and cook, whisking, over very low heat 10 minutes until smooth and thick. Put in bowl, cover with wax paper and cool.

Jere Rieser

Swedish Pineapple Cake

Cake:

1 (20 ounce) can crushed pineapple, undrained
2 cups flour
2 cups sugar
2 eggs
½ cup chopped nuts
2 teaspoons baking soda
1 teaspoon vanilla

Cake:

Combine pineapple, flour, sugar, eggs, nuts, baking soda and vanilla; mix until moistened. Pour into greased and floured 9 x 13-inch pan. Bake at 350°F for 40 to 45 minutes. Makes 1 cake.

Frosting:

1 (8 ounce) package cream cheese, softened
½ cup butter, softened
1¾ cups confectioners' sugar
1 teaspoon vanilla

Frosting:

Blend butter and cream cheese. Add sugar and vanilla. Mix until smooth.

Garie Perry

Mississippi Mud Cake

Cake:

2 cups sugar
1 cup butter, softened
4 eggs
1½ cups flour
¼ cup cocoa
¾ teaspoon salt
1½ cups coconut
1½ cups chopped pecans
1 teaspoon vanilla
1 (7 ounce) jar marshmallow creme or halved marshmallows

Cake:

Cream butter and sugar. Beat in eggs, one at a time, with spoon. Sift flour, cocoa and salt together. Stir into creamed mixture. Stir in coconut, pecans and vanilla. Pour into greased and floured 9 x 13-inch pan. Bake at 350°F for 30 to 35 minutes. Spread marshmallow creme or halved marshmallows on hot cake. Cool and ice. Makes 1 cake.

Mississippi Mud Cake

Icing:

½ cup butter

1 (1 pound) box confectioners' sugar

⅓ cup cocoa

⅛ teaspoon salt

⅓ cup milk

½ teaspoon vanilla

Icing:

Cream butter; add sugar, cocoa and salt. Add milk and vanilla; stir until smooth.

Jean Deckelman

Little Pecan Cakes

Cake:

1 cup sugar

⅔ cup butter, softened

2 eggs

1 teaspoon vanilla

1¾ cups sifted flour

1½ teaspoon cinnamon

1 teaspoon baking powder

½ teaspoon baking soda

Pinch salt

1½ cups coarsely chopped pecans

½ cup raisins, plumped and drained

1 Tablespoon grated fresh lemon rind

Cake:

Cream sugar and butter; beat in eggs and vanilla. Sift together flour, cinnamon, baking powder, baking soda and salt; add to butter mixture. Stir in pecans, raisins and lemon rind. Divide batter among 24 well buttered 2½-inch muffin tins and bake at 375°F for 20 minutes or until toothpick inserted in center comes out clean. Cool on racks. Remove from tins and spread tops with glaze.

Glaze:

½ cup sugar

⅓ cup sifted cocoa

¼ cup heavy cream

2 Tablespoons butter

¼ teaspoon vanilla

Glaze:

Combine sugar, cocoa, cream and butter in heavy saucepan, and simmer, stirring, for 5 minutes until smooth and thick. Remove fro het and stir in vanilla. Makes 24.

Mrs. Clarence Henry

7-UP Cake

Cake:

1 (18½ ounce) package lemon cake mix

1 (3¾ ounce) package vanilla instant pudding

¾ cup vegetable oil

1 (10 ounce) bottle 7-UP

4 eggs

Cake:

Combine cake mix, pudding, oil, 7-UP and eggs in large bowl. Blend until moistened. Beat with electric mixer at medium speed for 2 minutes. Pour into 3 greased and floured 9-inch cake pans. Bake at 350°F for 25 to 30 minutes or until toothpick inserted in center comes out clean. Cool for 15 to 20 minutes before removing from pans. Spread cooled icing between layers and on top and sides of cake. Makes 1 cake.

Icing:

2 cups sugar

1 (20 ounce) can crushed pineapple

½ cup butter

5 Tablespoons flour

2 egg yolks

1 cup coconut

1 cup chopped nuts

Icing:

Combine sugar, pineapple, butter, flour and egg yolks in saucepan. Bring mixture to a boil and cook until thick. Stir in coconut and nuts. Cool.

Mrs. Ralph Countryman Jr.

Apricot Angel Food

1 (10 inch) angel food cake

Slice cake into 3 layers.

Filling:

2 Tablespoons unflavored gelatin

2 Tablespoons cold water

2 cups heavy cream

2 teaspoons vanilla

¼ cup confectioners' sugar

Filling:

Soften gelatin in cold water, place dish in very warm water until gelatin liquifies. Add liquid gelatin to cream while whipping. Add vanilla. Add confectioners' sugar. Spread filling between layers.

Apricot Angel Food

Icing:

1 (12 ounce) package dried apricots
Water
½ cup sugar

Icing:

Cut apricots in small pieces, cover with water and cook slowly for 15 minutes. Add sugar and cook slowly for 10 minutes. Put mixture through food mill or in blender until smoooth. Cool. Spread over top and sides of cake. Refrigerate overnight. Makes 1 cake.

Mildred Merkle

Nutmeg Cake

Cake:

1⅓ cups sugar
½ cup butter
3 eggs
1 teaspoon vanilla
2 cups flour
2 teaspoons freshly grated nutmeg
1 teaspoon baking powder
1 teaspoon baking soda
½ teaspoon salt
1 cup buttermilk

Cake:

Cream butter and sugar. Add eggs, one at a time, beating well after each. Add vanilla. Sift flour, nutmeg, baking powder, baking soda and salt together; add to creamed mixture alternately with buttermilk. Pour into greased and floured 9 x 13-inch pan. Bake at 350°F for 25 to 30 minutes. Makes 1 cake.

Topping:

1 cup brown sugar
½ cup flaked coconut
6 Tablespoons butter
¼ cup cream
½ teaspoon vanilla

Topping:

Combine sugar, coconut, butter and cream in saucepan. Bring to a boil, and boil ½ minute. Add vanilla. Pour topping over warm cake and bake at 350°F an additional 5 minutes.

Pauline Jones

est Chocolate Cake

Cake:

2 cups boiling water

4 (1 ounce) squares unsweetened chocolate

½ teaspoon instant coffee

3½ cups dark brown sugar

1 cup butter

2 teaspoons vanilla

1 teaspoon red food color

1 cup eggs

1 cup sour cream

4½ cups sifted cake flour or 4 cups sifted flour

2 teaspoons baking soda

½ teaspoon salt

Cake:

Combine water, chocolate and instant coffee in bowl. Stir occasionally. Cool to room temperature. Cream brown sugar and butter. Add vanilla and red food color. Add eggs, one at a time, beating well after each addition. Add sour cream and blend well. Sift flour, baking soda and salt together. Add flour in three parts, mixing thoroughly, but do not overbeat. Add cooled chocolate mixture. Blend well, scraping sides of bowl frequently. Mixture will be thin. Pour into a 10-inch tube pan which has been greased and the bottom lined with wax paper. Bake at 340°F for 60 to 65 minutes or until tester inserted in highest part comes out clean. Cool 15 minutes in pan. Invert onto cake rack. Cool and ice. Makes 1 cake.

Chocolate Frosting:

4 (1 ounce) squares unsweetened chocolate

½ cup butter

1 egg

1 teaspoon vanilla

¾ teaspoon strong coffee (optional)

1 or 2 drops maple flavoring

⅛ teaspoon salt

1 (1 pound) box confectioners' sugar

¼ cup sour cream

Chocolate Frosting:

Melt chocolate and cool to room temperature. Cream butter, egg, vanilla, coffee, maple flavoring and salt together. Add half the sugar. Stir in sour cream and add the remaining sugar. Blend in cooled chocolate. Adjust texture by adding 1 Tablespoon sour cream, extra confectioners' sugar or 1 Tablespoon cocoa to your taste.

Sharon Winstein

Cookies, Bars and Squares

Chocolate Crunches

2 Tablespoons sifted flour
⅛ teaspoon baking powder
Pinch salt
1 (4 ounce) bar German sweet chocolate
1 (1 ounce) square unsweetened chocolate
1 Tablespoon butter
⅓ cup brown sugar
1 egg
1 Tablespoon water
1 teaspoon vanilla
1 (6 ounce) package semisweet chocolate morsels
1 cup chopped pecans
Pecan halves

Sift flour, baking powder and salt together. Melt sweet chocolate, unsweetened chocolate and butter in top of double boiler over simmering water. Cool. Stir in sugar, egg, water and vanilla. Add flour mixture. Mix in chocolate morsels and pecans. Chill until firm enough to drop by spoonfuls. Drop Tablespoons of dough onto greased or foil-lined cookie sheets 2 inches apart. Press a pecan half in center of each. Bake at 350°F for 12 minutes or until they are springy. Cool on racks. Store in airtight containers. Makes 24.

Mary Merten

Lemon Coconut-Snow Bars

Crust:

2⅔ cups flour
1 cup unsalted butter, softened
½ cup sugar
½ cup finely ground pecans
¼ teaspoon salt

Topping:

5 eggs
1½ cups sugar
¼ cup flour
½ teaspoon baking powder
Pinch salt
¾ cup Hawaiian Coconut Snow
½ cup lemon juice
1 teaspoon grated lemon rind
Confectioners' sugar

Crust:

Combine flour, butter, sugar, pecans and salt in large bowl and mix until well blended. Put into ungreased jelly roll pan. Bake at 350°F for 15 minutes to 20 minutes until brown on edges.

Topping:

Mix eggs and sugar together in large bowl. Sift flour, baking powder and salt together and combine with egg mixture. Mix in Coconut Snow, lemon juice and lemon rind. Pour over baked crust. Bake at 350°F for 18 to 20 minutes or until set. Sprinkle liberally with confectioners' sugar. Cool. Cut into bars. Makes 32. Hawaiian Coconut Snow is available in liquor stores.

Charlene Bazier

Tri-Level Brownies

Bottom Layer:

1 cup uncooked rolled oats
½ cup flour
½ cup brown sugar
6 Tablespoons melted butter
¼ teaspoon baking soda
¼ teaspoon salt

Bottom Layer:

Combine oats, flour, brown sugar, butter, baking soda and salt; mix well. Pat into 7 x 11-inch pan. Bake at 350°F for 10 minutes.

Middle Layer:

¼ cup butter, melted
1 (1 ounce) square unsweetened chocolate
¾ cup sugar
⅔ cup flour
¼ cup milk
1 egg
½ teaspoon vanilla
¼ teaspoon baking powder
¼ teaspoon salt
½ cup chopped walnuts

Middle Layer:

Combine butter and chocolate in large saucepan and cook over low heat until chocolate is melted. Remove from heat. Add sugar, flour, milk, egg, vanilla, baking powder and salt. Stir well. Stir in walnuts. Spread over first layer. Bake at 350°F for 20 minutes.

Top Layer:

1 (1 ounce) square unsweetened chocolate
2 Tablespoons butter
1½ cups confectioners' sugar
1 teaspoon vanilla

Top Layer:

Melt chocolate and butter in small saucepan over low heat. Remove from heat. Add sugar and vanilla. Add water if necessary. Spread over cooled brownies. Cut into squares. Makes 24.

Vicki Short

Sugar Cookies

¾ cup sugar
½ cup butter, softened
1 Tablespoon milk
1 teaspoon vanilla
1¾ cups flour
1¼ teaspoons baking powder
Sugar (garnish)

Combine sugar, butter, milk and vanilla in large bowl; mix thoroughly. Sift flour with baking powder and stir into sugar mixture. Chill well. Drop by heaping teaspoons onto foil-lined cookie sheets. Flatten by pressing with glass covered with damp cloth. Sprinkle with sugar. Bake at 350°F for 5 minutes, or until slightly brown. Makes 4 dozen.

Kelley Leopold

Chocolate Cheesecake Squares

Crust:

1 cup flour
½ cup sugar
3 Tablespoons cocoa
1 teaspoon baking powder
¼ teaspoon salt
½ cup butter, softened
1 egg yolk
½ cup finely chopped walnuts
1 teaspoon vanilla

Filling:

1 (8 ounce) package cream cheese
½ cup sour cream
⅓ cup sugar
1 egg
1 egg white
1 Tablespoon flour
2 teaspoons grated orange rind
½ teaspoon vanilla
¼ teaspoon salt
Semisweet chocolate curls (garnish)

Crust:

Combine flour, sugar, cocoa, baking powder and salt in large bowl. Cut in butter. Stir in egg yolk. Add walnuts and vanilla and mix well. Turn dough into a 9-inch square baking pan which has been lined on the bottom and 2 sides with a strip of foil that overlaps sides and press firmly over bottom. Bake at 325°F for 15 minutes.

Filling:

Combine cream cheese, sour cream, sugar, egg, egg white, flour, orange rind, vanilla and salt in large bowl. Beat until well blended. Pour over hot crust and bake at 325°F for 20 to 25 minutes or until filling is set. Cool in pan for 1 hour, then garnish top with chocolate curls. Cover and refrigerate. Cut into 1¾-inch squares. Makes 25.

Mrs. Richard McGillis

Pecan Cups

½ cup butter
2⅔ cups graham cracker crumbs
1 (13 ounce) can evaporated milk
1 (12 ounce) package semisweet chocolate morsels
1 cup brown sugar
1 cup chopped pecans
1 teaspoon vanilla

Melt butter over low heat. Add graham cracker crumbs, milk, chocolate morsels, sugar, pecans and vanilla; toss together with spoon. Place paper liners in miniature cupcake tins. Fill with batter to top of liners. Bake at 350°F for 12 minutes. Let stand 5 minutes before removing from pan. Makes 4½ dozen.

Nancy Lee Huck

Chocolate Oatmeal Bars

Crust:

2 cups brown sugar
1 cup butter, softened
2 eggs
1 teaspoon baking soda
1 teaspoon salt
2½ cups flour
2 cups uncooked rolled oats

Crust:

Cream sugar, butter, eggs, baking soda and salt until smooth. Stir in flour with spoon. Add oats. Batter will be stiff. Spread ⅔ of batter into greased 8 x 12-inch pan. Cover with chocolate filling, spreading to edges. Flatten pieces of remaining batter between hands and cover chocolate mixture. Bake at 350°F for 25 minutes. Cool for 30 minutes; cut into very small squares. Let stand, covered, overnight for ease in handling. Makes 6 dozen.

Filling:

1 (14 ounce) can sweetened condensed milk
1 (12 ounce) package semisweet chocolate morsels
3 Tablespoons butter
2 teaspoons vanilla
½ cup chopped nuts

Filling:

Combine condensed milk, chocolate morsels, butter and vanilla in top of double boiler and cook over hot water until chocolate melts. Stir in nuts. Cool while making crust.

Maria Schweizer

Nutmeg Butter Balls

Cookies:

1 cup butter, softened
¾ cup sugar
1 egg
2 teaspoons vanilla
3 cups flour
¾ teaspoon nutmeg

Cookies:

Cream butter and sugar until fluffy. Stir in egg and vanilla. Combine flour and nutmeg; add to creamed mixture gradually. Roll into 1-inch balls and place on cookie sheet. Bake at 350°F for 13 to 15 minutes. Ice when cool. Makes 6 dozen.

Frosting:

⅓ cup butter, softened
2 cups confectioners' sugar
2 Tablespoons cream or milk
2 teaspoons rum (optional)
1 teaspoon vanilla
Nutmeg

Frosting:

Cream butter until fluffy. Stir in sugar and mix until smooth. Add cream, rum and vanilla and blend thoroughly. Sprinkle iced cookies with nutmeg.

Tricia Reay

Troc-Tin Fudge Squares

Crust:

2 cups flour

1 cup butter, melted

½ cup confectioners' sugar

Crust:

Mix flour, butter and sugar together and pat over bottom and slightly up sides of 9 x 13-inch ungreased glass baking dish. Bake at 350°F for 10 to 12 minutes or until golden brown.

Filling:

1 (12 ounce) package semisweet chocolate morsels

2 Tablespoons butter

2 Tablespoons milk

⅔ cup sugar

2 teaspoons vanilla

2 eggs, well beaten

2 cups chopped pecans

Filling:

Melt chocolate, butter and milk over low heat. Stir in sugar and vanilla. Remove from heat and quickly beat in eggs. Pour over baked crust and cover heavily with pecans. Bake at 350°F for 20 minutes. Cool. Cut into squares. Makes 4 dozen.

Mrs. Ben Kenneth

Health Nut Peanut Butter Cookies

½ cup vegetable oil

½ cup chunky peanut butter

2 eggs

1 cup uncooked rolled oats

¾ cup flour

¾ cup brown sugar

½ cup instant nonfat dry milk

½ teaspoon baking powder

½ teaspoon salt

½ teaspoon cinnamon

1 cup shredded raw carrots

½ cup raisins

Combine oil, peanut butter and eggs in small bowl and stir until smooth. Combine oats, flour, sugar, dry milk, baking powder, salt and cinnamon in large bowl. Stir in peanut butter mixture until moistened. Stir in carrots and raisins. Drop heaping teaspoons of batter 2 inches apart onto ungreased cookie sheets. Bake at 350°F for 15 minutes or until light brown. Makes 4 dozen.

Roberta Tureen

Shortbread

2 cups butter, softened
1 cup sugar
5 cups flour

Cream butter and sugar in large bowl with electric mixer until light and fluffy. Beat in flour, 1 cup at at time, and beat until mixture is smooth. Roll dough out ¼-inch thick on lightly floured surface. Cut lengthwise into 1-inch strips, then cut at a diagonal to form diamonds. Prick all over with fork. Carefully place on greased cookie sheet. Bake at 350°F for 15 minutes or until lightly browned. Makes 6 dozen.

Kathryn C. Allison

Thumbprint Seed Cookies

1 cup butter
½ cup sugar
2 egg yolks
1 teaspoon vanilla
2 cups sifted flour
3 Tablespoons poppy seeds
⅛ teaspoon salt
Red currant jelly

Cream butter and sugar in large bowl. Add egg yolks and vanilla; beat until light. Stir in flour, poppy seeds and salt. Mix well. Chill for 2 to 3 hours. Shape into 1-inch balls. Put on ungreased cookie sheets. Press in center of each cookie with thumb. Bake at 375°F 10 to 12 minutes or until lightly browned. Press in center of each cookie again as you remove from oven. Fill centers with jelly just before serving. Makes 4 dozen.

Betty Suttle

Raisin Crisps

½ cup raisins
½ cup butter
¼ cup water
¾ cup sifted flour
½ teaspoon baking soda
½ teaspoon salt
¼ teaspoon cinnamon
¼ teaspoon nutmeg
1½ cups uncooked rolled oats
1 cup brown sugar
½ cup chopped nuts
1 teaspoon vanilla

Heat raisins and butter in water until butter is melted; cool. Sift flour, baking soda, salt, cinnamon and nutmeg into large bowl. Add oats, brown sugar and nuts and mix well. Add cooled raisin mixture and vanilla and blend well. Chill. Drop teaspoons of dough onto greased and floured baking sheet, then flatten cookies with glass covered with damp cloth. Bake at 350°F for 8 to 10 minutes. Makes 4 dozen.

Delores Wagenfuehr

Mint Stick Brownies

Brownie Layer:

½ cup butter
2 (1 ounce) squares unsweetened chocolate
1 cup sugar
½ cup sifted flour
2 eggs, well beaten
¼ teaspoon peppermint flavoring
⅛ teaspoon salt
½ cup chopped nuts

Brownie Layer:
Melt butter and chocolate over hot water. Cool. Add sugar, flour, eggs, peppermint flavoring and salt. Mix well. Stir in nuts. Pour batter into well-greased 9-inch square pan. Bake at 350°F for 20 to 25 minutes. Cool.

Mint Frosting:

1 cup sifted confectioners' sugar
2 Tablespoons butter, softened
1 teaspoon light cream
½ teaspoon peppermint flavoring
Few drops green food coloring

Mint Frosting:
Combine confectioners' sugar, butter, cream, peppermint flavoring and green food coloring. Mix until creamy and spread on cooled brownies. Refrigerate while making glaze.

Glaze:

1 (1 ounce) square unsweetened chocolate
1 Tablespoon butter

Glaze:
Melt butter and cocolate over hot water and blend well. Drizzle glaze over frosting and carefully spread to cover. Refrigerate to set glaze. Cut into small bars. Makes 4 dozen.

Melanie Bascom

Apricot Bars

1½ cups flour
1 teaspoon baking powder
¼ teaspoon salt
1½ cups uncooked rolled oats
1 cup brown sugar
¾ cup butter
1 (12 ounce) jar apricot preserves

Sift flour, baking powder and salt together in large bowl. Stir in oats and sugar. Cut in butter until crumbly. Pat ⅔ of mixture into 9 x 13-inch pan; spread with preserves and cover with remaining crumbs. Bake at 375°F for 25 minutes. Cool; cut into squares. Makes 36.

Deni Whitworth

Ginger Thins

1 cup unsalted butter
2 cups dark brown sugar
1 egg, beaten
2 cups flour
2 rounded teaspoons ginger
½ rounded teaspoon allspice
½ rounded teaspoon cinnamon
½ rounded teaspoon cloves
1 teaspoon vanilla

Cream butter until fluffy. Add sugar and cream until fluffy. Add egg and mix well. Sift flour, ginger, allspice, cinnamon and cloves together. Add gradually to butter mixture with mixer on low speed. Add vanilla and mix. Shape dough into 2 rolls 1½ inches in diameter. Wrap in wax paper. Refrigerate overnight. Slice into thin rounds. Bake on greased nonstick cookie sheets at 350°F for 9½ minutes; remove from sheet immediately. Store in airtight container. Makes 8 dozen.

Madeline Stribling

Florentines

⅔ cup brown sugar
½ cup butter
⅓ cup light corn syrup
2 Tablespoons frozen orange juice concentrate, thawed, undiluted
1 Tablespoon grated orange rind
1 cup sifted flour
1 cup finely chopped pecans
1 (12 ounce) package semisweet chocolate morsels

Combine sugar, butter, corn syrup, orange juice concentrate and orange rind in saucepan. Cook and stir over low heat until mixture boils. Remove from heat. Stir in flour and nuts. Melt chocolate morsels in top of double boiler, over simmering water. Drop batter 2 inches apart on well-greased cookie sheets. Bake at 350°F about 5 minutes in bottom third of oven. Cookies should be light brown. Cool a minute on cookie sheet. Finish cooling on rack. Spread melted chocolate on backs of cooled cookies. Let dry on rack. Makes 5 dozen.

Frances Copeland

Almond Crescents

1 cup butter
½ cup sugar
1¼ cups unblanched almonds, ground
2 cups flour
1 teaspoon vanilla
½ teaspoon salt
Confectioners' sugar

Cream butter and sugar. Blend in almonds. Add flour, vanilla and salt. Blend well. Chill until firm. Form small balls and roll into ½-inch thick sticks. Bend into crescent shape and place on greased cookie sheet. Bake at 350°F for 15 to 20 minutes. Roll in confectioners' sugar. Makes 36.

Evelyn Downing

Start-Your-Own-Bakery Cookies

1⅓ cups sugar
1 cup brown sugar
1 cup shortening
½ cup butter
4 eggs
1 Tablespoon vanilla
1 teaspoon lemon juice
3 cups flour
½ cup uncooked rolled oats
2 teaspoons baking soda
2 teaspoons salt
1 teaspoon cinnamon
2 (12 ounce) packages semisweet chocolate morsels
2 cups chopped pecans

Cream shortening, butter and sugars in large mixer bowl until thoroughly blended, about 5 minutes at high speed. Add eggs, one at a time, beating well after each addition. Add vanilla and lemon juice. Combine flour, oats, baking soda, salt and cinnamon. Add to creamed mixture and beat until well blended. Mix in chocolate morsels and pecans. Drop dough by scant ¼ cup on lightly greased cookie sheet about 3 inches apart. Bake at 350°F for 15 minutes. Leave cookies on sheet about 30 seconds, then put on wire rack to cool. Makes 36.

Suzy Wahl

Kentucky Brown Sugar Pecan Bars

1¼ cups flour
½ teaspoon baking powder
½ teaspoon salt
1 cup chopped toasted pecans
⅓ cup sugar
½ cup cold butter
3 eggs
1¼ cups dark brown sugar
¼ cup butter, melted and cooled
3 Tablespoons bourbon
1 teaspoon vanilla
Pinch salt

Sift flour, baking powder and salt together in bowl. Stir in pecans and sugar. Cut butter into small pieces and blend mixture until it resembles cornmeal. Press dough into well-buttered 8-inch square baking dish and bake at 350°F for 15 minutes. Combine eggs, brown sugar, butter, bourbon, vanilla and salt in bowl and beat well. Pour mixture over baked layer and bake at 350°F for 25 minutes. Cool and cut into 2x1-inch bars. Makes 32.

Carol Winkelmeyer

Acorns

1 cup butter, melted
¾ cup brown sugar
1 cup chopped pecans, divided
1 teaspoon vanilla
2¾ cups sifted flour
½ teaspoon baking powder
1 (6 ounce) package semisweet chocolate morsels

Combine butter, brown sugar and ¾ cup pecans in large bowl; blend well. Sift flour and baking powder together and stir into butter mixture; blend well. Shape cookies by pressing lightly into teaspoon. Place on ungreased cookie sheet and bake at 375°F for 15 minutes. Cool on wire rack. Melt chocolate morsels over hot water. Dip large end of cooled cookies in melted chocolate, then in remaining chopped nuts. Makes 36.

Jacqui Thompson

Nitey-Nite Cookies

2 egg whites, at room temperature
Pinch salt
⅔ cup sugar
1 cup chopped pecans
1 cup semisweet chocolate morsels
½ cup coconut

Beat egg whites and salt until stiff. Add sugar very gradually and beat until stiff. Stir in pecans, chocolate morsels and coconut. Drop teaspoons of batter onto foil-lined cookie sheet. Put sheet in 350°F oven and turn off oven. Leave in oven overnight or for 8 hours. Makes 3½ dozen.

Kay Ellen Thurman

Monte Carlo Squares

¾ cup butter
⅓ cup sugar
2 eggs, separated
1½ cups flour
⅛ teaspoon salt
1 cup apricot preserves
½ cup sugar
2 ounces sliced almonds

Cream butter and sugar. Add egg yolks and blend. Stir in flour and salt. Press into buttered and floured 9-inch square pan. Bake at 350°F for 20 to 25 minutes. Remove from oven and spread with apricot preserves. Beat egg whites with sugar until stiff and spread over apricot preserves. Sprinkle with almonds. Bake at 350°F for 25 to 30 minutes. Cut into squares. Cool before removing from pan. Makes 16.

Peggy McClellan

English Tea Cakes

Base:

1 cup flour
2½ Tablespoons confectioners' sugar
½ cup butter

Base:

Combine flour and sugar in bowl. Cut in butter. Pat in 9-inch square baking dish. Bake at 350°F for 15 minutes.

Filling:

1½ cups brown sugar
1 cup chopped nuts
½ cup coconut
2 eggs
2 Tablespoons flour
1 teaspoon vanilla
½ teaspoon salt
¼ teaspoon baking powder

Filling:

Combine sugar, nuts, coconut, eggs, flour, vanilla, salt and baking powder. Spread onto baked crust. Bake at 350°F for 25 minutes. Cool.

Lemon Icing:

3 cups sifted confectioners' sugar
⅓ cup butter
4½ teaspoons fresh lemon juice

Lemon Icing:

Cream 1 cup sugar and butter. Stir in lemon juice. Add remaining sugar and mix until smooth. Spread on cool cookies. Cut into squares. Makes 16.

Barbara Ferrenbach

Cookie Mounds

1½ cups sugar
½ cup butter, softened
½ cup shortening
3 eggs
1¾ cups flour
⅓ cup milk
1½ teaspoons cinnamon
1 teaspoon salt
1 teaspoon baking soda
2 cups rolled oats
2 cups raisins
1 cup chopped pecans

Cream sugar, butter, shortening and eggs until light and fluffy. Blend in flour, milk, cinnamon, salt and baking soda gradually and mix well. Stir in oats, raisins and pecans. Drop by rounded Tablespoons onto greased cookie sheets. Bake at 350°F for about 15 minutes or until golden brown. Makes 4 dozen.

Jennifer Murdock

Almond Kringler

1 cup flour
1 cup sugar
½ cup butter, softened
1 Tablespoon water
1 cup water
½ cup butter
1 cup flour
3 eggs
½ teaspoon almond extract

Combine flour and sugar in large bowl. Cut in ½ cup butter until crumbly. Add 1 Tablespoon water and stir. Pat into jelly roll pan. Bring 1 cup water to a boil in large saucepan. Add butter and stir to melt. Remove from heat and add flour, eggs and almond extract; blend well. Spread over the first layer. Bake at 350°F for 45 minutes. Ice while still warm. Sprinkle with almonds. Cool and cut into bars. Makes 4 dozen.

Icing:

¾ cup confectioners' sugar
1 Tablespoon milk
½ teaspoon almond extract
2 ounces sliced almonds

Icing:

Combine sugar, milk and almond extract. Beat until smooth.

Margaret Rhett

Chinese Almond Crisps

1¼ cups flour
½ teaspoon baking soda
½ teaspoon salt
¾ cup sugar
½ cup lard, softened
1 egg, lightly beaten
1 teaspoon almond extract
1 cup chopped blanched almonds
36 whole blanched almonds
1 egg yolk
2 Tablespoons water

Sift flour, baking soda and salt together into a small bowl. Cream sugar and lard until light in a large bowl. Beat in egg and almond extract. Beat in flour mixture, a little at a time, to form a soft dough. Stir in chopped almonds. Chill dough for 2 to 3 hours. Form dough into walnut-sized balls and place 1½ inches apart on lightly greased cookie sheets. Press a blanched almond into each cookie. Beat egg yolk with water and brush cookies lightly. Bake at 350°F for 10 to 12 minutes or until golden. Cool on racks. Makes 36.

Marie Crawford

Frosted Pecans

3½ cups pecan halves
½ cup butter
2 egg whites
Pinch salt
1 cup sugar
Cinnamon

Place pecans in jelly roll pan. Brown in 325°F oven for 5 to 10 minutes, shaking pan frequently. Do not let pecans burn. Melt butter in 9 x 13-inch pan. Add salt to egg whites and beat very stiff, adding sugar gradually. Fold pecans into egg white mixture. Spread mixture evenly in butter. Bake at 325°F for 30 minutes, stirring frequently. Remove and sprinkle with cinnamon. Makes 4 cups.

Tina M. Burke

Chocolate Truffles

8 ounces semisweet chocolate, cut up
3 Tablespoons boiling water
1 Tablespoon instant espresso
½ cup unsalted butter, cut up
3 Tablespoons brandy
Unsweetened cocoa or chocolate shot

Combine semisweet chocolate, water and espresso in top of double boiler over hot water. Heat over medium heat until chocolate is melted. Remove from heat. Beat in butter, one piece at a time, and blend well. Beat in brandy. Refrigerate for 4 to 5 hours or until firm. Shape into ¾-inch balls and roll in cocoa or chocolate shot. Store in cool place in airtight container. Makes 30 pieces.

Didi Wilson

Pecan Pralines

1½ cups brown sugar
1½ cups sugar
1 cup milk
1 teaspoon salt
¼ teaspoon cream of tartar
¼ cup butter, softened
1 teaspoon vanilla
2 cups chopped pecans

Combine sugars, milk, salt and cream of tartar in saucepan. Cook to soft ball stage, 238°F. Remove from heat and cool to 220°F. Add butter and vanilla. Stir in pecans. Cover chilled marble slab with foil. Spoon small mounds of mixture onto foil. Press into circles with fork or spoon back. Remove from foil when cooled and firm. Makes 24.

Eli Strassner

Nutty Crunch

1¼ cups sugar
¾ cup butter
½ cup whole unblanched almonds
¼ cup water
1½ teaspoons salt
½ cup chopped pecans
½ cup chopped blanched almonds
½ teaspoon baking soda
⅓ cup semisweet chocolate morsels, melted
½ cup finely chopped nuts

Combine sugar, butter, unblanched almonds, water and salt in saucepan. Boil, stirring frequently, until candy thermometer reads 290°F or until a drop in cold water is brittle. Stir constantly at end to prevent burning. Stir in pecans, blanched almonds and baking soda. Pour into well greased jelly roll pan. Spread melted chocolate over top and sprinkle with finely chopped nuts. Cool and break into pieces. Makes 1½ pounds.

Ann Kraft

Candy Apples

8 medium red apples
2 cups sugar
¾ cup water
½ cup light corn syrup
1 teaspoon red food color

Stick wooden skewers in leaf end of apples. Combine sugar, water, corn syrup and food color in top of double boiler. Heat to boiling. Continue boiling over direct heat, without stirring, until candy thermometer registers 280°F. Place immediately over boiling water in bottom of double boiler. Dip apples quickly in syrup and twirl until completely coated. Place on very well greased cookie sheet to cool. Makes 8.

Didi Wilson

Confection Fruitcake

2 pounds pecan halves
1 pound dates, chopped
1 pound candied cherries
½ pound candied yellow pineapple
½ pound candied green pineapple
½ pound shredded coconut
1 (14 ounce) can sweetened condensed milk
1 teaspoon rum

Combine pecans, dates, cherries, yellow pineapple, green pineapple and coconut in large bowl. Add milk and rum and mix well. Spread in greased jelly roll pan. Bake at 250°F for 2 hours. Put pan of water in oven to keep cookies from drying out. Makes 8 dozen.

Tricia Reay

Peanut Butter Cups

1 (1 pound) box confectioners' sugar
1½ cups graham cracker crumbs
1 cup peanut butter
1 cup butter, melted
1 (12 ounce) package semisweet chocolate morsels

Mix sugar, graham cracker crumbs, peanut butter and butter together well. Press evenly and firmly into buttered 9 x 13-inch pan. Melt chocolate morsels in top of double boiler over hot water. Spread melted chocolate over top of first mixture. Cool. Cut in squares. Makes 6 dozen.

Carmen Davidson

Kentucky Bourbon Balls

1 (1 pound) box confectioners' sugar
½ cup butter (do not substitute)
¾ cup finely chopped pecans
4½ Tablespoons straight bourbon
1 (8 ounce) box unsweetened chocolate
1 teaspoon paraffin
Pecan halves

Cream sugar and butter, stir in pecans and bourbon. Chill until firm. Roll into small balls and return to refrigerator for 30 minutes. Melt chocolate and paraffin in top of double boiler over hot water. Dip each ball separately with ice pick. Put on wax paper and top with pecan half. Chill for at least 2 hours. Wrap separately in plastic wrap and keep in a cool place. Makes about 4 dozen.

Mrs. Charles W. Freeman
Mrs. Ernest S. Clarke

Apricot Coconut Balls

1½ cups dried apricots, chopped
2 (3½ ounce) cans flaked coconut
⅔ cup canned sweetened condensed milk
Confectioners' sugar

Combine apricots and coconut in large bowl. Add milk and mix well. Shape into balls and roll in confectioners' sugar. Store in refrigerator. Makes 32.

Alberta Greenberg

Coconut Joys

3 cups coconut
2 cups confectioners' sugar
½ cup butter, melted
2 (1 ounce) squares unsweetened chocolate, melted

Combine coconut, sugar and butter until well mixed. Shape into balls. Make indentation in center of each ball and fill with chocolate. Chill until firm. Store in refrigerator. Makes 36.

Jolene Browne

Syrup

1 cup brown sugar
1 cup sugar
1 cup white corn syrup
1 cup evaporated milk

Combine brown sugar, sugar, syrup and milk in large saucepan. Cook until heated through. Store in refrigerator and reheat as needed. Makes 4 cups.

Jennifer Dean

Cappuccino

6 cups light cream
6 cups coffee
1 cup dark crème de cacao
½ cup rum
½ cup brandy

Mix cream, coffee, crème de cacao, rum and brandy in saucepan. Heat over low heat. Serve hot. Serves 10 to 12.

Alice Jefferson

Patio Potion

6 Tablespoons light rum
2 Tablespoons coffee liqueur
2 Tablespoons sweet cream
Crushed ice

Pour rum, coffee liqueur, cream and ice into cocktail shaker. Shake well. Pour into chilled glasses. Serves 2.

Sheldon Jackman

Lemon Sangria

3½ cups dry white wine, chilled
3 lemons, sliced
1 orange, sliced
1 green apple, peeled, cored and cut in wedges
Green grapes
½ cup cognac
¼ cup sugar
1 (10 ounce) bottle club soda, chilled
Ice cubes

Mix wine, lemons, orange, apple, grapes, cognac and sugar in large pitcher. Refrigerate overnight. When ready to serve, add soda and ice cubes and stir gently. Fruit can be added to glasses. Makes 1½ quarts.

Thelma Rhodes

Banci

3 scoops French vanilla ice cream
3 Tablespoons banana liqueur
2 Tablespoons crème de cacao
1 Tablespoon Amaretto

Combine ice cream, banana liqueur, crème de cacao, and Amaretto in blender. Blend until smooth. Serves 2.

Phyllis Brent

Hot Eggnog

1 quart vanilla ice cream
4 jiggers brandy

Warm ice cream in saucepan over moderate heat until just below boiling point. Blend in brandy. Serve hot. Serves 8.

Mrs. Brian Kennedy

Coffee Liqueur

6 cups water, divided
3½ cups sugar
1 (2 ounce) jar instant coffee
2 cups 190 proof grain alcohol
¼ cup vanilla
1½ Tablespoons chocolate syrup

Combine sugar and 3 cups water in saucepan, bring to a boil and boil 3 minutes. Cool to room temperature. Put 3 cups water in another saucepan and bring to boil. Add coffee and stir. Cool to room temperature. Combine both mixtures and add grain alcohol, vanilla and chocolate syrup. Stir well. Bottle in brown bottles or store in dark. Age 30 days. Makes 2¼ quarts.

Gwen Springett

Cranberry Sparkle

1 (1 quart) bottle cranberry juice cocktail, chilled
2 cups orange juice, chilled
3 (16 ounce) bottles 7-UP
Orange slices (optional)

Place ice ring in punch bowl. Add cranberry and orange juices. Pour 7-UP carefully down side of bowl. Float orange slices on top. Makes 3 quarts.

Leslie Maxwell

Champagne Punch

1 cup maraschino liqueur
1 cup cognac
2 oranges, thinly sliced
1 lemon, thinly sliced
1 teaspoon orange bitters
Ice block
3 (750 ML) bottles domestic champagne, well chilled

Put maraschino liqueur, cognac, orange slices, lemon slices and orange bitters in punch bowl; stir well. Let stand at least 1 hour. Place ice block in bowl. Pour champagne over ice. Stir well. Makes 3½ quarts.

Sue Leatherwood

Party Punch

1 (750 ML) bottle white catawba grape juice, well chilled
1 (750 ML) bottle dry white wine, well chilled
1 (750 ML) bottle white rum, well chilled
1 (28 ounce) bottle club soda
Claret to color
Ice block

Combine grape juice, wine, rum, club soda and claret in punch bowl. Add ice block to bowl. Makes 1 gallon.

Betsy Enslin

Champagne Brandy Punch

2 (28 ounce) bottles ginger ale, well chilled
1 (750 ML) bottle champagne, well chilled
1 (750 ML) bottle brandy, well chilled
1 orange, sliced
Ice

Combine ginger ale, champagne and brandy in punch bowl. Float orange slices on top. Fill bowl with ice. Makes 1 gallon.

Barbara Vandivort

Fancy Iced Tea

2 oranges
2 lemons
8 cups boiling water
1 scant cup sugar or artificial sweetener to equal
2 tea bags
1 bunch mint or 2 whole cloves

Remove rind and juice from oranges and lemon. Combine rind and juice with water, sugar or artificial sweetener, tea bags, and mint or cloves. Makes 2 quarts.

Mrs. Leigh Gerdine

Sippin' Cider

3 gallons apple cider
3 cups Meyers Dark Rum
1 (1 ounce) jar cinnamon sticks
⅔ (1½ ounce) jar whole allspice

Combine cider, rum, cinnamon and whole allspice in large kettle and heat over medium heat, stirring occasionally. Serve warm. Makes 3 gallons.

Kay Clements

Halloween Batch of Hot Buttered Rum

96 whole cloves
96 whole allspice
24 (3 inch) cinnamon sticks
1 cup sugar
12 cups boiling water
9 cups light rum
3 cups dark Jamaican rum
1 cup unsalted butter

Put cloves, allspice, cinnamon and sugar in very large souppot or kettle with a little of the boiling water. Let stand for 10 minutes. Add rums, boiling water and butter. Stir over very low heat until butter melts. Add more sugar if desired. Serve hot. Makes 3 gallons.

David C. Wahl

Hot Buttered Rum Batter

1 pound brown sugar
½ cup unsalted butter
¼ to ½ teaspoon nutmeg
¼ to ½ teaspoon cinnamon
¼ to ½ teaspoon cloves
Pinch salt
Puerto Rican rum
Jamaican rum
Hot milk
Nutmeg (garnish)

Cream sugar and butter until smooth and fluffy. Add nutmeg, cinnamon, cloves and salt to creamed mixture. Store in glass jar in refrigerator until ready to use. For each serving, preheat a 6-ounce mug. Put a heaping teaspoon of batter into mug. Stir in 3 Tablespoons Puerto Rican rum and 1 Tablespoon Jamaican rum. Fill with hot milk. Top with nutmeg.

Winifred Jeep

Index

A

B

C

D

E

F

G

H

I

J

N

O

P

Q

R

S

T

V

W

Y

Z

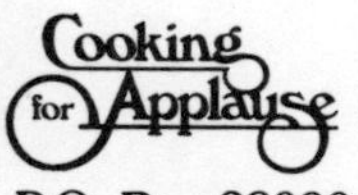

P.O. Box 28090
St. Louis, MO 63119

Please send me ________ copies of ***Cooking for Applause*** at $12.95 per copy.
I am including $1.50 each to cover postage and handling.

Name ______________________________

Address ______________________________

City ____________________ State __________ Zip __________

Make checks payable to ***Cooking for Applause***
All proceeds will be used to support The Repertory Theatre of St. Louis.

Cooking for Applause

P.O. Box 28090
St. Louis, MO 63119

Please send me ________ copies of ***Cooking for Applause*** at $12.95 per copy.
I am including $1.50 each to cover postage and handling.

Name ______________________________

Address ______________________________

City ____________________ State __________ Zip __________

Make checks payable to ***Cooking for Applause***
All proceeds will be used to support The Repertory Theatre of St. Louis.

Cooking for Applause

P.O. Box 28090
St. Louis, MO 63119

Please send me ________ copies of ***Cooking for Applause*** at $12.95 per copy.
I am including $1.50 each to cover postage and handling.

Name ______________________________

Address ______________________________

City ____________________ State __________ Zip __________

Make checks payable to ***Cooking for Applause***
All proceeds will be used to support The Repertory Theatre of St. Louis.